Child sexual abuse in Victorian England

Women's and Gender History

General Editor:
June Purvis
Professor of Women's and Gender History, University of Portsmouth

Published

Lynn Abrams and Elizabeth Harvey (editors)
Gender relations in German history: power, agency and experience from the sixteenth to the twentieth century

Paula Bartley
Prostitution: prevention and reform in England, 1860–1914

Elizabeth Crawford
The Women's Suffrage movement: a reference guide 1866–1928

Shani D'Cruze
Crimes of outrage: sex, violence and working women in Victorian England

Carol Dyhouse
No distinction of sex? Women in British universities, 1870–1939

Bridget Hill
Women, work and sexual politics in eighteenth-century England

Sandra Holton and June Purvis
Votes for women

Linda Mahood
Policing gender, class and family: Britain, 1850–1940

Jane McDermid and Anna Hillyar (editors)
Midwives of the revolution: female Bolsheviks and women workers in 1917

June Purvis (editor)
Women's history: Britain, 1850–1940

Wendy Webster
Imagining home: gender, 'race' and national identity, 1945–64

Barbara Winslow
Sylvia Pankhurst: sexual politics and political activism

Forthcoming titles include:

Elizabeth Edwards
Women in teacher training colleges: a culture of femininity, 1900–1960

The Central Criminal Court at the Old Bailey. Photo: M. J. S. Jackson.

Child sexual abuse in Victorian England

Louise A. Jackson

London and New York

First published 2000
by Routledge
11 New Fetter Lane, London EC4P 4EE

Simultaneously published in the USA and Canada
by Routledge
29 West 35th Street, New York, NY 10001

Routledge is an imprint of the Taylor & Francis Group

© 2000 Louise A. Jackson

Typeset in Garamond by Taylor & Francis Books Ltd
Printed and bound in Great Britain by Clays Ltd, St Ives plc

British Library Cataloguing in Publication Data
A catalogue record for this book is available from the British Library

Library of Congress Cataloging in Publication Data
A catalog record for this book has been requested

ISBN 0–415–22649–X
ISBN 0–415–22650–3

Contents

Figures

Acknowledgements

The research and writing of this book would not have been possible without the support of the School of Cultural Studies, Leeds Metropolitan University, where I now teach and the Department of History at Roehampton Institute, London, where I undertook my doctoral study from 1993 to 1997. The content of this book has been influenced by discussions in a wide variety of seminar groups and conference sessions and by conversations with individuals too numerous to mention. I am, however, particularly indebted to Meg Arnot (who supervised my thesis on sexual abuse in London, 1870–1914) and to Carolyn Steedman (who acted as moderator) for their encouragement and inspired suggestions. I am grateful to Anna Davin, Simon Gunn, Gordon Johnston, Peter King, John Seed, Heather Shore, Deborah Thom and Cornelie Usborne for their constructive comments at various points in the research; also to Lesley Hall for her proficiency as reader of the final manuscript. I should also like to thank Ian Wakeling of the Children's Society, Jewish Care, Nicholas Malton of the NSPCC, Gordon Taylor of the Salvation Army, and the Wellcome Trustees for granting access to their archives, for help and advice, and for permission to publish extracts from source material. The staff of the West Yorkshire Archive Service, the London Metropolitan Archive, the Public Record Office and the British Library have provided an invaluable service. Pat and Mike Jackson have been stalwart in their support, encouragement and affection for more years than I can remember.

The names of all children, defendants and non-expert witnesses have been changed in order to protect their identity.

1 Introduction

'The children of the poor'

Social and cultural contexts

The Central Criminal Court at the Old Bailey in London, England, is renowned world-wide for its iconography; most particularly for the symbolic figure of Justice, rising above the domed roof, holding her golden scales and sword outstretched to judge good from evil with clarity and equity.[1] Less well known is the inscription carved in stone above the main entrance to the present court: 'Defend the Children of the Poor and Punish the Wrong-Doer'. Taken from the Bible – Psalm 72, verse 4 – this text evokes justice as a Christian principle in contrast to the neo-classical presence of the female statue. The court building, designed by Edward de Montford and rebuilt on the original site of Newgate Prison, was officially opened in February 1907; construction had begun in 1902 and the design plans date back to the turn of the century.[2] The inscription can, therefore, be seen as a snapshot of the ideals of the late Victorian/early Edwardian paternalistic State and gives an insight on attitudes to criminality and victimology in this period. The older biblical understanding of the 'Children of the Poor' as all whom Christ would save had acquired new layers of meaning in relation to nineteenth-century ideas about children and childhood.

On a literal level, the inscription identified working-class children as the immediate beneficiaries of justice and their protection as the primary purpose of the judiciary. Its significance, however, cuts far deeper. As Anna Davin has demonstrated, children were, by the end of the nineteenth century, seen as the future of the nation, their welfare a vital part of the imperialist project.[3] The late Victorian notion of children's rights was delineated in relation to their role as future citizens; the association of children with justice can, therefore, be seen as a statement of State-building, of defending citizenship. The child had also, by this time, come to play a vital symbolic role in terms of the individual. Carolyn Steedman has drawn attention to the emergence, from the Enlightenment onwards, of the child figure as a personification of 'ideas about the self and its history'.[4] In this light, the evocation of the child in relation to the concept of justice is a bid for psychological security: the child must be protected to guarantee all our pasts and indeed all our futures.

The association is also a gendered one.[5] One could say that, on the symbolic level, it is maternalism rather than paternalism that is invoked as protection; it is the female figure of Justice who is defending her children. However, as Marina Warner has written, female allegorical figures had very little to do with 'the actual order' which consisted of male judges and statesmen.[6] In practical terms, justice was undeniably masculine. What of the child? Steedman has also argued that, by the end of the nineteenth century, 'when the child was watched, written about and wanted, it was usually a feminised set of qualities (if not a female child) whose image was left behind for our analysis'.[7] These 'feminised qualities' are apparent in the inscription's positioning of the child as a weak passive victim rather than active doer (of either right or wrong); caught in a double bind of 'littleness' and poverty, she is defenceless. As a child she represents innocence, in opposition to, on the one hand, the experience and knowledge of adult self-determination, and, on the other, the guilt of the wrongdoer. She is object/victim in relation to the subject figures of both the wrongdoer and her 'defender', the masculine mechanism of State power. The association of the feminine with the victim is apparent in the very names of the 'Societies for the Protection of Women and Children' which proliferated throughout the nineteenth century.

By the turn of the century, therefore, the figure of the (female) child had become an important symbol of the innocent victim of crime. The prevention and punishment of child abuse was deployed as a paradigm for the ideals of the English criminal justice system.[8] This book will concentrate its attentions on one specific form of abuse: child sexual abuse, portrayed by child savers as the most sinister, examining its treatment within the law, and in relation to wider social, political and cultural agendas.

Crime and the law

It is usually acknowledged that the sexual abuse of children was both discovered and constructed in the late 1970s within a very particular framework of aetiology, diagnosis, treatment and cure.[9] In other words, sexual abuse is a late twentieth-century phenomenon, located specifically within contemporary culture and society. Historians, however, have been quick to demonstrate its historical antecedents and to point to the late nineteenth century as a period when mass campaigning and parliamentary legislation were mobilised over the emotive topics of child prostitution, incest and the age of consent.[10] Victorians used a wide collection of euphemisms – 'moral corruption', 'immorality', 'molestation', 'tampering', 'ruining', 'outrage' – to refer to sexual abuse, which was prosecuted in the courts as indecent assault, rape, unlawful carnal knowledge or its attempt. Although not widespread, the term 'sexually abused' was indeed used by Scottish surgeon George

William Balfour in his 1864 translation of a work on forensic medicine by Johann Ludwig Casper.[11] Although Victorians had no umbrella term that was uniformly applied, they would certainly have recognised the term 'child sexual abuse'. Indeed, Jan Lambertz has made a similar deduction in relation to sexual harassment cases in her study of gender relations in the cotton factories of Lancashire during the 1890s.[12] Victorians had a clear concept of inappropriate sexual attention that constituted abuse of power and which, on various occasions, was brought to public attention as an issue. It clearly makes sense to talk of both 'sexual harassment' and 'sexual abuse' in a nineteenth-century context. Recognising that child abuse is, nevertheless, a socially and historically constructed category, this book explores the specific meanings attached to sexual abuse in Victorian and Edwardian England, demonstrating how the actualities of criminal cases intermeshed with the symbolic delineation of the child.

Nineteenth-century parliaments enacted a long string of statute laws concerned with the regulation of sexual offences, many of them affecting the way in which child abuse was treated and dealt with in the courts. The death penalty was lifted in cases of rape in 1841, the statutory age of consent for girls was raised twice – from 12 to 13 in 1875 and from 13 to 16 in 1885 – and incest was finally made a criminal offence in 1908.[13] It was in this period, too, that many of the legal practices and principles which govern the way child sexual abuse is treated in the courts today were established and negotiated. This book focuses on the period c.1830–1914, in order to assess the immediate impact of the changes in statutory law and court practice. Historians who adopt the notion of a long nineteenth century see the First World War rather than changes of monarch as a cultural and social watershed. While dominant attitudes towards sexual abuse that were developed and promoted during Victoria's reign continued to influence twentieth-century interpretations, the rising interest in psychoanalysis and child psychology after 1914 suggests that the post-war period requires separate evaluation.[14]

Although the number of crimes tried on indictment in England and Wales was falling in relation to population between 1830 and 1914, the number of sexual offences sent for trial – a large proportion of which involved the sexual assault of children – increased drastically (see figures 1.1 and 1.2). News reports, witness statements and the records of voluntary agencies all defined the sexual corruption of children as crimes of 'the most aggravated and serious character'.[15] But, throughout the period, only a small proportion of reported cases of sexual abuse – probably less than a third – resulted in conviction.[16] Why this paradox? Why the contrast between the vehement rhetoric and the apparent leniency of magistrates and judges? In solving this central conundrum, this book grapples with a list of related questions regarding the perception and treatment of sexual abuse, the impact of shifts in legislation, and the experiences of those involved in the criminal justice system. How were child witnesses treated in the courts?

What stories did they have to tell? How did relations or neighbours deal with abuse in their midst? How were abusers judged? What happened to the children concerned after proceedings? I shall demonstrate throughout that the ambiguities and complexities surrounding sexual abuse were related to Victorian constructions of gender difference, childhood, sexuality and social class.

Child welfare and social purity

It is vital to stress that sexual abuse was, throughout the period, associated with female children. English child-saving agencies almost always spoke of offences against 'young girls' (rarely boys), usually committed by men (although female accomplices might be implicated). Court proceedings, as this study demonstrates, reflected this specificity: 99 per cent of defendants tried on charges relating to the sexual assault of children were male, while 93 per cent of victims in these cases were female. While French forensic specialists had researched and debated the signs of sexual abuse on male as well as female bodies during the 1850s, their findings were never translated into English.[17] The 'discovery' of sexual abuse in England from the 1860s onwards was the product of a coalition of interests between the social purity

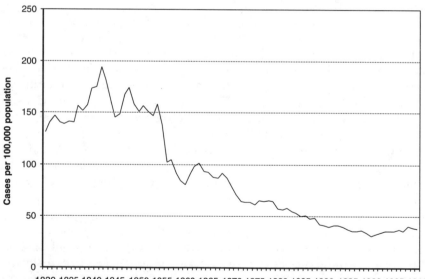

Figure 1.1   Criminal cases tried on indictment in England and Wales in relation to population, 1830–1910

Sources: (Parliamentary Papers, annual judicial statistics, 1830–1910; B. R. Mitchell, *British historical statistics* (Cambridge: Cambridge University Press, 1988))

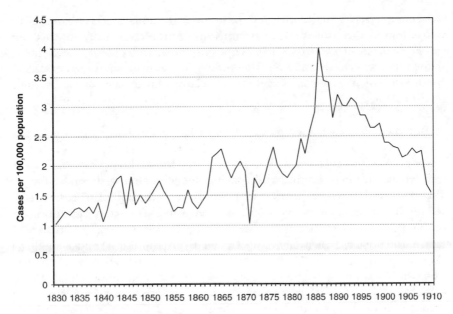

Figure 1.2 Sexual assault cases tried on indictment in England and Wales in relation to population, 1830–1910

Sources: (see figure 1.1)

Note: The term 'sexual assault' encompasses all charges of rape or unlawful carnal knowledge, attempted rape or unlawful carnal knowledge, assault with intent to rape, and indecent assault

societies and the burgeoning child welfare movement. The reason for the invisibility of boys (despite police knowledge of a market for adolescent boy prostitutes) lies in the emergence of the issue from the social purity and rescue societies' preoccupation with 'fallen' women and young female prostitutes. A woman's character, unlike a man's, was judged in relation to her sexual reputation. Girls and women could 'fall' but boys could not, according to the Victorian sexual schema. Sexually abused girls, as a group, constituted a specially targeted social problem. Boys did not and their futures were rarely discussed.

A growing body of interdisciplinary studies has drawn attention to the emergence of the romantic concept of childhood and its increasing hold on nineteenth-century minds.[18] In the sixteenth and seventeenth centuries, the Calvinist notion of original sin had stressed that children were evil by nature, requiring rigorous discipline to resist temptation. From the end of the eighteenth century, however, this was replaced with the idea, promoted by Wordsworth and the romantic poets, that children, born as innocents, were innately virtuous. As Steedman has demonstrated, the figure of the romantic child, reproduced and reworked through a variety of genres during the course of the nineteenth century, became the object of a great deal of psychological investment as a personification of the essence of self, as a key aspect of personal identity; our view of childhood today is still profoundly shaped by this inheritance.[19] The romantic child represented the ideal condition which, as Jacqueline Rose and Carol Mavor have shown in their studies of the work of J. M. Barrie and Lewis Carroll, adults might long for but never return to.[20]

But the newly identified romantic child had a sinister or ugly twin: the juvenile delinquent. It is no coincidence that the concept of juvenile delinquency also emerged between 1780 and 1820, as a by-product of romanticism.[21] Ideas of childhood innocence and juvenile delinquency must also be linked to the formation of middle-class cultural identities in this period and to demonstrations of status and respectability in opposition to both a debased aristocracy and an uneducated labouring poor.[22] If the child was born innocent, then environment led to corruption. Amidst concerns about social unrest, the 1830s and 1840s saw a proliferation of investigations into the living conditions, demeanour and behaviour of labouring children in the mining and manufacturing industries and in agricultural gangs.[23] Delinquency was related to social class; delinquents were the children of the poor. As one member of parliament put it in 1885: 'the conditions of life in which a large proportion of the population was placed brought young girls into contact with vice, and gave them experiences to which women of 20 in a higher class were strangers'.[24] The effects of delinquency were clearly gendered.[25] In boys, corruption began as petty thieving and led into a downward spiral of criminal activity. For girls it took the form of immorality or sexual precocity. The associations between delinquency, corruption and sexual knowledge had a significant impact on the treatment of the girl victim of sexual abuse.

Although the meanings of sexual abuse were also constructed in relation to feminist, radical and socialist epistemologies, this book will emphasise the dominance within the legal and welfare systems of a discourse of Christian moral economy, promoted by the middle classes, that produced an area of confusion around the girl victim's status. Although the rape of the innocent was defined, theoretically and symbolically, as the most heinous crime which could be committed against children or childhood, the real female victim of sexual abuse was viewed as problematic. The act of sexual abuse was deemed to have corrupted the girl and effected her 'fall' from innocence; once 'fallen', her moral status was dubious. The sexually abused girl was seen as a polluting presence, and was a particular danger to other children. The construction of childhood in terms of sexual innocence was dependent on the association of adulthood with knowledge and experience. Girls who lost their innocence could no longer be deemed 'children' and, instead, became social misfits who needed retraining and reforming in a specialist institution. In terms of age, body and appearance they were still children but, in terms of mentality and morality, they were seen as 'unnatural' beings, premature adults who had not had the benefits of a 'healthy', 'normal' development. Harry Hendrick has suggested that the history of child welfare policy in the nineteenth and twentieth centuries can best be understood in relation to shifting and overlapping narratives of children as both victims and threats; the 'children of the poor' were clearly both.[26] This dualism can be used to explain the problematic position of the sexually abused girl child in Victorian and Edwardian society. At the same time as she was constructed as the helpless victim of an individual act of brutality, she was, simultaneously, seen as a wider social threat to those around her.

The term 'Christian moral economy', used here to describe a fluid currency or exchange of moral and immoral influences within a social body, had its origins in the evangelical revival and unitarian movement of the late eighteenth century.[27] The moral condition of society was dependent on the regulation and containment of immorality, which could contaminate those with whom it came into contact. In 1794 unitarian physician and medical jurist Thomas Percival had argued that 'political and moral economy can subsist in no community, without the steady execution of wise and salutary laws'.[28] He went on to argue that: 'the criminal ... who evades the sentence of justice, like one infected with the pestilence, contaminates all whom he approaches'.[29] Percival pinpointed precise links between sexual abuse, the corruption of the child, and wider notions of social contamination:

> In all civilized countries the honour and chastity of the female sex are guarded from violence by the severest sanctions of the law. And this protection is at once humane, just and necessary to social morality ... it is essential to morality that licentious passion should be restrained, that modesty should not be wounded, nor the mind contaminated, in some instances, before it is capable of forming adequate conceptions of right and wrong.[30]

While theories of moral contamination shifted and changed during the course of the nineteenth century – the panic about the expansion of the 'great unwashed' in the early Victorian period was replaced by more localised concerns about hygiene and immorality in the slums of the 1890s – the notion of a sexual/moral economy, in which immorality was 'catching', was still resonant.[31] In the worst cases of immorality it was necessary to invoke the criminal justice system.

Since gendered notions of sexual morality were intertwined with perceptions of social class, the socio-economic standing of victims and defendants played an important role in sex abuse trials. The reports of social investigators and parliamentary committees portrayed brutality, immorality, incest and, therefore, deviancy as the norm amongst the poorest sections of society who lived in dirt and squalor. The middle and upper-working classes were depicted, in contrast, as respectable and morally righteous. Whilst seeking to deconstruct these mythologies – by demonstrating, for example, that the poor were clearly not desensitised to morality – I shall also expose their currency within the criminal justice system. The likelihood of conviction was linked to the social class, reputation and status of, on the one hand, the defendant and, on the other, the victim. The reputation of the girl child was gauged in terms of sexual knowledge and experience; that of a male defendant in relation to his occupational status and position as a family man. Perhaps because child sexual abuse was defined as such a horrible and brutal crime, juries found it harder to believe that a 'normal', 'respectable' male, with a permanent job and family responsibilities, should wish to molest a child. The middle-class male and, indeed, the middle-class home, was less likely to be the subject of surveillance or scrutiny.

Histories and theories of abuse

The first histories of rape, domestic and sexual violence emerged in the late 1970s and early 1980s as a result of the emphasis, in radical feminist theory, on the importance of sexual politics in structuring gender relations. Feminist writers Susan Brownmiller and Florence Rush had a very specific agenda: to demonstrate that the sexual abuse and rape of women and children was a continual process throughout history which had served to maintain the basis of male power.[32] As Brownmiller famously put it: 'From prehistorical times to the present I believe rape has played a critical function: it is nothing more or less than a conscious process of intimidation by which *all* men keep *all* women in a state of fear.'[33] While recognising that Brownmiller's work was groundbreaking, subsequent historians of sexual violence have criticised her for projecting her reading of contemporary society back into the past.[34] Most significantly, Brownmiller failed to allow for the historical and cultural specificity of rape and sexual violence; that is the notion that acts can carry different meanings over time and that the power dynamics of class, race and gender relations shift and change. Her work seems to be underpinned, to some extent, by an essentialist assumption that rape is part of the male biological condition. The notion of 'conscious process', which Brownmiller deployed to describe a collective patriarchal operation across time and space, has become untenable as a way of thinking about historical events. In many ways the 'conscious process' has become the historian's, as an aspect of the process of self-reflexive history-writing in which we are constantly engaged.

Indeed, it could be argued that the key words in Brownmiller's statement are the subjective, personal and passionate 'I believe', which acts as a negation of any claim that history is an objective, positivistic science. The 'self-conscious' historian is faced with the proposition that history can never be anything other than his or her personal account, or even, as Hayden White has described it, the 'translation of fact into fictions'.[35] In relation to a topic like sexual abuse, there is of course very little in the way of 'fact', as it is traditionally understood, in the primary source material. The historian is confronted with a sea of stories all claiming to be 'truths', a series of contestations in courtroom or street, words of anger, bitterness, reproach, pain. However, although the sequences of 'truths' may have been framed in line with certain pre-existing narrative structures and in relation to a wider cultural and symbolic framework, there is also blood, pain and tears which make it impossible to forget there is a 'real' child, father or mother involved. Even within a coded and ordered witness statement transcribed by a court official, there is nevertheless something that appertains to the indelibly personal. This means that the historian's methodology is inevitably based on a particular type of hermeneutics, on interpreting statements and uncovering diverse and complex series of meanings in relation to wider political, cultural and linguistic structures, but also with an awareness of individual initiative, agency and resistance. In this way histories are products of an interactive process, of dialogue between historians and historical subjects, and, as such, are able to suggest new insights on both past and present.

Sensitivity to historical meanings of language, to the cultural specificity of legal and welfare practices, and to the historical construction of self and identity is necessary in order to avoid anachronism. In a study of rape in seventeenth-century England, Garthine Walker has provided a cogent warning against the use of psychoanalysis as an interpretative methodology for the early modern self.[36] She has argued that gaps or silences in women's narratives of rape and abuse cannot be interpreted as 'the repression of traumatic memories' since such a hypothesis cannot be tested historically.[37] It can be argued that the modern psyche in its various incarnations is as much a cultural creation as witches or demons. Even if psychoanalysis does offer, as a last surviving grand narrative, some kind of 'transhistorical' truth about emotional and psychological development, one has to ask where, exactly, its relevance lies in relation to history as a discipline. History's interest in the emotions centres on their specific cultural articulations, on the ways in which love, fear and anger were experienced and described historically. We know those emotions are there because people talked about them; the point is to listen carefully to their words. We need to be reticent about projecting psychical states based on a contemporary social and cultural landscape on to a different topography.

Children and the family

Histories of abuse also deal with the relationship between force, power and authority in personal relations, and with the domains of the individual, family, neighbourhood and State. Studies of sexual violence by Anna Clark, Linda Gordon and Judith Walkowitz have sought to engage with a more sophisticated analysis of power dynamics and of the operation of gender in society than that offered by Brownmiller and Rush.[38] Gordon, for example, in her groundbreaking study of welfare agencies working with family violence clients in Boston, Massachusetts, has argued that:

We need concepts of male supremacy that can explain the power that women have managed to exert ... the compromises that men have often made. ... and the extremely complex struggles, negotiations, and co-operation with which the sexes have faced each other and the social/cultural institutions that define gender relations.[39]

She foregrounds this important analytical issue and ably demonstrates that abuse is constructed through time in relation to notions of gender, ethnicity and class. In considering child abuse, however, it is also vital to examine categories based on age, on notions of adulthood/childhood, and to examine how relations between adults and children have been shaped in the past both within families as well as outside of them.

Michel Foucault's identification of different 'technologies' of power that act on the body – in particular the juridical (where power is vested in a sovereign authority enforced through force/fear) and the disciplinary (where power is a relationship that is constantly re-negotiated through discourse) – is helpful in considering the dynamics that lead to abuse.[40] Although Foucault did not himself discuss how power was gendered, these models have been adapted by feminists.[41] The notion of disciplinary power as a complex, strategic and shifting relationship, where both resistance and hegemonic domination are part of the dynamics, allows historians to build up a more complex picture of the interactions between age, gender, class and ethnicity in the formation of social positioning.

Foucault's main aim, however, was to chart the transformation from the dominance of the juridical model to that of the disciplinary model with the emergence of the modern State. Such a mapping has very little relevance at the level of family and neighbourhood (which Foucault ignored) where both models continued to operate together. As Vikki Bell and Shani D'Cruze have argued, physical aggression and its threat remained a central constituent of the power dynamics of interpersonal relations.[42] Material and economic conditions are also important considerations in histories of sexual violence. James Hammerton and Linda Gordon have both chosen to make use of the term 'patriarchy' to describe the gendered system of power/authority prevalent in the nineteenth-century family, in which 'fathers control families and families are the units of social and economic production'.[43] It is important to identify any subtle changes in the structuring of male supremacy and their impact on the treatment of abusers and victims in cases of incest and family violence. Jeff Hearn has argued that 'private patriarchy' was slowly being replaced from the 1850s onwards by what he has called 'public patriarchy', the supremacy of a State dominated by male politicians and public servants which attempted to 'police' the previously private realm of the family.[44] Yet the effects of the shift to an interventionist State policy should not be over-stated. Women's and children's positions of economic dependency, coupled with discursive constructions of family respectability and reputation, meant that they were often powerless to act against violent husbands or fathers.

In examining the relationships of adults and children it is also important to consider the affective: the emotional ties between individuals. Davidoff, Doolittle, Fink and Holden have drawn attention to the concept of intimacy within family and kin – involving the physical and the emotional as well as issues of power and control – as an important area for historical investigation.[45] Histories of child abuse also need to consider the residential provision offered for child victims, first by philanthropic bodies and later by the State. In examining the institution of the children's home, the intimacy of the adult/child relationship remains a point of focus. Londoner Arthur Harding, discussing his experience in a Dr Barnardo's home at the turn of the century, reflected that: 'In smaller homes children could meet with kindness and understanding. In large ones, authority was impersonal and strict discipline, loneliness and even bullying were likely.'[46] In both institutional homes and the family sphere children's experience was, inevitably, diverse. Such a truism leads to a series of complex questions. How did children and adults share social space? How were the different relationships of children and adults negotiated on a daily basis? In what circumstances did the close social proximity of children and adults lead, on the one hand, to affection and, on the other, to abuse? What sort of physical proximity was seen as appropriate for adults and children? Were there different notions of what was appropriate for men than for women? In what sets of circumstances were boundaries crossed? These are all-important questions if attention is focussed on intimacy and the affective nature of interpersonal relationships.

As sociologist Chris Jenks has written, 'all contemporary approaches to the study of childhood are clearly committed to the view that childhood is not a natural phenomenon ... childhood is a social construct'.[47] Who, exactly, is a child, is a philosophical rather than an historical question. The historian's task is to delineate how decisions on this question were reached in the past and how they impacted on the lives of ordinary children. Yet most historians who look at child sexual abuse have to deal with intense personal beliefs that childhood does mean something different from adulthood and that sexual acts between adults and children are wrong. If childhood, the body, sexuality, morality are cultural constructs, what are we to do with our own sense of ethical judgement?

In 1978 Foucault took part in a debate in which he argued that sexual relations between adults and children should not be restricted by the law.[48] He maintained that 'French laws ... relied upon a historically specific notion of childhood which had links with a whole network of disciplinary power/knowledge relations'; the child was denied the right of consent since it 'was never listened to, its desires just presumed'.[49] As Vikki Bell has pointed out, however, Foucault's stance could only be predicated upon his exclusion of gender, race, class and age as vital categories of analysis.[50] We are not all 'equal players' in the pursuit of pleasure. Some individuals do have more power than others, while discourse itself creates dominations based on gender, age and class which are, frequently, backed up by fear. The backlash in academia against the concept of a post-modern hyper-real world devoid of morality and ethical judgement is already well underway. Jeffrey Weeks, for long the exponent of Foucauldian methodology in his work on homosexuality and gay politics, has also argued for the creation of a morality which is alternative to traditional articulations of family values but which restores ethics of responsibility and care for others.[51] Such an approach has never been off the feminist agenda; now, however, and mainly as a response to AIDS, the issue of ethics is being taken seriously by other radical voices in the field of sexual politics.

Richard Evans has suggested that it is the job of the reader rather than the historian to condemn or condone, to make moral judgments.[52] However, as sociologists working on contemporary societies are very aware, there is such a thing as ethical responsibility in research. Researchers, even historians, working on topics of this nature, must treat their subjects with the utmost care and sensitivity. We have a duty to our subjects to 'use them as a source' in a responsible way, to render their accounts with subtlety, to acknowledge the interconnectedness of body, pain, experience, voice. Meanwhile, if discourse is linked to power, and indeed, to the experiences of men, women and children in the social world, feminists and other concerned groups can recognise the importance of creating alternative discourses to those judged morally reprehensible.[53] Studies of sexual abuse also contribute to a broader historiography since they can be used to explore important questions about the meanings of childhood and adulthood and the interplay of family, community, law and the State.

The age of consent

As well as reflecting Victorian debates on childhood and sexuality, statute law effectively brought new groups of 'children' into being as it attempted to re-label, repackage and re-educate. While, historically, rape as a crime was based on the issue of consent or resistance, girls under a certain age were deemed incapable of giving their consent to sexual acts. Ideas of exactly when a girl child became a responsible adult woman moved dramatically but certainly not uniformly in nineteenth-century England. As Anna Davin has pointed out, the age of responsibility/protection was judged differently in statutes referring to guardianship, work, marriage or property ownership.[54] With regard to the age of consent, a girl of 12, considered a mature sexual agent in 1870 was, by 1885, labelled in terms of vulnerability, as unable to defend herself from sexual advances. Age-of-consent legislation was extremely complicated and subject to considerable variation depending on the gender of the victim, the specific charge pursued, and changes over time. A cursory outline of statute law will be followed by a brief analysis of the factors that influenced parliamentary opinion.

The legislation

There was considerable confusion surrounding the age of consent to sexual intercourse for girls although it was, technically, 12 until 1875. The confusion dated back to the reign of Elizabeth I and resulted from distinctions between felony and misdemeanour and between common and statutory law. Under Edward I, forcible rape had been made a felony in 1285 while the act of carnally knowing a female 'within age' (the legal age of marriage, which was 12 according to common law) was considered a misdemeanour.[55] Under Elizabeth, both rape and the carnal knowledge of a girl under the age of 10 were redefined as felonies without benefit of clergy in 1576.[56] Matthew Hale argued that sexual intercourse with females under 12 should, nevertheless, be considered statutory rape and therefore felony.[57] Blackstone, however, took the line that offences involving girls under 10 were felony by Elizabethan law and merely misdemeanours, under common law, if they involved girls aged 10–12.[58] Anthony Simpson has argued that, although the Elizabethan statute aimed to amend rather than replace the medieval law, the notion of a common law age of consent was gradually set aside as a dead letter during the eighteenth century up until 1875.[59] In only one of the Old Bailey cases he has examined was an attempt made to try, as misdemeanour, a case involving a girl in the 10–12 age group. Simpson's argument is not entirely convincing for the nineteenth century. Early Victorian legal experts cited 12 as the legal age of consent, and charges of unlawful carnal knowledge involving girl victims aged 10–12 were tried at the Old Bailey and Assizes throughout the 1840s and 50s.[60] Indeed the Offences Against the Person Acts of 1828 and 1861 stated categorically that the carnal knowledge of females under 10 was a felony and of girls aged 10–12 a misdemeanour, eradicating the distinction between common and statutory law and removing what were undoubtedly grounds for dispute.[61]

As a result of pressures put on parliament by social purity and feminist campaigners to raise the age of consent, carnal knowledge of girls aged 12–13 became a misdemeanour in 1875, and a felony if it involved females under 12.[62] Finally, in 1885, the Criminal Law Amendment Act raised the female age of consent to its present level of 16; carnal knowledge was considered a felony if the girl was under 13 and a misdemeanour if aged 13–16.[63] Thus the distinction between felony and misdemeanour remained. The unwitting discrepancy between common law and statute law after 1576, which distinguished between different age bands of female child, was, during the course of the nineteenth century, formalised, institutionalised and justified on the grounds of moral, physical and mental development. Even today, age-of-consent legislation still accords a different legal status to girls under 13 than to those in the 13–16 category, enshrining in law the belief that the sexual assault of younger children is more serious than that of adolescents and that an abuser should be protected from girls in a transitional age band who might appear to be older than they actually are.[64]

The law was made more complicated by the fact that the age of consent for indecent assault (which could encompass all sexual acts not based on vaginal penetration) gradually moved out of kilter with that for unlawful carnal knowledge. It seems to have been assumed, in the early nineteenth century, that indecent assault of girls or assault with intent to ravish came within the remit of the 1285 and 1576 Acts.[65] The 1861 Offences Against the Person Act clarified the age of consent as 12 for any attempt to have unlawful carnal knowledge and there was some increase at a national level in the prosecution figures for sexual offences against females during the 1860s.[66] Although the 1861 Act did not refer to boys, they were present in legal deliberation. Since sexual acts between men were essentially illegal, prosecuted as sodomy, attempted sodomy, or assault with intent to commit an unnatural offence, to 'consent' meant to be criminally liable.[67] For boys, the age of criminal responsibility – 14 – functioned for much of the century as an age of consent.[68] However, by the Assault of Young Persons Act of 1880, the age of consent to indecent assault for both boys and girls was fixed at 13, some five years after it had been raised to 13 in cases of unlawful carnal knowledge.[69] It was not until 1922 that the age of consent in cases of indecent assault was raised from 13 to 16 for both boys and girls, bringing it in line with the age of consent to full sexual intercourse for girls.[70]

Incest – sexual intercourse between blood relatives – was not made a crime in England and Wales until 1908, although it had been an offence punishable before the church courts until 1857.[71] The 1908 Punishment of Incest Act, whose passage has been widely discussed by historians, outlawed intercourse between siblings, parents and their children, grandparents and grandchildren.

Thus the legislation for prosecuting child sexual abuse was confusing and complicated; the question of which charge was most appropriate varied across time. With regard to girls aged 10–12, for example, the charge of indecent assault tended to replace the charge of assault with intent to ravish from 1880 onwards. Successful prosecution depended on the knowledge and experience of the law of individual magistrates, lawyers and police.

The campaigns

The nineteenth-century changes in age-of-consent legislation have usually been delineated as a response to increasing concerns about juvenile prostitution. As Edward Bristow has shown, a proliferation of societies such as the London Society for the Protection of Young Females, the Rescue Society, and the Reform and Refuge Union came into existence to save and reclaim 'fallen' women.[72] They increasingly turned their attentions to the issue of juvenile prostitution, which they said was common in the big cities. As early as the 1830s rescue societies expressed concerns about what they called a 'white slave trade' which involved the abduction of young country girls who, lured to London with promises of work in domestic service, were then drugged and trapped in brothels.[73] In the 1870s and 1880s these myths were revived, by active feminist and social purity movements concerned with the moral state of the nation, in relation to a perceived European traffic involving the decoying of English girls to Brussels.[74] A succession of parliamentary committees, meeting to consider the problem of containing and regulating prostitution, heard evidence from police, clergy and philanthropists, who spoke of the prevalence of juvenile prostitution at home and abroad.[75] Howard Vincent, director of criminal investigations with the Metropolitan Police, told a House of Lords Select Committee in 1881 that juvenile prostitution was 'rampant' in London so that, at night, in the streets round Haymarket and Piccadilly there were 'children of 14, 15 and 16 years of age, going about openly soliciting prostitution'.[76] In 1882 Anglican purity campaigner Ellice Hopkins told the committee of her work with prostitutes as young as 9.[77]

Social purity groups argued that one of the ways to curb juvenile prostitution was to introduce legislation to raise the age of consent to at least 16. After a string of bills to amend the law failed to pass through parliament in 1857, 1873, 1883 and 1884, the societies concerned with the protection of women and children organised rallies and meetings around the country and sought to develop a new heightened media profile. In July 1885 W. T. Stead, editor of the *Pall Mall Gazette*, who had already used every possible opportunity to promote the campaign in the pages of his newspaper, printed the results of his own private investigation into 'juvenile prostitution' in London in a series of articles entitled 'The maiden tribute of modern Babylon'.[78] The articles included a number of interviews and stories but one tale overshadowed all others: that of 'Lily' (whose real name was Eliza Armstrong), the child of 13 who, Stead claimed, was bought for £5 from her mother. It was this story which led to Stead's arrest, trial and conviction at the Old Bailey in the autumn of 1885 on charges of abduction and indecent assault (which related to a medical examination carried out by a French midwife to check whether the girl was a virgin).[79] This story, too, seems to have captivated the popular imagination, and the increased pressure for new age-of-consent legislation culminated in the successful passage of the 1885 Criminal Law Amendment Act. The campaigning did not end there; the National Vigilance Association, founded in the fervor of August 1885, went on, with other feminist and social purity groups, to continue lobbying parliament to close the loop-holes in the Act, to raise the age of consent further, to outlaw incest and to close remaining brothels.

Certainly the narrative of the juvenile prostitute, which had been repeated many times over the course of the century, played a dominant role in the age-of-consent campaign. It was, as Judith Walkowitz has demonstrated, a gripping but familiar melodramatic story, involving an array of colourful characters: the dissolute mother, the evil procuress, the innocent girl child, and a phantom-like aristocratic client.[80] It is clear, however, if we examine the details of the parliamentary debates and committee reports, that the problem of the sexual assault of children, by fathers, neighbours or employers as well as by strangers, was an issue of concern that was closely related to the issue of 'juvenile prostitution'. Indeed the 'Maiden tribute' articles also contained an emotive description of Stead's visit to the shelter run by the National Society for the Prevention of Cruelty to Children (NSPCC) where he met little girls of 5, 6 and 7, who had been sexually assaulted, one of them by her mother's lodger.[81] Stead went on to use his defence speech at the Old Bailey to list the cases of indecent assault and unlawful carnal knowledge of children which had been tried over the previous month.[82] Walkowitz has argued that the issue of juvenile prostitution was over-exaggerated by campaigners: that most prostitutes were over 16 and that there is very little evidence that younger girls were regularly soliciting.[83] Indeed, judges and magistrates who sat in the London courts could recollect very few occasions where they had dealt with prostitutes under the age of 16.[84] They were, however, extremely concerned about the number of cases which came for trial involving the sexual assault of children, often by fathers or brothers.[85] It is clear that the term 'juvenile prostitution' had become, by the late Victorian period, yet another euphemism – along with those of 'moral outrage', 'corruption' and 'immorality' – to refer to what we now describe as child sexual abuse. The story of the child prostitute was simply the most acceptable articulation of the problem; it was clear who was 'good' and who was 'evil' and it did not open up the moral and emotional can of worms that a narrative of incest would have involved.

The legislature

The blocking of a whole series of criminal law amendment bills in the House of Commons and the reluctance of the Home Office to push legislation must be linked, as Frank Mort has argued, to a desire to maintain the existing double standard without questioning male sexual behaviour.[86] Contrary to the suggestion of subsequent historians, no MP was prepared to admit to using child prostitutes.[87] But many of those who opposed the raising of the age of consent did so on the grounds that it would increase the possibilities of blackmail by girls who were already corrupted, worldly-wise, and able to dress themselves up to appear older. Yet, as Mort has demonstrated, liberal MPs such as James Stuart, who had campaigned for the repeal of the Contagious Diseases Acts, also opposed the criminal law amendment bills because they were concerned that increased police surveillance would be used against the poor.[88] As Mort has suggested, the successful passage of the 1885 Bill must be attributed to the frenzied demonstration of public support for the measure as well as to the increased profile of non-conformist purity MPs, such as Samuel Smith and Henry Wilson, within the Liberal party.[89]

Mort does not discuss at any point, however, how parliamentary debates related to shifting notions of childhood. When the age of consent did become the focus of specific discussion it raised three central questions. When, in sexual terms, did a girl become a woman? What was the difference between girl child and woman? What marked the transformation? Answers were discussed in terms of physical, mental, social and moral development. In 1880 Mr Hastings, stipendiary judge and MP, maintained that the age of consent should be lowered to 10 on the grounds that cases had arisen where girls under 12 were 'sufficiently developed in body to become pregnant'.[90] In 1885 Mr Macartney MP argued that it was the average rather than the extreme which must stand as point of reference. He supported the move to raise the age of consent for a misdemeanour to 16 and for a felony to 13 since 'it was said that the age of puberty was between 13 and 15'.[91] The pubescent girl, by virtue of her body's transitional state (from child to woman), required some protection but not the full arm of the law.

The importance of mental/moral development was also closely elaborated as a separate issue from that of bodily development. There were concerns that 'bad' living conditions led to a precocious mental disposition (not necessarily accompanied by physiological prematurity) amongst girls of the labouring classes and some MPs used this claim to argue for a lower age of consent.[92] Significantly, however, precocity tended to be viewed as 'unnatural' and 'abnormal'. Childhood was identified as, in essence, a state of mental weakness and vulnerability which, given its potential for abuse, required absolute protection. Lord Mount-Temple identified this vulnerability as both a natural state and a cultural product when he argued that:

> In ordinary cases, a girl of 15 was more a child than a woman. Trained to obedience, she found it difficult to say 'no' to those who spoke with the authority of age and station. ... She could not resist the terrible results of the traps and nets set for her more than goldfinches could avoid the nets concealed from their sight.[93]

Like wild birds, the 'ordinary' or 'normal' child, as naturally ingenuous, was unsuspecting prey to her predators; she was, as several MPs described her, an 'innocent'. Education and socialisation had also, however, instilled her with the notions of trust and obedience seen as central to the adult–child relationship. Innocence and ignorance could, therefore, be maintained and, indeed, contrived by controlling the different forms of knowledge available to child and adult. The emergence of child sexual abuse as a burning social issue and its discussion within and without parliament can be seen as a culmination of Victorian desires, social and psychological, to define and contain both childhood and sexuality. It was part of a move to naturalise and normalise the childhood condition amongst all social classes.

Collating data

Trial by jury

For the purposes of this book a total of 1,146 sexual assault cases, tried on indictment before courts in Yorkshire and Middlesex (including metropolitan London), have been collected. The court registers of the Central Criminal Court at the Old Bailey, the Middlesex Quarter Sessions, the County of London Sessions, the Yorkshire Assizes and the West Riding Quarter Sessions were sampled at five-yearly intervals for the years 1830–1910.[94] Historical records have been passed down to us in a piecemeal and haphazard fashion. Some indeed have not stood the tests of time: the records of the North Eastern circuit for the period 1890–1921 were erroneously destroyed by the clerk of the Assize during the Second World War. Furthermore, the questions we now ask of historical sources might not fit with legal or contemporary categories. Cases of child sexual abuse were tried as indecent assault, rape, assault with intent to rape, unlawful carnal knowledge or its attempt, sodomy and its attempt. In some periods the age of the victim is specified in the charge and in others it is not. By gleaning court registers, depositions, indictments, appeal petitions and newspaper reports (both local and national) for information, it was possible to discover that at least 602 of these cases involved child victims (see figures 1.3–1.7).

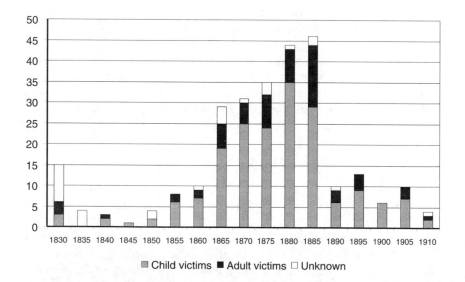

Figure 1.3   Sexual assault cases tried at the Middlesex Sessions, 1830–1910

Sources: (London Metropolitan Archive, MJ/CP/B and MJ/SPE; local and national newspapers)

Note: See figure 1.2 for definition of sexual assault

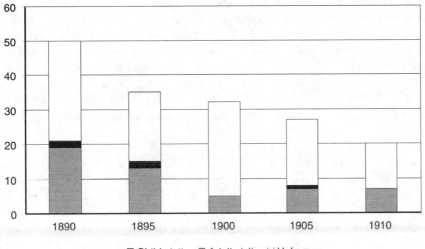

Figure 1.4 Sexual assault cases tried at the London County Sessions, 1890–1910
Sources. (LMA, Acc. 2385 and LJ/SR; local and national newspapers)

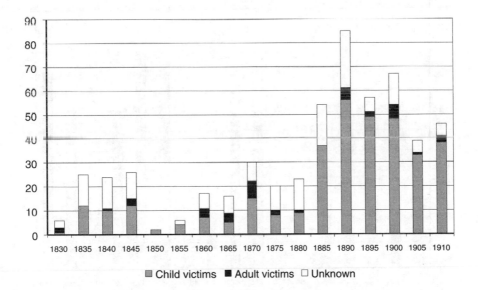

Figure 1.5 Sexual assault cases tried at the Old Bailey, 1830–1910
Sources: (Public Record Office, CRIM 9, CRIM 4 and CRIM 1; local and national newspapers)

An extremely accurate profile of the Middlesex Quarter Sessions cases was compiled as a result of both good survival of court records and substantial press coverage (see figure 1.3).[95] This profile shows that an overwhelming majority of cases of sexual assault – some 67 per cent – definitely involved child victims. In 22 per cent of cases the victim was known to be an adult and in only 11 per cent of cases was it impossible to identify the age of the victim. Similarly, at the Old Bailey, at least 64 per cent of cases involved child victims (see figure 1.5). Figures are less stark in the Yorkshire cases: we know children were victims in at least 46 per cent of sexual assault cases tried at the Yorkshire Assizes and 41 per cent of West Riding Quarter Sessions cases (see figures 1.6 and 1.7). It is clear, therefore, that two-thirds of all metropolitan court trials for sexual assault and possibly half of all Yorkshire trials involved what we would now term the sexual abuse of children under 16.

Anna Clark's study of rape trials on the North Eastern circuit has demonstrated the increased prominence of child victims in the period 1770–1845. She has written:

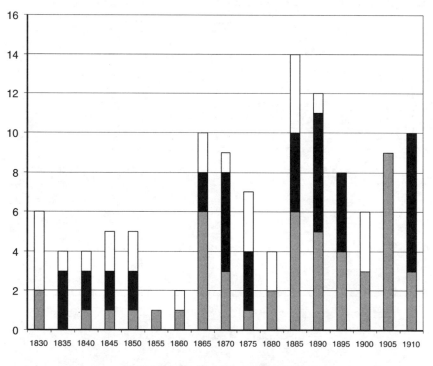

□ Child victims ■ Adult victims □ Unknown

Figure 1.6   Sexual assault cases tried at the West Riding Quarter Sessions, 1830–1910

Sources: (West Yorkshire Archive Service, QS7 and QS1; local and national newspapers)

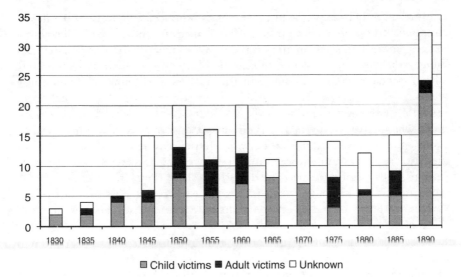

Figure 1.7 Sexual assault cases tried at the Yorkshire Assizes, 1830–1890

Sources: (PRO, HO27/112; local and national newspapers)

While sexual assaults on girls under thirteen accounted for only two per cent of the depositions in the late eighteenth century Assize records, they provide 27 per cent of the depositions from 1800 to 1829, and 30 per cent of the sexual assaults reported in the northern newspapers between 1830 and 1845.[96]

The profile of the metropolitan and Yorkshire courts undertaken for the present survey shows that probably at least half of all cases already involved children in the period 1830–45, rising in the Middlesex and Old Bailey cases to 75 and 70 per cent respectively for the period 1870–1910. The shift from adult to child victims is extremely interesting. Although nineteenth-century commentators ascribed a perceived increase in 'immorality' to children's employment in factories and to overcrowded living conditions, this is, as Clark has observed, an unsatisfactory deduction.[97] Clark, however, holds short of offering an explanation for the shift. It is important to distinguish between reported crime and 'real' crime. The statistics do not necessarily indicate that more children were being abused; they do suggest, however, that these cases were more likely to be prosecuted and tried in the courts.

The processes that brought a case to trial were many and varied, involving a whole range of personnel – victims, parents or prosecutors, police (after 1830), magistrates and grand juries – making it impossible to draw simple conclusions about causation. The shift from adult to child victims can only be explained in terms of a complex set of social and cultural factors. Most significantly, it must be linked to the increased emphasis placed on childhood as an important developmental stage, articulated not merely through the writings of middle-class officials and the reports of parliamentary commissions but also through more popular genres of cheap entertainment such as melodrama. The shift to prosecute child sexual abuse was also, perhaps, a response to the publicity generated by the rescue societies who increasingly turned their attentions to 'juvenile prostitution'. Given that it was usually mothers who first discovered signs of abuse, one can also speculate about women's increasing desire to use the new police to protect their children rather than themselves.

Summary jurisdiction

Because sexual abuse was prosecuted through such an array of different charges, it is important to examine all levels of jurisdiction. Charges of rape or unlawful carnal knowledge were, throughout the period, only triable on indictment at the Assizes or Old Bailey. Indecent assault charges could be tried on indictment at the County Quarter Sessions as well as the Assizes (in London they came before the Middlesex Quarter Sessions until 1890 and, after then, the County of London Sessions). But it is also important to consider the business of the magistrates courts, so often neglected by historians because records have not survived or remain uncatalogued. As soon as a charge was made, the Police Court or Petty Sessions was the first port of call, where magistrates would deliberate as to whether there was a case to answer. Sexual abuse cases might be dismissed at this stage, committed for trial to a higher court, or tried as 'common assault'. Furthermore, as a result of the 1908 Children Act, magistrates were permitted to try cases of indecent assault involving young persons under 16 at a summary hearing.[98] Magistrates were extremely important decision-makers.

Additional surveys have, therefore, been conducted of two Middlesex police courts – Thames Police Court 1885–1910 and Hampstead Petty Sessions 1870–1914 – for periods which are fully documented.[99] Although selection criteria included the survival of good-quality sources, Hampstead and Thames are also useful comparisons because they represent very different demographies and environments. Hampstead was still very much a village in an outlying area of Middlesex throughout the nineteenth century. It is interesting with regard to sexual offences because of the heath, which was used for recreational purposes by Londoners as well as locals, and which, among other parks and open spaces, was cited as a problem area for 'public indecencies'.[100] Thames Police Court, on the other hand, covered the area of the East End that included Whitechapel, Stepney and Limehouse, a densely populated urban district which included slums inhabited by the poorest London residents as well as more affluent working-class households. The Thames Police Court area had its fair share of families who dwelt in one room, living in conditions which moral reformers suggested could only lead to depravity and incest.

Both these surveys show that a large number of child sexual abuse cases referred to magistrates were never committed for trial on indictment even before 1908; instead they were dismissed outright or dealt with as common assault charges. Out of thirty-nine cases of sexual abuse which came before the Hampstead magistrates in the period 1870–1914, only a quarter were committed for trial. Three-quarters were dealt with summarily, 60 per cent of these receiving a conviction for common assault or indecent exposure (usually involving a fine) and 40 per cent having their cases dismissed. The keenness of Hampstead magistrates to deal with cases themselves and to provide some type of salutary deterrent (in the form of conviction for minor offences) must be linked to their desire to 'clean up' the heath. The statistics for Thames Police Court, which dealt with a much greater body of business than Hampstead, are equally provocative. Out of a total of fifty-four cases of sexual assault known to have involved child victims, referred to the court in 1885, 1890, 1895, 1900, 1905 and 1910, a third were discharged without trial, and three were convicted, by magistrates, of common assault. The remaining thirty-three cases were committed for trial at the Old Bailey or Quarter Sessions, twelve of which were either acquitted or dismissed by the grand jury. Overall, therefore, a total of thirty out of the fifty-four cases – 53 per cent – were acquitted or dismissed.

The evidence for Thames Police Court and Hampstead Petty Sessions reveals inconsistencies of practice based on personal opinion and parochial concern. They also provide a worthy warning against placing too great a statistical emphasis on indicted crime. Furthermore, they suggest that most sexual abuse cases were either acquitted or trivialised and convicted as minor public order offences. The inconsistency between the abhorrence of sexual abuse (reflected in age-of-consent campaigns and legislation) and the apparent ease with which defendants were discharged or acquitted needs to be reconciled. Such a task cannot be achieved through the analysis of data alone but, rather, requires a detailed qualitative analysis of the intricacies of individual courtroom hearings. Much of this book will, therefore, be concerned with a close reading of newspaper reports and witness statements or depositions (available for the Middlesex and West Riding Quarter Sessions) in an attempt to understand the wider social and cultural 'knowledges' that influenced courtroom decisions and the treatment of witnesses.

Patterns of settlement

The two regions – Yorkshire (with a particular focus on the West Riding) and Middlesex (including London) – were chosen in order to build up elements of a national picture across a diverse range of settlement types. The industrial conurbation of Leeds, Bradford, Halifax and Huddersfield provided employment in textile mills and then, with their contraction, in clothing manufacture; iron and steel was the basis for industry in Sheffield and Rotherham, and coal provided substantial employment around Barnsley.[101] Yet patterns of settlement were complex within the West Riding. Industrial workers also lived in smaller mill townships or mining villages, surrounded by rural and semi-rural landscapes. Agriculture – hill-farming, dairying, or arable – offered significant employment in many areas. In Middlesex the city and business districts of London provided employment in the service industries connected with commerce, while industrial development was mainly concentrated around the Thames docks.[102] The casual sweated businesses of London's East End offered very different patterns of employment to the mills of the West Riding, although sweating also appeared in the West Riding as tailoring replaced textiles towards the end of the century.[103] During the course of the nineteenth century rural Middlesex was increasingly colonised by the metropolis as a suburban dormitory, but outlying areas remained rural and semi-rural in character even in 1900.

The diversity and complexity of settlement types, their relationship to specific regional patterns of industrial development or contraction, and their fluid and changing configuration in this period of migration and demographic growth makes it very difficult to produce neat, compartmentalised categories for analysis.[104] Dichotomies based on urban/rural, metropolitan/provincial, industrial/commercial are clearly too simplistic for such a task.[105] It is also important to recognise that the number of cases of sexual assault reported remained, on a *per capita* basis, small throughout the period. Even in 1886, when the reporting of rape and indecent assault (against both children and adults) was at its highest level, only four cases were tried nationally per 100,000 people.[106] Indeed, in Cornwall, where population was very sparsely dispersed, fewer than ten cases – and sometimes as few as one or two cases – were tried each year.[107] The level of statistical information that is available is simply not robust enough to support a sustained analysis based on settlement type, local economy and land-use; I shall therefore focus on changes over time, seeking to identify elements of similarity across regions.

Definitions

Any age of consent or attempt to fix an age on childhood is of course an artificial categorisation although it might, for many reasons, be a necessary one. Children are individuals who grow and develop into adults; there is no one obvious moment when the transformation is effected. In writing about 'children' and searching for them in court records, I am referring to those whom the Victorians and Edwardians came to define as children as a result of the 1885 Criminal Law Amendment Act: those under the age of 16. It has been necessary, too, to adopt the Victorian term 'victim' to refer to those who experienced abuse although the term 'survivor' is utilised as a form of resistance and empowerment in contemporary rehabilitation strategies.[108] Since the concept of 'survivor' is linked to processes of self-definition and identification, its application would be problematic in a historical context. The term 'victim' is adopted because it was used historically, because it had a specific legal meaning in court, and for want of a satisfactory alternative. It is important, nevertheless, to consider its loaded and nuanced meanings, which served to construct women and children as vulnerable dependants in need of protection.

Since its rediscovery in the late 1970s, social workers and care agencies have attempted to produce working definitions of the elements that constitute child sexual abuse. The NSPCC, for example, has defined sexual abuse as: 'the involvement of children in sexual activities they do not fully comprehend, to which they are unable to give informed consent, or which violate the social taboos of family life or are against the law'.[109] The search for a definition of sexual abuse is, however, something of a red herring in a historical study. Rather than starting with an underlying and absolute notion of what is and what is not abuse, I shall examine how sexual abuse was constituted historically, focusing on those acts that were described as indecent, illegal, corrupting or abusive by Victorians. Carolyn Conley has suggested that there were no clear established guidelines in the nineteenth century as to when, exactly, an act became indecent. She has quoted the words of Justice William Brett, who remarked to one jury that 'I cannot lay down the law as to what is or is not indecent beyond saying that it is what all right-minded men, men of sound and wholesome feelings would say was indecent.'[110] To some extent we have moved no nearer to an all-encompassing definition than Brett; the labelling of an act as abuse and the evaluation of consent are still, arguably, subjective practices.

The hidden figure

The very nature of sexual violence makes the gathering of source material extremely difficult. We are frequently told that rape and sexual abuse are the most under-reported of crimes.[111] Statistics for present-day western societies show that most sexual violence is committed by someone close to its victim – by a friend, carer or relative. It is so often secret because it takes place behind closed doors.[112] The secret may be kept a whole lifetime and it may be blocked from memory. Historians trying to uncover this secret find fragments of events and experiences but the whole picture will always evade us. While social workers and sociologists have attempted to use detailed survey and interview work to predict figures for the amount of sexual violence in existing societies, we cannot even begin to guess about historical figures. As Carol Ann Hooper has pointed out, citing the work of David Finkelhor and Diana Russell, even oral history projects which give researchers the chance to put their questions directly to their subjects are problematic in this context.[113] Russell has suggested that incestuous abuse, as opposed to abuse outside the family, increased in the period 1916–1960; Finkelhor argued there was no consistent trend over time.[114] Both, perhaps unsurprisingly, have detected a marked drop during the First and Second World Wars and a sharp rise immediately after. As a whole, however, the reliability of oral interviews is questionable. What sort of memories are we tapping into and how have they been altered or shaped over time? Are a younger generation, who have been brought up in the midst of international awareness and sometimes hysteria about sex abuse, more likely to categorise experiences as such?

When it comes to examining history before the 1920s, the task is even harder. There are, of course, few people to ask. Sources are at best random, at worst non-existent. Court records provide an extremely useful body of material; unfortunately, by their very nature, they can only tell us about those cases of rape and abuse that led to criminal proceedings. Rare documentation does however exist of cases that were never reported to the police, preserved in the records of philanthropic societies and welfare organisations. This book also examines, therefore, the records of children's homes run by the Church of England Waifs and Strays Society, the Salvation Army, and the Jewish Association for the Protection of Women and Children, enabling us to follow the paths of those children who were placed in institutional care whether or not they were involved in court proceedings.

Content and overview

The book is structured in relation to the different stages involved in the legal process, beginning with the detection of abuse and the making of a charge, moving on to the giving of evidence in court, and culminating with verdict, the sentencing of defendants and the issue of child custody. From the point of view of the child, this framework relates, too, to personal chronology and life-cycle: the experience of abuse, the retelling of that experience in court, the possible removal of the child from parental home to institution, and, finally, retraining (moral, spiritual and industrial) for employment on reaching the age of 16.

Chapter 2 demonstrates the existence of a common set of codes, meanings and understandings surrounding the disclosure and treatment of the sexual abuse of children in working-class neighbourhoods. Chapter 3 examines the work of the welfare societies and organisations that were involved in rescuing children and prosecuting cases of sexual abuse in the courts, stressing the dominance of the social purity paradigm. Chapters 4 and 5 examine two controversial forms of evidence that were nevertheless vital in court proceedings: the testimony of medical experts and of child witnesses.

Chapter 5, which focuses on the problematic moral status of the child witness, also intersects with chapter 6, which examines the gendered discourses that positioned the male defendant. The decisions of judge and jury involved a weighing up of the perceived character and status of each, victim and alleged abuser, which was closely connected to notions of gender, class and sometimes to ethnicity and religion. Finally, chapter 7 examines the children's homes which emerged to take 'fallen' girl children, uncovering the systems of rehabilitation and training which dominated institutional daily life. Once again, the moral status of the sexually abused child was seen as dubious, necessitating her separation from 'normal' children. This chapter will examine the opinions and motives of welfare workers as well as the experiences of their child clients.

The trajectory is also a circular one since, from the 'Homes' of chapter 7, the girls returned to the 'homes' or families of chapter 2 (whether they were sent back to their parents or themselves later became parents). These chapters are also closely related since they discuss a level of social interaction – the intimate daily relationships of child and carer/parent – that is very different from the impersonal detachment of the 'expert' judge, doctor, or policy-maker for whom the child was a case to be solved. It is important to acknowledge that differences of perception are related to degrees of personal intimacy. Historians tend to disregard the significance of affective relationships, those ties that cannot be interpreted purely in terms of power. The 'fallen' or 'corrupted' child of official publications, welfare policies and courtroom discourse was still, to those who knew her intimately, a unique and special individual.

2 Family, neighbourhood and police

Introduction

In March 1895 Yorkshire labourer James Wright appeared before Harrogate magistrates as a key witness in a case involving the indecent assault of his 9-year-old niece. He described how he had gone to visit his married sister, Maria, one morning at her home in the town. The door was closed but, as he pushed it open, he thought he heard a child's voice shouting 'be quiet ... or I shall tell my mammie'.[1] His niece, Polly, was lying on the floor in a state of disarray; a young man, who worked as a local errand boy, was moving quickly away from her. Maria was nowhere in sight. Wright told magistrates: 'I picked him up, gave him three cuffs across the face & twice hit him with the broad of my foot. I then took him to my mother's, where my sister was washing. My sister told me to fetch the police.'[2] James Wright's story tells us about the daily routine of a close-knit working family, about its disruption through the discovery of abuse, and about the responses of family members. Wright's immediate reaction was one of aggression and violent retribution, while his sister turned to the official mechanism of the law. Witness statements such as this, recorded in court depositions when cases were committed for trial, make it possible to examine the attitudes of working-class families and neighbours. How did labouring communities view the abuse of their children? How did they deal with it? What role did they envisage for the police force and for official modes of punishment? In what circumstances were incidents most likely to be reported to the police?

While there has been considerable discussion of the ways in which the sexual mistreatment of children was constituted as a social problem by the middle-class élite, very little attention has been given to popular and working-class views. Judith Walkowitz has focused on the newspaper exposé of juvenile prostitution which editor W. T. Stead published in the *Pall Mall Gazette* in July 1885 as part of the campaign to raise the age of consent from 13 to 16.[3] Couched in the language of melodrama, Stead depicted the vices of a corrupt aristocracy as a threat to the people, uniting working and middle classes in a shared defence of morality and respectability. Other historians have drawn attention to official reports and middle-class social commentaries that emphasised the immorality of the poor rather than the rich.[4] During the 1830s and 1840s government inspectors produced descriptions of mills and factories as 'seminaries of vice' and described the 'promiscuous crowding of the sexes' in agricultural areas.[5] These concerns were revisited in official and philanthropic texts of the 1880s as a way of articulating renewed fears of social disorder.[6] In 1883 the Rev. Andrew Mearns published the results of his own private investigations into the state of the poor in London.[7] He identified 'incest' as 'common' on account of the crowded living and sleeping arrangements that resulted when families inhabited one room.[8] Similarly, Lord Shaftesbury told the 1885 Royal Commission on the Housing of the Working Classes that 'the effect of the one-room system is physically and morally beyond all description ... it is totally destructive of all benefit from education'.[9] There has been a tendency, within certain histories of child abuse, to take the accounts of inspectors and reformers at face value, to assume that the nineteenth century working classes *were* immoral. In an influential 1978 essay which is still frequently cited, Anthony Wohl argued that 'there is much that we can learn from the upper and middle-class responses'; he concluded that incest was indeed common amongst the urban poor because reports said so.[10] Such an account is deeply problematic. Middle-class representations of the labouring classes should not be confused with the experiences of the poor themselves.

The court depositions prepared for the Middlesex and West Riding Sessions show that working people did not turn a blind eye to the abuse of their children as Mearns and Shaftesbury suggested. On the other hand, Stead's myth of the aristocratic impostor, who seduced the daughters of the poor, had very little factual basis. The majority of abuse cases involved complainants and defendants of similar social rank: working class and petite bourgeoisie. As historians of crime continually point out, depositions are complex documents with no clear authorial voice.[11] Each witness testimony was shaped by the questions of police officers, lawyers and judges. The courts required the production of a narrative that was structured and coded in a certain pre-ordained mould, which used very different language patterns to those of everyday speech. The story that James Wright told in court might have been very different from the one he told at home or in the public house. Yet it contains intense feelings and emotions as well as very particular details about himself and his family. Wright's own investment and involvement in the account cannot be overlooked.

The statistics for England and Wales show a series of banded increases in the number of cases of rape, unlawful carnal knowledge and sexual assault of females (the majority involving child victims) which were sent for trial by jury during the course of the nineteenth century (see figure 2.1). From the low plateau of the 1830s, national prosecution levels rose slightly in the 1840s, increased once again in the 1860s, suddenly peaked in 1885 and declined gradually in subsequent years (see also figure 1.2). The meaning of these statistics is far from obvious. Were more offences being committed?

Were more offences being reported to the police? Were the police more likely to act on complaints? Were magistrates more likely to send cases for trial by jury instead of settling them at petty sessions level? It is significant that the shifts in prosecution level appear to have occurred in conjunction with changes in statute law. The repeal of the death penalty for rape and unlawful carnal knowledge in 1841 seems to have inaugurated the first increase. The second can be linked to the 1861 Offences against the Person Act, which clarified previous age-of-consent legislation (although the effects of this Act were not obvious in Yorkshire, suggesting that in some areas the common law age of consent had always been upheld). Finally, the 1885 peak can be tied to the much-publicised raising of the age of consent from 13 to 16 in August of that year. It can be assumed that the prosecution figures do not, therefore, represent any increase in actual crime. The answer lies in shifts in attitudes, responses and behaviour patterns of prosecutors, police and magistrates respectively. These shifts are far from quantifiable and can only be analysed through a close reading of newspaper reports and witness statements.

Depositions can provide a useful indication of the way in which responses and experiences were commonly articulated. They will be used here to draw

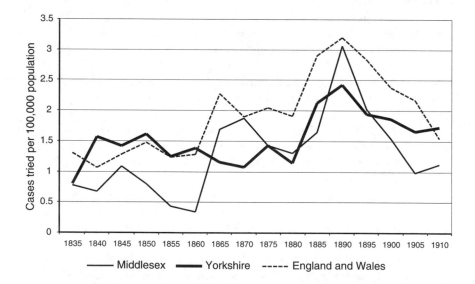

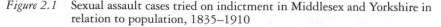

Figure 2.1   Sexual assault cases tried on indictment in Middlesex and Yorkshire in relation to population, 1835–1910

Sources: (Parliamentary Papers, annual judicial statistics, 1835–1910; Mitchell, *British historical statistics*)

Note: See figure 1.2 for definition of sexual assault

attention to strong elements of continuity over time, suggesting that reactions like those of James and Maria were common throughout the nineteenth century. A whole range of both formal and unofficial strategies for dealing with sexual abuse existed within working-class areas long before either the founding of the NSPCC in 1884 or the moral panic over the abuse of girl children that reached a crescendo in 1885. The number of cases which were tried in court was low even in 1885. Although changes in the law and systems of policing meant that official sanctions were more likely to be used as the century progressed, older informal practices continued to be deployed throughout the period.

This chapter will also argue that, throughout the Victorian and Edwardian period, the law was most likely to be invoked in allegations involving abuse outside the nexus of the nuclear family: by strangers, employers, lodgers or neighbours. Cases involving incestuous abuse were much more likely to remain secret or, if they were revealed, to be dealt with through unofficial community sanctions. The articulation and interpretation of abuse as well as the factors that affected strategical choices will be examined in relation to the structures and socio-cultural identities of both neighbourhood and family.

The terms 'neighbourhood' and 'community' are notoriously problematic, so embedded as they are in a nostalgic sentimentality for something which is now lost.[12] It is important not to use them indiscriminately, but it is practically impossible to discuss the social/cultural/spatial networks of nineteenth-century working people without making reference to these terms. The term 'neighbourhood' will be used here to refer to geographically defined areas of 'neighbours', including relatives, who lived in close spatial and social proximity, often in the same or an adjacent street, who used common facilities (shops, public houses or places of worship) and who provided practical support for each other on a daily basis.[13] The term 'community' will refer to the presence of a further set of identifications – the sharing of values and beliefs – and the way in which individuals interacted to support and protect these systems.[14] The term 'police' (as used in the chapter title) refers not only to official police constables but to other informal systems of social and moral regulation within communities.

Finally, it is important to stress that regional and local diversity, resulting from different patterns of settlement, working practices, customs and traditions must be taken into account. The aim of this chapter is not to homogenise working-class reactions and strategies but, rather, to make some general points of comparison whilst allowing for the complexity of regional variation. An examination of the collective responses that were evinced in cases of extra-familial abuse will lead on to an analysis of difference and specificity in cases of incest.

Collective responses

Whether witness statements record what was really said, what witnesses would like to have thought they said, or a toned-down version avoiding profanity, they do, nevertheless provide some general indication of popular attitudes and beliefs. When parents and other adult witnesses confronted abusers they articulated their sense of shock and horror through a shared vocabulary: 'you contaminating villain' (1840), 'a bad wicked man' (1865); 'nasty scoundrel' (1865); 'you dirty beast' (1870); 'dirty old man' (1875); 'old beast' (1882); 'What a wicked thing for an old wretch like you to do to a baby' (1880); 'You beastly man' (1880); 'dirty devil' (1895) 'dirty pig' (1900); 'dirty goat' (1910).[15] Others used extreme threats: '[I] said to him if that child had been mine I would have killed him' (1830); 'You vagabond, I'll kill you' (1870).[16] As Mary Douglas has pointed out in her anthropological study *Purity and danger*, concepts of dirt and contamination act symbolically to define social and moral boundaries.[17] The insults of witnesses reinforced the existence of a *cordon sanitaire*, which positioned abusers as an abject group and expelled them from the otherwise respectable and civilised community. Just as W. T. Stead was to describe the child abuser as a monster or minotaur stalking London, so too witnesses labelled those who molested their children as beasts or hybrids. As unclean, bestial, evil and villainous, abusers were defined as inhuman and unnatural, outside of the norms of civilised society.

Douglas has also suggested that notions of dirt and pollution help to iron out ambiguities: 'ideas about separating, purifying, demarcating and punishing transgressions have as their main function to impose system on an inherently untidy experience'.[18] The notion of the abuser as 'dirty beast' detracted from the possibility that he might be, after all, just a man, somebody's father or uncle or son. The language of pollution and bestiality drew attention away from the family as a site of sexual danger by positioning the abuser safely outside of the social circle.

The insults used by witnesses also made reference to the language of melodrama in their typecasting of the abuser as an evil or wicked villain seducing innocent and vulnerable children. Martha Vicinus has made a very similar point to Douglas in her analysis of the psychological and emotional impact of the 'melodramatic fix':[19]

> Melodrama places the most profound problems in a moral context and thereby makes them manageable ... the good is made visible in the passive suffering of virtuous characters, while evil is embodied in the villain, who is constructed as an amalgamation of lust, violence and avarice.[20]

This ruse is particularly obvious in the response 'what a wicked thing for an old wretch ... to do to a baby' (the baby being, in fact, a 9-year-old).[21] The power of this statement is dependent on the juxtaposition of the corruption of age and the innocence and powerlessness of extreme youth. As Vicinus has pointed out, this process of stereotyping means the blame can be fixed firmly on the individual: 'the villain, with his insatiable desires, is cordoned off and treated as an aberration'.[22] The abuser was defined in opposition to the norms of working-class masculinity. Indeed, his deviance was seen as a negation of his gender; he was beast rather than man. The suggestion that there was a beast in *every* man only emerged in feminist rhetoric at the end of the nineteenth century as a subversion of melodrama.[23] Thus the language of insult cited in the depositions indicates the presence of a strong moral code, of strategies of surveillance and regulation. Sexual abuse was seen as brutal outrage but, at the same time, removed from the intimate sphere of the familial.

Parents, relations and neighbours were vital figures in the discovery and reporting of abuse and in the catching of offenders. As Ellen Ross has demonstrated in her study of late nineteenth-century London, it was mothers who were responsible for family survival and subsistence.[24] As well as the central duty of providing food for the family, mothers' domestic work also included sewing, cleaning and nursing the bodies of their husbands or children when sick.[25] Brought into intimate physical contact with their children as they cared for them on a daily basis, mothers were the first to notice tell-tale signs of abuse such as marks on the body or stains on linen. A Halifax mother told magistrates in 1850: 'Before she went to bed I had her stockings off to mend. I observed the top of one of them had blood on it – When she had taken her chemise off it was covered with blood. I asked her what it meant.'[26] When children came home with sweets, money or other gifts suspicions would also be alerted: 'She came in with a halfpenny and a bit of glass and chalk. The child was crying and she made a communication to me.'[27] Mothers then proceeded to examine their children's bodies for injuries, inflammation or venereal disease, sometimes calling female neighbours to assist.

Angry mothers often went in pursuit of assailants, confronting and challenging them with verbal insults, violence and the threat of the police:

> I went to ... [his] house, saw him and asked him how dare he take such a liberty with my child and he said 'You cow, I'll serve you the same' and I struck him and he hit me back and I hit him several times and I may have scratched his face. After that ... my husband met a policeman and told him.[28]

Because the detective role of the police was slow to develop, the onus was on the prosecution to track down and catch offenders for much of the century.[29] Fathers were more likely to become involved in these later stages. Complaints were lodged with magistrates or parish constables in the earlier decades of the nineteenth century and, with the gradual development of the new police forces, at a police station or office.[30]

Witnesses at the Quarter Sessions somewhat inevitably told a story of recourse to the law as the obvious strategy for dealing with abuse. A 10-year-old girl, who was assaulted on a highway to the south of Huddersfield in 1865, screamed at her attacker: 'I called out I should tell the police.'[31] In 1905 an Enfield father, who had gone with his daughter to search for her assailant, told magistrates how the man started to 'whimper and cry' when he took him into custody.[32] The arrested man begged him to resolve the dispute informally but the father refused: 'He said "I did it sir, I'll never do it again, give me a good hiding and let me go"; I said "oh no" and I took him to the station and charged him.'[33] Witnesses like this father revealed clear views about the role of law and punishment, which were probably conceived in terms of protection as well as retribution.

In melodramatic fiction, justice is always guaranteed and good triumphs over evil in a simple resolution of conflict. However, witnesses seem to have put rather more faith in the law's ability to lock people up than was actually merited. There are rare reports of the after-trial comments of witnesses who displayed acute disappointment at verdict and sentencing. Such was the experience of a 'gipsy' and his wife who, asleep one summer night in a van parked in fields between Kilburn and Edgware, were roused by a child's screams.[34] Outside, a man was threatening a girl at knifepoint and tearing at her underclothes. The gipsy fought the man and chased him away, informing the police the next day. At Hampstead Petty Sessions, the judge sentenced the man to six months' imprisonment for aggravated assault, commending his interceptors for their actions. The gipsy thanked the Bench 'but said he did not think the prisoner had got what he deserved. He should have liked to see him get ten years'.[35]

The gipsy's actions demonstrate another important point: the existence of a notion of collective responsibility towards children. In addition to mothers, court depositions show that grandmothers, aunts, cousins, and an extended network of female friends played an important role in the detection of sex abuse cases. In this 1880 case, a widow lodging in a house in St Pancras described how concern for her landlady's daughter led to discovery of assault:

> I came downstairs and heard the little girl crying, the prisoner was in the kitchen and the girl was standing crying on the sofa, I asked her what was the matter, but she could not answer, she seemed very agitated and frightened. He did not say anything. I went upstairs to another lodger and we called the child upstairs and asked her what she was crying for and she then made a complaint against [the] prisoner.[36]

As Ross has demonstrated, childcare was a collective practice in working-class areas, with neighbours functioning as auxiliary parents.[37] Within a neighbourhood women kept a close eye on each others' children, particularly when mothers were known to be out at work.

The sense of collective responsibility towards children was not just evidenced in self-defined neighbourhoods. Court narratives tell frequent stories of strangers stepping in to challenge men found abusing children in public spaces. In 1890 the butler and gardener of Cusworth Hall near Doncaster told the magistrates that they had heard a child's cries when they were returning home one Saturday afternoon.[38] They saw a man abusing an 8-year-old boy beneath the bridge and they set a trap for him, moving either side of the arch to block both ways of escape. They proceeded to secure the man and hand him over to the police. In another Yorkshire case two labouring men spotted a man who had decoyed some children into the woods, chasing after him until he jumped into a canal.[39] He stayed in the water for a full ten minutes and was arrested and taken to the police station when he finally emerged. Passers-by, both male and female, intervened to help children assaulted in public places, whether they knew them or not, and sometimes large groups were involved. One defendant was pursued by what the local press described as a 'crowd of enraged people', who chased him into a house which they proceeded to search from top to bottom, eventually discovering him hunched up in a corner of the loft.[40] Court depositions, therefore, reveal a wider sense of responsibility for the protection of children. The sexual assault of children was viewed, in terms of popular morality, as extremely serious and in the cases sampled, as a matter for the law.

Patterns of prosecution

The evidence provided by the qualitative source material on the one hand and quantitative data on the other seems to be highly contradictory. There appears to be an enormous discordance between the absolute condemnation of child sexual abuse revealed in the depositions and the extremely small incidence of cases tried. Even in 1886, when 1,091 cases of rape, sexual assault and unlawful carnal knowledge were tried in English and Welsh courts, this still only represented four cases for every 100,000 of the population.[41] This figure is diminutive compared to recent estimates that up to a half of all women experience abuse at some point in their lives.[42] Historians of crime are aware of the looming shadow of the 'dark figure' which signifies all those cases which were never reported to official bodies.[43] Given that modern sociologists and social workers have suggested that the vast majority of sexual abuse cases remain secret, the incidents reported to the police and indeed tried in the nineteenth century must have been a very small tip of a very large iceberg.[44] How does this affect the conclusions that can be reached? To what extent did working people really trust the courts or the police? If there was a popular culture which articulated outrage at the brutality of abuse, why were prosecutions so few and far between? These questions will be pursued by considering, firstly, the relationships of neighbourhood, police and magistracy and, secondly, the types of offences that were most likely to be prosecuted.

Community and law

Robert Storch and David Philips have argued that the new police was viewed with hostility by working-class communities in the industrial north and west midlands, who resented attempts to survey and eradicate traditional sports and recreations.[45] Storch has depicted the police as an official agency attempting to impose the values of the middle-class élite on working people. In his memoirs of Salford slum life at the turn of the nineteenth century Robert Roberts described the attitude of the poor towards the police as one of 'fear and dislike'.[46] Working men and women continually came into conflict with the law and police over strikes, riots and demonstrations. In London mounted police and life-guards brutally lashed into a crowd of unemployed labourers demonstrating in Trafalgar Square on 'bloody Sunday', 13 November 1887.[47] Durham mining villages were notorious for assaults on police as a result of hostilities engendered during industrial disputes.[48] There were undoubtedly urban 'ghetto' areas – such as 'The Nichol' in London's East End – which outsiders, including the police, were reluctant to enter.[49]

Yet, as Jennifer Davis and Carolyn Conley have demonstrated, law and police were not always seen as a threatening mechanism of élite control; they could also be used by working people to retain and enforce the moral codes and values of their own community.[50] As Davis has written, in her study of Jennings' Building, a west London rookery: 'it was possible for the same individual to use the law to prosecute wrong doing but also to experience the intervention of the law as oppressive'.[51] Prosecution was a possible strategy when other methods of solving disputes proved unsatisfactory. The relationship between police and working people was a complex and ambiguous one with a great deal of regional and temporal variation; experiences differed from neighbourhood to neighbourhood, street to street and even on a day-to-day basis.[52] It is clear, however, that the vast majority of court business was brought by working people – whether gipsies, slum dwellers or 'respectable' and well-to-do elements – and that they used the courts with confidence to settle disputes about property or the person. Hence, a wide variety of settlement types are represented in the depositions and newspaper reports sampled for the present study. The West Riding courts were used by residents of mining villages and mill towns, of urban Leeds and Bradford, and of the rural districts to the north of Leeds itself. In Middlesex, cases of sexual abuse were reported from rural areas of the county as well as from metropolitan London and the mushrooming suburbs. For the metropolis itself, the list of the addresses given by victims can be checked with the colour-coded maps of London produced by Charles Booth in 1889 to demonstrate that all categories of working people from the 'well-to-do' to those described as 'vicious and semi-criminal' turned to the courts to seek redress.[53]

It is worth examining the details of a London case, tried by the Lord Mayor at Mansion House Petty Sessions in 1865 and reported at length in *The Times*, as a demonstration of the social diversity of those using the courts to police moral offenders. On 21 June 1865 9-year-old Caroline Hawkins went missing after setting off for school from her father's grocer's shop in a 'respectable' street in the city of London.[54] Her parents were unable to trace her until the following Sunday when she was found as a patient in the London Hospital. Subsequent investigations revealed that she had been decoyed and abducted by William Hubbard, described as a labourer, who had forced her to wander the streets all week. At night they slept in lodging-houses, Caroline sharing a bed with the landlady's little girl. On the Saturday night, however, Hubbard took her to another lodging house in Flower and Dean Street, Whitechapel, where he allegedly asked the Irishwoman in charge for a double bed. The woman said she had refused, told the man the child must sleep with one of the female servants, and asked him 'if he was not ashamed of himself'.[55] The matter did not end there since 'some of the lodgers, indignant at the prisoner bringing the child there, set upon him and struck him, upon which he ran out of the house leaving the child behind'.[56] They took the child to the hospital because she seemed ill and stupefied and summoned the police, who arrested the man in a crowd.

These then were the reponses of dwellers in a common lodging house, the type of people whom journalist Henry Mayhew had identified in 1849 as 'licentious' and 'promiscuous' in their practice of vice.[57] The notorious Flower and Dean Street was later coloured black on Booth's maps to represent the terrain of the 'vicious and semi-criminal'.[58] According to Booth's report 'the evil character of the black streets is ... to be seen on the faces of the people – men, women and children are all stamped with it'.[59] Yet this newspaper story presents a very different picture of the character of lodging-house dwellers, of men and women with their own established moral codes and very clear ideas of what was right and wrong. There might not have been a bed for everyone but there were guidelines as to what was an appropriate arrangement for sharing. This story, like many others, shatters the image of the poor as immoral and depraved. It also demonstrates a range of strategies for dealing with abuse: the preventative and prohibitory actions of the landlady, the aggressive response of the lodgers who laid into him physically, the attempt to aid the child, and, finally, the move to call the police and assist with the arrest.

Like James Wright's narrative, with which the chapter began, this story had a number of possible endings which could have stemmed from any one of those strategies. Although prosecution was one option, depositions and newspaper reports provide firm evidence that cases could also be resolved through preventive interceptions, inter-personal and community violence, or financial settlement. Frequent references to 'a good hiding', to buy-off attempts, and to mothers keeping their children away from suspected men, suggest that these were widely used alternatives.[60] Davis has written 'although the working-classes brought a significant number of criminal prosecutions ... to a large extent their conflicts continued to be resolved ... informally in their neighbourhood'.[61] It was possible for communities to treat abuse as serious without dragging cases through the courts.

Robert Storch has suggested that the history of the nineteenth-century police and magistracy has to be understood in terms of a clamp-down on the communal practices of the working classes.[62] Aspects of such a clamp-down are, indeed, revealed in the sexual abuse depositions sampled for this study. Magistrates and judges were clearly changing their opinions about the role of unofficial mechanisms in resolving disputes as the nineteenth century progressed. While condoning and even encouraging community sanctions in the earlier part of the century, out-of-court settlement in criminal cases was increasingly associated with lawlessness. This can be demonstrated by examining the transformation in attitude in cases involving firstly community violence and, secondly, financial settlement.

Community violence

At Bow Street Police Court in September 1830 a shoemaker was acquitted of enticing girl children into the vaults beneath the Adelphi Theatre with the intent of abusing them. The magistrate said there was insufficient evidence to convict but he went on to tell the court: 'If I were the father ... and had a good horsewhip in my hand, I know where I should apply it.'[63] The shoemaker was left to the 'rough justice' of the mob that had gathered outside the courtroom:

> The hint of the magistrate was not given in vain, for the fellow no sooner escaped from the office, than he was met by a posse of women, who began to hoot and pelt him, and a sturdy coal-heaver tripping up his heels rolled him for several yards in the kennel, to the no small delight of the bystanders. Covered with mud and filth, he retreated in the direction of Holborn where his pursuers gave up the chase, fully satisfied with the speed and the substantial justice which had overtaken the old sinner.[64]

The mob continued to voice its opinion, through verbal and physical violence, as the century progressed, but police and prison guards were more likely to act in a protective capacity towards the prisoner. In May 1870 a crowd gathered outside Marylebone Police Court to voice their condemnation of a defendant accused of raping a 4-year-old girl: 'the mob surrounded him, and gave him some rough handling. Had he not been well guarded by the police he would have been lynched'.[65] The authorities increasingly saw the mob as an hysterical and violent monster rather than a vehicle for community justice. The extension of the jurisdiction and authority of police forces in the decades after 1830 must be seen as an attempt to replace community violence/justice with officially sanctioned controls.

Financial settlement

Clive Emsley has pointed to the continuation within the nineteenth century of a legitimate eighteenth-century practice, sometimes involving magistrates, whereby a financial payment could be made by an assailant to a victim in a case of assault but not theft.[66] It is also possible that the offering of payments in sexual assault cases was a reference to another very different tradition: the long-established conception of working-class women's bodies as property or commodity which could be bought or bartered for.[67] In some areas the practice of settling sexual assault cases through financial payment was still accepted by the courts at mid-century. In December 1860, for example, a mill overlooker was charged with the rape of one of his female workers, aged 14, in the township of Austonley near Doncaster. When the case was tried at the Yorkshire Assizes, the defence lawyer argued that no offence had been committed because the girl and her mother had accepted payment.[68] It was assumed that consent could be given retrospectively:

> Mr Maule contended that however immoral the conduct of the prisoner might have been, he could not be convicted of a charge of this description, and that the sum of £1 (which the mother said she received as a recompense for the loss of time of her daughter) was really paid as a compromise, it being understood that nothing further was to be said about the matter.[69]

The judge permitted this defence and the jury acquitted the prisoner.

Increasingly, however, attempts to settle a case financially were viewed as both illegal and as a declaration of guilt on the part of the defence. In 1875 a member of Hammersmith Board of Works who was 'well known in the district' tried to offer money to a young servant girl who claimed he had molested her.[70] Defence counsel was hard pushed to convince the magistrate that 'the offer to compromise the case was not done in consequence of any admission that Mr [Fletcher] had assaulted the girl, but for the purpose of avoiding publicity'.[71] In a Yorkshire case of 1885 a Rotherham mother was pressurised into continuing with the prosecution although she clearly preferred to settle the matter privately:

> [He] said 'I am very sorry and I hope you will not appear against me —
> It will leave me a lesson I shall not easily forget'. He paid me four
> shillings then and another sixpence afterwards for the cost of the

summons. I should not have proceeded with the case but the magistrates did not approve of me settling it.[72]

Thus unofficial modes of solving disputes were increasingly discouraged and discounted by police and magistrates and this may have been a factor leading to an increase in litigation for sexual abuse as the century progressed.

Community and 'respectability'

It would be misleading to view the very gradual shift from community justice to prosecution as uncontested, non-negotiated or unwanted by labouring people. Changes in strategies of policing were not simply imposed from above, whatever the aims and ambitions of officials. Ordinary people continued to play an active and participatory role in catching and challenging sex offenders but they did, increasingly, see the law as an appropriate final resolution. This could be interpreted as a result of the breakdown of community following the migration and dislocation associated with industrialisation. The evidence examined here, however, suggests a strong element of collective and community-based action in sexual abuse cases which ended up in court. It seems that, despite aspects of conflict, there was sufficient similarity between the articulation of moral codes in working-class neighbourhoods and attempts by the authorities to clamp down on moral offences.

The development of this shared ground and, therefore, any increase in prosecutions from the mid-century onwards can be linked to a remodelling of working-class masculinity. Anna Clark has described the development of radical and Chartist rhetoric that portrayed the working man as a morally upright, respectable and responsible breadwinner who supported and protected his wife and children.[73] She has argued that this new philosophy of masculinity had begun to break down previous notions of libertine manliness by the 1840s. John Benson has, similarly, pointed to the cultural transformation of mining villages during the course of the nineteenth century: chapel, temperance society and the reading room of the miners' institute provided strong competition for the public house.[74] Elements of the working classes shared with the petite bourgeoisie a claim to the culture of respectability and even, on occasion, competed for it. Wife-beating and child abuse obviously did not tally with the notion of respectable working-class manliness and men sought to recast themselves as the protectors of their wives and children. Yet this notion of 'respectable masculinity' must be treated with care. The work of Ellen Ross and Shani D'Cruze has done much to demonstrate that violence continued to be an important mechanism by which men attempted to exert control over their wives.[75] As a later section of this chapter will demonstrate, the notion of clinging on to 'respectability' amongst peers and neighbours could simply mean that women and children kept abuse secret.

'Moral panic'?

Increased willingness to prosecute was undoubtedly also linked to changes in statutory law which reflected as well as influenced popular attitudes. The removal of rape from the list of capital offences in 1841 unburdened prosecutors, juries and judges alike of the guilt of sending a man to his death. Although neighbourhoods voiced outrage at the actions of a child molester, death itself was viewed as too heavy a penalty. Where men were awaiting the gallows, families, friends and neighbours petitioned the Home Secretary for reprieve.[76] In July 1840 James Hepworth, aged 67, was sentenced to hang at the York Assizes for rape of a 12-year-old orphan girl at a beershop owned by her uncle and aunt in Barnsley, West Yorkshire. A petition was drawn up and signed by 51 Barnsley men protesting not against his conviction (since there was clear evidence of guilt) but against the sentence of death: 'It is the earnest wish and fervent prayer of his aged wife and disconsolate family as well as of a great portion of the loyal and dutiful inhabitants of Barnsley that the execution be dispensed with.'[77] The impact of execution was felt by family and community; petitioners were not condoning Hepworth's behaviour but expressing their belief that hanging was too serious a penalty. A similar petition was received from the 'inhabitants of the City of York', signed by 30 men, again requesting commutation of sentence in Hepworth's case.[78] Reference was made to the bill to lift capital punishment for rape that was currently held up in its passage through parliament. Aware that the law was about to change, these Yorkshiremen argued that it was wrong to hang a man because of delays in the parliamentary process. In other cases the parents of child victims, who had themselves initiated court proceedings, signed petitions for commutation of sentence.[79] The petitions to the Home Secretary demonstrate the complexity of rape cases; communities expressed outrage at the sexual abuse of their children but were frequently unwilling to see neighbours and friends hang for it. The abolition of capital punishment for rape clearly affected public attitudes towards prosecution.

The sudden increase of cases tried in 1885 was partly a result of the criminalisation of certain acts (sex with girls aged 13–16) which were previously deemed licit. Yet there was also a sizeable increase in the number of cases involving girl children under 13, acts which were already illegal.[80] The push to prosecute in 1885 must, therefore, be linked to the generation of a 'moral panic' as a result of W. T. Stead's newspaper exposé of the prevalence of juvenile prostitution, which attracted a great deal of attention in both London and the provinces. Over a quarter of a million Londoners attended a mass rally that was held in Hyde Park to call for the raising of the age of consent, and publicity permeated all classes and age groups.[81] The *Pall Mall Gazette*'s articles on juvenile prostitution were directly referred to in courts of law. In

August 1885 *The Times* reported a case at the Middlesex Sessions in which a 68-year-old man was accused of indecently assaulting two little girls aged 9 and 10. Adult and child witnesses alike were asked if they had read the 'horrible' stories in the *Pall Mall Gazette*:

> Besides the little girls mentioned, another girl, aged 13 years, and a plumber were called to give corroborative testimony. Mr Purcell elicited in cross-examination that the girl had read recent horrible publications and had discussed them with boys, and the plumber said he took part in the demonstration in Hyde Park on Saturday. Even the girl of nine years of age had heard these matters discussed by her playmates.[82]

The defendant received 'an excellent character' and the foreman of the jury stopped the trial. Judge Fletcher 'said the witnesses were not to blame for the evil knowledge which had been put in their way'.[83] Here, the possession of 'evil knowledge' (a theme which will be explored in much greater detail in chapter 5) was used to rubbish the evidence and suggest that all witnesses, including the adult male plumber, were guilty of fabrication. Two other important points, however, can be gleaned from this story. The first concerns the extent of public consciousness of the 'Maiden tribute' scandal: 9-year-old children were discussing the matter in the streets and London labourers were involved in the demonstration for a Criminal Law Amendment Act. Secondly, it is clear from this report that the scandal of 'juvenile prostitution' was commonly and popularly elided with the issue of sexual abuse. Although the newspaper articles had referred most obviously to prostitution, this was, in the public mind as well as in the discourse of purity campaigners, linked directly with other instances of abuse. It was clearly understood that 'juvenile prostitution' was a euphemism for sexual abuse.

Although London was located at the centre of the scandal, residents of provincial towns and cities also followed the debates and were emotionally caught up in them. A series of public meetings was held in Leeds and petitions were gathered in support of raising the age of consent.[84] The Salvation Army toured Yorkshire spreading its message of moral reform.[85] At the Warwick Assizes, reference was made to the campaigns to raise the age of consent. Justice Denman, trying a case in December of the year, pointed out the peculiar similarity between the allegations of the female defendant and the publicity material that had surrounded the new Criminal Law Amendment Act: 'the tale told by the prosecutrix ... did marvellously gather up in the course of it a great many of the very topics which were prominently dealt with by the act'.[86] Thus the scandal of July 1885 was certainly more than metropolitan in scope. It was discussed at public meetings and in courts of law throughout the country; the press reports made reference to a common vocabulary of euphemism. It would be misleading, however, to claim that Stead's newspaper reports were responsible for the creation of a moral climate. Although the publicity clearly served to focus public attention on the matter, Stead was also mobilising grass-roots concerns that had been in existence long before 1885.

Extra-familial abuse

It has been suggested, so far, that prosecutions for sexual abuse were relatively infrequent during the nineteenth century because of the retention of traditional informal mechanisms of moral regulation alongside official strategies; but it is important to ask further questions about the circumstances that influenced the choice of strategy. It is significant that, where details of specific circumstances are available, a large proportion of court cases involved allegations of abuse in public places by total strangers (see figure 2.2). When cases involving men known to their victims were reported, they tended to implicate male lodgers, neighbours and employers rather than blood relatives. Only a relatively small number of reported cases involved incest: that is abuse by relatives through blood or marriage. This does not mean that incest was less likely in the Victorian family. Rather, given that the results of recent sociological research suggest that most abuse takes place within home and family, it is appropriate to conclude that incest was least likely to be resolved through the courts.[87] It was in cases of extra-familial abuse that the courts became a favoured option.

Differences between the types of offences prosecuted in London and Yorkshire are illuminating for the light they shed on police practices and social identity (see figures 2.3 and 2.4). A third of cases in the Middlesex sample involved strangers (where the abuser/victim relationship can be

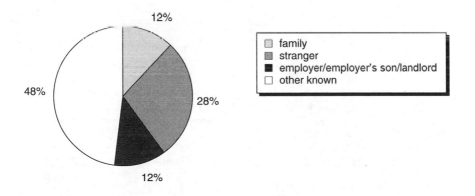

12%

48%

28%

12%

☐ family
▨ stranger
■ employer/employer's son/landlord
☐ other known

Figure 2.2   Relationship of defendant to victim where known (sexual assault of children), 1830–1910

Sources: (Cases tried on indictment, Yorkshire and Middlesex. See figures 1.3–1.7 for details of sampled sources)

identified) whereas in Yorkshire they constituted the smallest category (14 per cent). In Yorkshire, on the other hand, prosecution of employers was much higher: 23 per cent compared to 10 per cent. These statistics do not have the credibility of hard data since they are based on inconsistent patterns of information (and, indeed, there are many cases for which there is no information about the relationship of abuser to victim);[88] they can, however, be seen as suggestive and perhaps indicative. In both samples, the proportion of cases involving family members (16 per cent in Yorkshire and 12 per cent in Middlesex) and members of the wider neighbourhood (47 per cent in Yorkshire and 46 per cent in Middlesex) are fairly consistent. While cases involving incest tended to be surprisingly low, it is not, however, surprising that individuals who offended in their local neighbourhood were likely to end up in the courts; witnesses were easily able to identify and locate them after the event.

The large proportion of child sexual abuse cases involving strangers which came before the Middlesex courts can be linked to a wider Metropolitan Police agenda: to curb public order offences and cases of indecency. During the 1830s plain-clothes policemen patrolled Hyde Park, which had become a notorious pick-up area for men seeking sex with other men.[89] Throughout the century men appeared in court in connection with charges of indecent exposure, attempted sodomy, indecent assault and (after 1885) gross indecency as a result of police vigilance in parks and open spaces. Finally, the surveillance of parks within the jurisdiction of the Metropolitan Police Commissioners was stepped up through the Parks Regulation Act of 1872 whereby uniformed park-keepers, employed as additional constables, were given the powers, privileges and immunities as well as the duties and responsibilities of a normal police constable.[90] These park constables, in

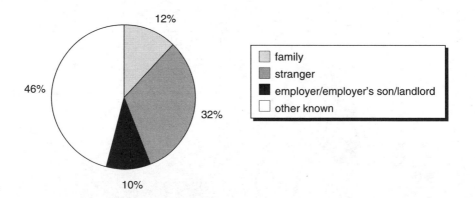

Figure 2.3   Middlesex: relationship of defendant to victim where known (sexual assault of children), 1830–1910

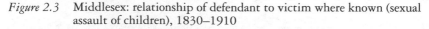

Sources: (Middlesex cases tried on indictment. See figures 1.3–1.5)

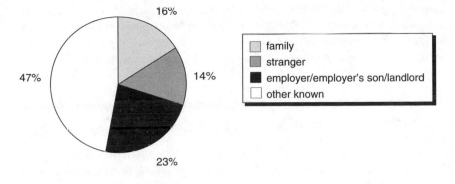

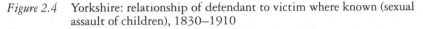

Figure 2.4   Yorkshire: relationship of defendant to victim where known (sexual
assault of children), 1830–1910

Sources: (Yorkshire cases tried on indictment. See figures 1.6–1.7)

patrolling their beat, were clearly aiming to stop all forms of 'indecent
behaviour' as well as to eradicate the 'park pest' who molested children.[91]
This is not to say that police divisions in Yorkshire were indifferent to
public order offences; a number of cases came before the West Riding
Quarter Sessions involving indecent assaults on girl children in the public
park at Wakefield, where prosecution was dependent on alert gardeners or
their assistants.[92] Indecent exposure does not, however, appear to have been
constructed as a serious and endemic public problem as it was in London.
The official status and responsibility of the London park constable was not
duplicated elsewhere.

   In Yorkshire, on the other hand, a substantial proportion of cases relate to
the employer/employee configuration, particularly to masters and servants,
although there were also cases involving the prosecution of factory over-
lookers by young female textile workers. Up until the Education Act of
1870, it was common practice for girls as young as 10 to be sent out to work
as domestic servants, sometimes living on the premises; in the later decades
of the nineteenth century girls over 14 were in regular employment.[93]
Separated from their families and friends they were particularly vulnerable,
as Shani D'Cruze has demonstrated, to abuses of the authority and economic
power which masters held over servants.[94] Girls who worked for lower-
middle-class employers who could only afford one servant were in a double
bind. They were unable to fall back on the advice and support of other
employees and often found themselves in the house alone with their master
(or, indeed, his son). The majority of servant/master cases involved working-
class parents prosecuting those just above them on the social ladder.

   Traditions of radicalism rather than deference, embedded in particular in
the working-class cultures of the West Riding, made it possible to report
master/servant cases.[95] Radicalism made use of the melodramatic myth of

aristocratic seduction (already outlined), describing economic and political oppression through the metaphor of sexual exploitation. Terry Eagleton has analysed the operation of the rape myth in *Clarissa* to suggest that in Richardson's novels 'sexuality, far from being some displacement of class conflict, is the very medium in which it is conducted'.[96] In *Clarissa* the bourgeois sensibility of the female protagonist finally triumphs over the old-style libertine behaviour of an out-moded aristocracy. For Eagleton, *Clarissa* is an allegory 'of class warfare ... between a predatory nobility and a pious bourgeoisie'.[97] Anna Clark has shown that the myth of aristocratic seduction was transferred from the middle-class novel of the eighteenth century to the radical writings of Godwin and Wollstonecraft, finally emerging into the political arena as part of the rhetoric of the anti-Poor Law and Chartist movements of the 1830s and 40s.[98] Myths of seduction could be shifted onto different social groups without affecting the significance of the social conflict at stake. Thus the seduced maiden and the libertine became a 'class metaphor' which represented working class against capitalist, as well as bourgeoisie against aristocracy. The courtroom became an arena in which the 'politics of seduction' could be played out, servants and their families clearly undeterred by any notion that court practice might be shaped by a very different ideology. As Douglas Hay has argued in his study of eighteenth-century justice, even though the courts might have seemed to be just, it did not necessarily mean that they were.[99] Whilst a significant number of sexual assault prosecutions featured children and young women who worked as servants, only half resulted in conviction. Many cases may have been thrown out by magistrates without ever coming to trial. The employers themselves took the view that they were more likely to be believed, asserting their own claim to a position of respectability.[100]

Incest

The same cultural agenda which made it possible to prosecute master/servant abuse also kept familial abuse out of the courts. As Clark has written, the myth of seduction, which depicted rape in class terms 'falsified reality' since it obscured issues of gender.[101] Most significantly, it failed to recognise that most women and children were probably abused by men of their own class and drew attention away from the family as a site of abuse. Incest, although stigmatised as the most serious form of sexual abuse, was also the most under-reported. In his account of his childhood in the Manchester slums, Robert Roberts wrote: 'I don't recall a single prosecution: strict public silence saved miscreants from the rigours of the law.'[102] There were legal impediments which, as the NSPCC pointed out, made it very difficult to prosecute cases of child abuse that occurred within the private space of family life: 'Atrocities committed on a child in the presence of the mother only are seldom punishable. A mother's evidence against a father on behalf of their child, magistrates and judges are forbidden to admit.'[103] This was not altered until 1889 with the passage of the Prevention of Cruelty to Children Act, which at last made the evidence of wives legally admissible.[104]

Despite the legal restriction, mothers and children developed a brave and resourceful range of preventative strategies when sexual abuse occurred at home. Elsa Hammond, aged 15, begged her mother not to leave her in the house alone and her mother arranged to keep watch on her husband's activities.[105] Elizabeth Chubb, aged 11, regularly slept next door at her cousin's house if her stepfather began to harass her. Her mother sought refuge there too when he seemed particularly violent.[106] Grandmothers, neighbours and family friends provided vital networks of support. A mother might well be prohibited from giving evidence in court but she could always set her neighbours up as witnesses. Mary Smith, who suspected her husband Robert was abusing 7-year-old Flora, arranged for her landlady and a female friend to spy on him from an adjacent room.[107] The two women later gave evidence against him.

The way in which incest was dealt with depended on the specific nature of each individual husband and wife relationship. In a significant proportion of cases that did come to court, the mother and father of the child were estranged or there was reference to quarrelling and animosity. In March 1870 a Hoxton engraver was found guilty at the Middlesex Sessions of indecently assaulting a 7-year-old girl, Emily, whom he had fathered. The parents, who had never married, were estranged and, so *The Times* tells us, 'he had not paid anything towards her maintenance for the last five years or seen her since she was eight months old until, shortly after Christmas, he saw her at his mother's house'.[108] Subsequently, he turned up at the house, uninvited, where the woman and child lodged in a room. The mother deposed that she had put her daughter to bed before going out for the evening, returning shortly before midnight:

> I went up into my room and it was quite dark. The prisoner was there. I asked him who opened the door to him & he said a woman & he said he had been kissing [Emily] & cuddling her & said I did not thank him for it & was rather cross & he said I see you want me to go & I said yes and he went away. On Thursday morning my child complained to me & I examined her and on the evening I took her to a doctor.[109]

The tension and animosity between them is even apparent in the short staccato phrases of the deposition account.

Husbands tended to argue that allegations were false and that wives had made them out of malice. As one Halifax man put it: 'the charge is made at the instigation of my wife who wants me back in prison. I have had a very unhappy life since my marriage'.[110] The quarrels that are detailed in the depositions seem to be symptomatic of severe family problems, deep economic hardships and whole sequences of brutalities. The 15-year-old daughter of the Halifax man told a very different story to her father: 'He has not been a kind father to us, he beats us all. He goes away for long periods and we have to get parish relief.'[111] In a case involving a Wakefield mining family, tried at the West Riding Quarter Sessions in 1840, the children described fights between their parents and the father's threats that he would break his daughter's neck by throwing her downstairs.[112] For these families, made to suffer on a prolonged basis because of neglectful or violent behaviour, the possibility of prosecution and a lengthy prison sentence provided a glimmering hope of escape from the darkness and brutality. In her study of family violence in Boston, USA, Linda Gordon has suggested that beaten wives, reluctant to turn to the authorities for self-protection, would seek legal or philanthropic assistance when their children were endangered; there was a line of brutality which mothers refused to see crossed.[113] Similarly, in the incest cases which came before the Middlesex and West Riding sessions, women with violent husbands saw the sexual abuse of their daughters as a final deciding moment in the sequence of atrocities.

Yet there were wives who acted in protection of their husbands. The newspapers commented on cases where mothers refused to give evidence against their husbands after the law changed, where mothers actively supported their husbands in court, and where daughters failed to appear to give vital evidence.[114] Although melodrama in the theatre concentrated very much on the domestic locus, often even on parent–child relations, and indeed functioned so as to 'solve' wider social problems in terms of the familial, it was when abuse took place inside the home that melodramatic language was less likely to be deployed to describe events. This must be because systems of polarity break down if the divide between 'us' and 'them' is no longer clear. Incest was one of those moments when, according to Christina Crosby, 'the history of the people thwarts identification and breaks the melodramatic fix'.[115] It was reasonably simple to classify abuse by strangers or acquaintances in clear black-and-white terms, to categorise it in line with the melodramatic tradition of evil and bestiality. When the abuser came from within the family itself, was known as a husband and father, standard conceptualisations could break down, loyalties could splinter. One London father was said to have urged his family to reconsider their decision to turn him over to the police, warning them to 'consider what you are doing, think of the exposure of the family'.[116] Issues of family honour, respectability, shame and humiliation were coupled with the severe financial burden of losing the male breadwinner. Many families must have known they would end up in the workhouse, condemned as paupers or figures of pity.

Despite the attempts to maintain secrecy within the family and the financial and legal restraints that made prosecution an impossibility, cases of incest did, nevertheless, come to light. When mothers remained silent or, indeed, when fathers were acting as single parents, the whistle was blown by neighbours who overheard shouts, cries and threats, or became the confidantes of children with no-one else to turn to.[117] Furthermore, as Carl Chinn has suggested, although cases of incest were unlikely to end up in the courts, they might nevertheless be dealt with through a range of community sanctions. Chinn, who has used oral history to build up an account of life in the Birmingham slums at the beginning of the twentieth century, has written that:

> The punishment of men such as this was usually ostracisation … although the belief persisted that where incidents of incest were blatant, the neighbours would give the man 'a bloody good hiding' and hold his head under the communal stand-pipe while he was doused in cold water.[118]

Although these oral histories refer to a later period, it is likely that the strategies involving gossip, shaming and punishing were long-standing traditions that were consolidated during the course of the nineteenth century.

A re-reading of the parliamentary blue-books can provide similar insights to Chinn's oral histories for other areas of the country. While the final report of the 1885 Royal Commission on the Housing of the Working Classes chose to make direct links between overcrowding and incest, highlighting Lord Shaftesbury's description of the immorality of the poor, other 'expert' witnesses who gave evidence to the commission held very different views. Clergy and school board officials working in the urban slums argued that the one-room system was no more likely to lead to incest than any other sleeping arrangement. London School Board inspector T. Marchant Williams, who had visited homes in Finsbury and Marylebone where the one-room system was prevalent, said that, even in the poorest districts, men who had committed incest, were 'marked men' in the district and viewed with 'peculiar horror'.[119] His comments suggest the strategies of shunning and ostracisation which Chinn has mentioned. Clerkenwell vicar Rev. Alfred Fryer told the commission that reports about the prevalence of incest in overcrowded areas had been exaggerated. Although children might be more knowledgeable about the realities of sexuality and pregnancy, this did not mean they were abused, corrupted or immoral:

> I know of one case of a girl of 12 or 13 who used to assist at her mother's confinements. She was one of a family of seven children, who with the father and mother were all living in the same room. … But that same girl refused to be tubbed before her brothers and sisters; she would never be washed before the other; she had a tremendous sense of personal modesty.[120]

Bristol vicar Ernest Adolphus Fuller, similarly, described systems whereby families partitioned their room with curtains to provide privacy.[121] Overcrowded neighbourhoods had their own moral codes and sensibilities, refusing to tolerate those who disregarded them.

Thus neighbours, relations and friends provided important support networks as well as strategies of censure for dealing with incest when it came to their knowledge. Yet a complex set of reasons – family status and respectability, economic vulnerability, fear of further brutality – might also lead to a conspiracy of silence within the family group. Discovery and, indeed, the necessary evidence to indict often depended on the type of co-incidence that resulted from close social proximity: from neighbours stumbling in at the wrong moment, hearing screams next-door through paper-thin walls, having conversations in the yard in a fleeting moment when a child was out of her father's view. Within the incest cases sampled, none have come to light that involved isolated families living in areas of scattered settlement. It is impossible to make specific deductions from this since the reporting of incest *per capita* was incredibly small even in areas of dense population. The sample would have to be extended drastically to produce any statistically meaningful conclusion. The equal lack of incest prosecutions involving middle-class defendants does, however, suggest a similar proposition: that incest was more likely to be prosecuted, and probably also unofficially policed, in close-knit working-class neighbourhoods. Linda Gordon has suggested that Boston women turned to official agencies 'when their informal networks could not protect them, adding these agencies to their reservoir of resistance strategies'.[122] It is striking that a high proportion of cases of incest that came before the Middlesex and Yorkshire courts also made reference to drunkenness, to wife-beating and to threats of assault on children. It would seem that these cases involved men who were too violent, too brutal, to be controlled by family or neighbourhood. In cases of incest, prosecution offered a desperate final measure.

This chapter has examined the role of informal mechanisms of detection and regulation (based on the interventions of family, friends and neighbours) as well as the circumstances in which working people turned to the official mechanism of the courts; the interventions of an increasing body of voluntary and semi-official welfare agencies will be considered next.

3   The child savers

Introduction

Three very different case histories can be juxtaposed to draw attention to the varied experiences of the parents and children who came into contact with the late Victorian/Edwardian child welfare system. In the first, 14-year-old Ena was placed under the legal custody of the NSPCC in 1906 after her stepmother was fined a shilling for kicking her and beating her with ropes. The society had been observing the family for some time; her father was described as a 'drunkard' and it was known that her brother had sexually assaulted Ena before she was 10 years of age.[1] Although legal action was not pursued over that matter, the society was able to remove Ena from her family at a later stage on grounds of cruelty. Since the NSPCC did not itself provide residential accommodation, it arranged for Ena to be sent to the Salvation Army home for children the Nest in Clapton, north London.

In a second case, 12-year-old Caroline gave evidence at the Leeds Assizes in May 1900 against the man accused of abusing her. The case broke down as a result of her 'unreliable evidence and contradictory statement', but the Leeds Rescue Committee (which ran a local rescue home for 'fallen' women) was intent on 'saving' the child.[2] The committee successfully challenged the mother's claim to custody on the grounds of 'immoral surroundings': the child was illegitimate, her mother was cohabiting with another man who was not the girl's father, and they were living in Quarry Hill, described by philanthropists as 'the worst part of Leeds. ... The surroundings are simply awful.' The Rescue Committee contacted the Church of England Waifs and Strays Society to arrange accommodation away from Leeds although there was no evidence that Caroline had suffered abuse or neglect at home. In a third case, a mother returned early from her visit to a Picture Palace in Hull one evening in 1914 to discover her husband sexually abusing their 10-year-old daughter Carrie. The father was sentenced to six months' imprisonment for the assault but Carrie's mother turned to the Salvation Army asking them to take her daughter and place her in institutional care before he was released from prison.[3]

These three cases, drawn from records kept by children's homes, show that prosecutions for sexual abuse were not always pursued, that other forms of intervention were attempted, and that child custody was just as important an issue as punishment of offenders. They demonstrate that child welfare was the concern of a proliferation of voluntary institutions and organisations, each with its own particular remit, each scrutinising parental conduct for signs of viciousness; moral indiscretions were viewed as part of a continuum of bad parenting which ended in brutality and violence. Yet, as well as being subject to their scrutiny, parents also saw welfare agencies as a useful resource in the care and protection of their children.

Histories of the child protection movement in the late Victorian period have tended to focus on the work of the NSPCC, founded in 1884.[4] Those who see child protection as part of a progressive march from savagery to civilisation have depicted the foundation of the NSPCC ahistorically as the inevitable and somewhat overdue climax of the development of the humanitarian impulse.[5] Certainly the NSPCC warrants detailed consideration. It was soon identified as the principal agency concerned with crimes against children and, in London at least, worked closely with police and magistracy. Its directors Benjamin Waugh and Robert Parr were regularly consulted by parliamentary committees as the leading experts in the field of child welfare. As Harry Ferguson has demonstrated, the NSPCC played an important role in the development of the techniques and practices associated with modern social and welfare work.[6] He has argued that the NSPCC, in setting up a nation-wide body of professional inspectors following a set of clear policy guidelines and answerable to a central head office, established a systematic programme of welfare intervention which was based on 'modern' notions of family surveillance: regular visits, advice and warning. For Ferguson, the society's development of the special preserve of the 'emergency case', which unusually warranted immediate and direct intervention (prosecution or removal from parental custody), is a key element in modern welfare practice.[7] Yet Ferguson's focus on NSPCC sources means that the activities of other societies are obscured.

This chapter will, in contrast, stress elements of continuity rather than change in the treatment of sexual abuse cases by child protection agencies in the mid and late Victorian periods. This is not to contradict Ferguson's thesis but to argue that sexual abuse must be analysed as a separate category of case. Constructed as a social problem during the 1860s and 1870s by rescue and social purity groups, its meanings were negotiated within a discourse of Christian moral economy. The influence of this social purity agenda can be clearly detected in early NSPCC publicity material produced under the aegis of director Benjamin Waugh. Similarly, while the development of a professional inspectorate and legal office is an extremely significant element in the NSPCC story, it was not without precedent. The legal case work undertaken by the NSPCC was pre-empted, on a metropolitan scale, by the Associate Institute for the Protection of Women and Children which prosecuted sexual abuse cases in the London courts on a regular basis during the 1860s and 1870s. Despite the high profile role of the NSPCC on a national level, it should not be assumed that the society monopolised child welfare work. Local rescue groups and private philanthropists as well as prominent social purity societies were actively involved in the work of saving 'fallen' girl children long after 1884. The NSPCC was simply the largest society of many.

This chapter will examine the attitudes and activities of welfare agencies handling sexual abuse cases c.1860–c.1914, emphasising the connections between rhetoric and practice. How was sexual abuse viewed? What factors affected the decision to prosecute? What strategies were employed in the courtroom and how successful were they? It will argue that social work with sexually abused children, viewed as a whole, was *ad hoc* and unsystematic. It was based on the activities of an abundance of societies and individuals but framed to a large extent within a social purity paradigm that tended to view all sexual abuse cases in terms of 'emergency': 'fallen' children should be removed from their homes if possible, to be retrained and reformed in a specialist institution. The prosecution of sexual abuse offenders was often closely linked with attempts to gain custody which arose as much from this desire to reform the 'corrupted' child as from the need to protect her from further abuses. It was only under the NSPCC directorship of Robert Parr, who succeeded Waugh in 1904, that attempts to shift this paradigm become detectable.

The rhetoric of abuse

In her study of welfare agencies working in Boston, Massachusetts, USA, in the late nineteenth and early twentieth centuries, Linda Gordon has highlighted the influence of first wave feminism on the practice of social work.[8] Gordon has argued that victims of incest and sexual abuse were treated with sympathy between 1880 and 1910; it was in the period 1910–60 that the girl victim was reconstituted as a threat and labelled as a juvenile delinquent.[9] This book contends, however, that the concept of the sexually precocious female 'juvenile delinquent' was a significant reference point, whether direct or indirect, in discussions of sexual abuse in nineteenth-century England. It is important to draw attention to feminist campaigns that exposed male sexual brutality and argued for a similar standard of moral behaviour for men and women, but it is also clear that feminist rhetoric cannot be separated from the social purity agenda.[10] While feminists such as Josephine Butler were extremely sympathetic to the plight of girl victims, their belief in an essential feminine moral virtue meant that the 'fallen' girl who did not repent remained a social threat.[11] The rhetoric that was deployed by the child savers to describe sexual abuse will be analysed here to draw attention to the complex meanings and configurations of 'victim' and 'threat' that drove welfare practice.[12] The influence of social purity ideas will be stressed throughout.

Both before and after the founding of the NSPCC, cases involving sexual abuse were publicised and prosecuted by a range of rescue societies set up to 'protect' women and children, initially from prostitution. For example, the Society for the Protection of Females, formed in London in 1835, had endeavoured 'to suppress (by law) houses which encouraged juvenile prostitution'.[13] From the mid Victorian period onwards attentions began to focus on child victims; discussions of prostitution were expanded to encompass wider concerns about the 'seduction' of children. The Society for the Rescue of Young Women and Children, set up in 1853 and usually known as the Rescue Society, argued that the number of children earning money through prostitution was in fact small. Rather, the issue of concern was the youthful age at which young girls were 'led astray from virtue' and 'once fallen, become an easy prey to subsequent temptation'.[14] Thus the Rescue Society began to shift the agenda from juvenile prostitution to what we now term sexual abuse, campaigning to raise the age of consent in order to protect children over 12. For the Rescue Society, sexual assault must be added to a list of factors, which included overcrowding and unsupervised social activity, that encouraged the 'germs of vice' and led to 'juvenile depravity'.[15]

If social purity, both feminist and anti-feminist, had helped focus attentions on sexual abuse, its agendas were also influential within the newly founded NSPCC and amongst other rescue societies with which it worked. The National Vigilance Association (NVA) and the Jewish Association for the Protection of Women and Girls, both founded in 1885, also saw the prosecution of offences of 'corruption' and 'immorality' as an important part of their work.[16] These groups had close associations with the NSPCC; the Rabbi elect sat on the committee of the NSPCC, and Benjamin Waugh was frequently invited to speak at NVA meetings. Waugh's social purity sympathies are also reflected in his friendship with *Pall Mall Gazette* editor W. T. Stead and his delineation of a highly moral and chivalrous form of masculinity in which men were to act as protectors of women and children (see chapter 6).

NSPCC rhetoric often categorised the different forms of crimes against children in a linear order of gravity, with sexual abuse, throughout the period, adjudged the most serious. In 1888 it was described as 'the vilest crime against childhood';[17] in 1908 as 'the most grievous form of cruelty'.[18] The annual reports stated 'Of all the corrupt things in life the corruption of morals of an unprotected child is the most dastardly and contemptible'[19] and that 'there is no more cowardly class of offence in the whole category of crime'.[20] Although the NSPCC used dramatic language to publicise its work whenever possible, other crimes against children were correspondingly portrayed as less serious. In one often-quoted 1885 case, a mother had locked her child in an orange box under her bed from morning to night to escape the attentions of the school board; the NSPCC described this practice as 'a milder form of crime'.[21] This language raises the question as to why, exactly, sexual abuse was seen as the 'most dastardly'. The purpose of this line of enquiry is not to trivialise incidents of sexual abuse but to ask why it was often treated, rhetorically, as more serious than the cases of chronic neglect and brutal beating that also regularly featured in the pages of the society's journal, the *Child's Guardian*.

Euphemism

The middle-class rescue and child-saving movement did not of course use the expression 'sexual abuse' but, rather, selected a whole set of euphemisms to describe the phenomena. The NSPCC, reporting its statistics for 1887, cited what it referred to as 'nameless outrages';[22] in 1889 these were described as 'cruel immoralities'.[23] By 1894 sexual abuse was covered by the legal terms 'indecent and criminal assault' in the official statistics; but the society continued to use the epithets 'corruption of morals', 'grave evils' and 'moral offences' in lengthier prose reports, sharing the language of morality/immorality which had been developed by social purity groups. Time and time again the NSPCC drew attention to the silence which must, so it argued, of necessity, surround it because the details of cases were too delicate to report. Such cases were instances of 'evil which is altogether unmentionable';[24] they were 'too sad and too dreadful to relate'.[25] Foucault has drawn attention to the way in which silence can function as a discursive practice;[26] within the nineteenth-century rhetoric of child-saving and social purity, euphemisms and well-posted silences spoke volumes.

As a coded expression, euphemism was dependent on the popular knowledge and understanding of its meanings. Ed Cohen has drawn attention to the paradox that, while none of the newspapers covering the Oscar Wilde trial printed the charges against him, everyone seemed to be aware of their implications.[27] Euphemisms are expressions that avoid the statement of the obvious and provide, instead, a highly interpretative and value-laden description. The term 'social evil', for example, in just two words, located prostitution within both society and a Christian moral tradition, blaming prostitution for everything that was wrong in civilisation, while at the same time suggesting that the process of civilisation had in fact made it necessary.

The rhetorical device of euphemism, rather than silencing or hiding incidents of abuse, in fact drew attention to them by turning them into sensation. NSPCC and social purity reports were highly coloured, emotive and suggestive, and were in some ways more explicit, as a result of their use of euphemisms, than any clinical or legal language could have been. This extract, taken from the NSPCC's 1908 annual report, demonstrates this point amply:

> Sad to say the most grievous form of cruelty, the cruelty of immorality, endangering the body and polluting the mind, stands higher than it has ever done. In 756 cases the classification is corruption of morals. Under this head the disclosures are of a revolting nature: little girls of tender

years, the age of some being as low as three, have been the victims of savage indecencies too terrible to relate. The depths of shame and disgrace revealed in these cases are quite beyond description. To many people they would be unbelievable.[28]

Silence becomes a highly meaningful space to which the imagination is conspicuously drawn and left to roam. Without actually naming sexual abuse, this passage articulates a highly developed account of both its cause and effect. It is caused by 'savagery'; it leads to shame and disgrace; it endangers the body and pollutes the minds of children. This framework of belief about sexual abuse was repeated in most promotional material.

The continual references which child savers made to the child's 'littleness' and, indeed, their choice of the word 'child' or 'girl' are also revealing. Although it was invariably female children who were seen as the recipients of sexual abuse, child-saving publicity often preferred the gender-neutral term 'children'. This was because of the specific associations that the words 'children' and 'childhood' conjured up in late Victorian minds. 'Children' were not merely individuals of a certain age, but were seen as inhabiting a specific state – the state of 'childhood' itself – which was associated with a condition of innocence, weakness and vulnerability. The legal label 'children of tender years', which was generally applied to those below the age of 8, similarly portrayed the child as delicate, defenceless and, through the suggestion of softness and malleability, open to impression and influence. Children, by virtue of their childish condition, were entirely dependent on the care and protection of others.

Carolyn Steedman has, indeed, described the 'complex register of affect that has been invested in the word "little"'.[29] The power of the labels associated with childhood and infancy – their ability to rouse the emotions – has already been demonstrated in chapter 1, where examples were cited of a 'baby' of 9 and a 'young woman' of 14. When child welfare campaigners spoke of 'little victims' or 'child victims' (or displayed them visually) they aimed to elicit a specific emotional response. By virtue of both her 'littleness' and her position as victim, the child was doubly wronged; the rape of the innocent was a double crime.

'Savagery' at home

Sexual abuse, like other forms of child abuse, was seen as threatening because it was the result of 'savage' impulses. The related oppositions of savagery/civilisation, immorality/morality, cruelty/humanity were regularly dwelt upon in both social purity and NSPCC publicity material. It was, of course, an important feature of W. T. Stead's articles 'the maiden tribute of modern Babylon', which exposed the presence of a heathen immorality within what appeared to be a modern Christian civilisation.[30] NSPCC director Benjamin Waugh himself penned a famous article on child cruelty in England entitled 'The child of the English savage' and popular adventure writer Henry Rider Haggard could always be relied upon to come up with similar allusions in the talks he gave for local NSPCC meetings.[31] He told a meeting in Norfolk in 1894 that:

> He had spent a good many years in contact with savages, whose habits were peculiar and in some ways immoral, but amongst them he had never heard of such atrocities practised upon helpless children as were reported in the English daily papers.[32]

As editor of the *Child's Guardian*, Waugh warned his readers in 1891 that England needed to get its own house in order before it began bragging of its superiority to its colonies. In a note concerning the brutality of 'peculiar wrongs done to girl children of tender age', he commented: 'Yet do we English get nationally agitated about child marriage in India. When shall we obey the command of our Master and *begin at Jerusalem*.'[33] Sexual abuse was a 'ghastly anachronism in a civilised and Christian country'.[34] The fear of savagery at home, bound up with imperial imagery, was clearly related to concerns about national degeneration and racial depletion.

Although the NSPCC often declared that cruelty knew no class and indeed was just as likely to be found among the rich as the poor, it was nevertheless the houses of the poor rather than the rich that its inspectors visited routinely. Indeed the society came more and more to focus on the poor and the problem of overcrowding as a cause of abuse. George Behlmer has suggested that the NSPCC had to rethink its ideas on poverty in the 1890s in response to Booth's study of *Life and labour of the people in London* which reported that whole neighbourhoods of the idle and vicious poor were governed by 'brutality within the circle of family life'.[35] The Society, as a result, increasingly depicted poverty as a contributory factor in cases of cruelty. The Blackheath branch report of 1904 echoed many of the concerns about incest which had been articulated in the 1885 Report of the Royal Commission on the Housing of the Working Classes:

> Where whole families of both sexes are herded together, the slightest restraint of decency being entirely disregarded, how is it possible that children brought up under such conditions can grow up into sober and respectable citizens?[36]

In a paper on 'Assaults and corruption of children' given in 1910 Robert Parr took a similar line, arguing that: 'It would be unwise to leave unmentioned the conditions under which a great many people live, for there can be no doubt that a lack of privacy in the home is followed by too great precocity in the family.'[37]

Although all child abuse was 'savage', sexual abuse was clearly the worst form of savagery. The children themselves were depicted as 'pitiable girlchild victims of monsters devoted to horrible sensuality'.[38] For the Victorian child savers, the true horror of sexual abuse lay not in the actual physical act of abuse but in the long-term effect it had on the child, physically and morally. Sexual abuse was described as an 'evil which is both mutilating and corrupting' as well as being 'horribly unnatural'.[39] Abuse polluted and corrupted the child; it effected the beginnings of her own transformation into savage or monster. Both were ostensibly monsters since both were 'unnatural' – the offender for his base and immoral desires, the victim for her fall from the innocent state of childhood which was judged her natural condition. Such a fall was a permanent one; children whose innocence was gone were 'ruined for life'.[40] As I shall demonstrate in chapter 7, the need to separate 'fallen' from 'unfallen' children provided the basis for the setting up of separate 'specialist' training schools and homes for this particular category of girl.

The language used by child savers had a significance and function beyond the merely descriptive. In analysing the words and categories which have been deployed in relation to abuse since the 1960s – 'battering', 'battered child syndrome', 'incest' – Ian Hacking has suggested that the choice of label indicates a certain aetiology or causation, and a resultant treatment, either medical, psychological or social.[41] At the end of the nineteenth century child sexual abuse was constructed as 'corruption of morals' within a discourse of social purity. Although there are significant references to the concept of children's rights as citizens in the *Child's Guardian*, most accounts of sexual abuse describe its effects in relation to notions of a Christian moral economy, to the battle of good over evil or wickedness. Today the effects of sexual abuse are often gauged in terms of long-term psychological trauma/damage. At the turn of the century child savers believed that the effect of sexual abuse was 'corruption' which would transform good to evil, childhood innocence into sexual precocity. Immorality was seen as catching, as a dangerously polluting presence, which would corrupt those with whom it came in contact. This was why sexual abuse was seen as more serious and more horrific than any other form of crime against children.

In 1893 the *Child's Guardian* reported on an Old Bailey case involving a 13-year-old girl who had seduced and corrupted a whole list of teenage boys, commenting that 'she was, what, alas! hundreds of girls are, a moral pest amongst the young'.[42] The language of 'childhood' and 'littleness', which suggested innocence was, in this report, replaced with references to girlhood and moral corruption. Once gendered as female, this child was clearly sexualised.[43] The abused child, once corrupted, could become immoral, delinquent and probably criminal; her protection was partly about imposing order and discipline on a society threatened by impending savagery and disorder.

The professionalisation of prosecution

The professionalisation of welfare work – the standardisation of procedure and the employment of a paid body of experts – was apparent in the development of an NSPCC inspectorate answerable to central office and also in the creation of a central legal office to oversee the prosecution of court cases. During the late 1880s London lawyer William Moreton Phillips acted as principal solicitor to the Society from his practice in Worship Street.[44] When the society moved its headquarters from Harpur Street to Leicester Square in 1902, Moreton Phillips also changed premises, establishing himself there as in-house solicitor. He was responsible for all legal matters, for overseeing all prosecutions nationally and for instructing all lawyers employed by the society. He retained a close personal involvement in London cases, continuing to appear in the courts on a regular basis, at the same time working closely with the director to develop a prosecution policy for the new society. While most studies of the NSPCC have concentrated their attentions on the inspectorate, this section of the chapter will, therefore, focus on the legal work of the NSPCC and other agencies.

The work of the society's legal office has largely been ignored because of the NSPCC's constant affirmation that it was 'not a mere prosecuting society anxious to serve convictions'.[45] In 1892 Asquith, as Home Secretary, said the society offered an essential and complementary role to the police force primarily because its main concern was not to punish the wrong-doer but to prevent crime.[46] This was indeed true of the bulk of NSPCC business, which increasingly took the form of neglect cases where offending parents would be advised, warned, and kept under the regular surveillance of inspectors.

Sexual abuse cases, however, stand in an unusual position within the society's work. For, while continually denying its desire to prosecute and its preference for other remedies, the NSPCC preferred to prosecute offenders in sex abuse cases if at all possible. It continually highlighted the problems surrounding children's evidence in cases of this nature, campaigning for the lifting of the oath, the holding of hearings *in camera*, and the necessary presence of women in the courtroom. In 1912 it prosecuted nearly a third of all cases of indecent or criminal assault which came to its attention, although only 4.5 per cent of its total business ended in court proceedings.[47] Sexual abuse cases, therefore, formed a significant body of the NSPCC's prosecution work. They were seen as key or 'emergency' cases in which the legal system must be invoked to 'defend the children' and to 'punish the wrong-doer' .

William Shaen and the Associate Institute

The creation of the NSPCC's legal office should be evaluated in terms of development rather than innovation. From the early 1860s another London lawyer, William Shaen, had begun to identify child welfare as a specialist branch of legal practice in his capacity as solicitor to the Associate Institute for the Protection of Women and Children, prefiguring the legal work of the NSPCC by some twenty-five years. Originally founded in 1843 as a rescue society, the Associate Institute was initially involved in lobbying parliament for a stepping-up of the laws against procurers and brothel keepers.[48] It soon, however, moved away from the emphasis on prostitution, campaigning to improve the legal protection of women and girls from acts of violence and attempting to ensure these were enforced in the courts. The Associate Institute prosecuted particularly vicious assaults by husbands on their wives and even defended girl children accused of petty theft.[49] In 1884 the Society claimed to have dealt with 700 cases of 'cruelty and injustice to women and children'; its aim was 'to act for the the welfare of the helpless, especially all those little ones who are too feeble to resist and totally unfit to plead their own cause'.[50]

Throughout the 1860s, 1870s and early 1880s, the Associate Institute was involved in prosecuting sexual abuse cases in the London courts on a regular basis. This legal work was conducted under the auspices of Shaen, who also played a leading role in the lobby work of the organisation, petitioning the Home Office to raise the age of consent from the 1860s onwards.[51] According to the biography written by his daughter Margaret, he espoused almost all of the burning social and moral issues of the day;[52] a non-conformist, he was active in the temperance and anti-vivisection movements and was an active supporter of higher education for women and female suffrage. As chairman of the National Association, he was centrally involved in the battle against the Contagious Diseases Acts and was called to give evidence before the 1871 Royal Commission.[53] Rather than focusing his evidence on the question of adult prostitution, he used the opportunity to highlight and publicise the inadequacy of the laws which dealt with sexual offences against children. He called for a rise in the age of consent to 16 and suggested that offences should be considered 'doubly criminal' when committed by someone who 'occupies a position involving special duties towards the injured person' such as 'parent against child ... master against servant, or by a medical man against a patient'.[54] He argued that seduction by master or father was a common cause of prostitution; once fallen, girls were more likely to take to the streets.

The Associate Institute was actively involved in the prosecution of at least thirty-four of the Old Bailey and Middlesex Quarter Sessions cases sampled for the study: six in 1860, nine in 1865, thirteen in 1870, two in 1875, three in 1880 and one in 1885 (the decline in figures indicating the emergence of other prosecuting societies, most significantly the NSPCC). It achieved convictions in 82 per cent of these cases, a substantial success rate which was markedly better than the average 67 per cent conviction rate for cases of sexual assault on children which came before the Middlesex Sessions in the period 1860–1885. Shaen either appeared in court himself or instructed a number of representatives with whom the Associate Institute worked regularly and it seems that, at least during the 1870s, cases were referred to the association by the police after allegations had been made.[55] The child victims of these cases tended to originate from very poor households unable to afford legal costs: four were the children of single mothers, four worked as servants or child-minders, and two lived in Little Clarendon Street, later described by Booth as an area inhabited by those reduced to poverty of 'a dismal, vicious type'.[56] Although it tended to concentrate its attention on metropolitan cases, the Associate Institute was also involved in the notorious prosecution of Lord Norbury in March 1865 for a sexual assault on a 15-year-old servant girl at his Kentish residence; Norbury was convicted of common assault and fined £5.[57]

There was a clear overlap between the activities of the Associate Institute and the NSPCC. Indeed the sharing of a similar name – the Associate Institute was also commonly known as the Society for the Protection of Women and Children – caused a great deal of confusion for contemporaries.[58] By 1885 the Associate Institute was appearing very infrequently in the courts and, despite attempts to benefit from the publicity created by the NSPCC, soon expired from view.[59] Its demise was perhaps also a result of Shaen's death in 1887. By 1891 the Institute had agreed to hand over all cases involving children to the NSPCC.[60]

George Behlmer has portrayed the Associate Institute dismissively as a disorganised, unprofessional body continually battling against impending financial collapse.[61] A detailed analysis of its day-to-day involvement in the London courts reveals a different picture. Albeit on a much smaller scale, the specialist work of the Associate Institute prefigured the procedures developed by the NSPCC. The role of William Shaen in championing the aims of the Institute both at the national parliamentary level and at the level of the local London court system – as an 'expert' in cases involving the sexual assault of children – foreshadowed the work of both NSPCC director Benjamin Waugh and solicitor William Moreton Phillips.

The NSPCC in court

The benefits of having an experienced in-house solicitor were apparent in the favourable record of convictions recorded by both William Shaen as we have seen and, later, by William Moreton Phillips. Barrister William Clarke Hall (later a London magistrate) was also employed as an experienced NSPCC counsel for a period of some twenty-five years.[62] In 1890 the NSPCC achieved convictions in 77 per cent of the sexual abuse cases it prosecuted at the Old Bailey, compared to a conviction rate of 64 per cent in non-Society cases involving child victims. Perhaps as a result of a backlash amongst judges and juries against the previous sympathy accorded the child victim, NSPCC conviction rates fell to 55 per cent in 1895; but this still compared favourably with the low conviction rate of 35 per cent in non-NSPCC cases. In 1900 a 77 per cent conviction rate was once again achieved. These successes could have been the result of either a more skilful approach in court or a pragmatic prosecution of only those cases that were most likely to end in conviction. Moreton Phillips' own personal annotated copy of the 1904 *Inspector's directory* suggests the latter, since he penned a comment that: 'where cases are going badly or in cases where substantial permanent improvement has been found, [the] solicitor must be instructed to apply for withdrawal rather than to allow cases to be dismissed'.[63]

In 1905 the NSPCC achieved a notable success in a very high profile, controversial and, indeed, very difficult case – the prosecution of a 57-year-old Baptist minister accused of indecently assaulting three girls in his own Brixton chapel.[64] The defence claimed an alibi and attempted to assert that the mothers of the girls were trying to blackmail the minister. The prosecution case rested mainly on the evidence of the three girls, aged 12 and 13, who claimed the minister had invited them to the chapel one evening for extra Bible classes. Moreton Phillips acted for the prosecution during lengthy committal proceedings at Lambeth Police Court and he later instructed Clarke Hall when the case was tried at the County of London Sessions. The courts were packed on every occasion and the atmosphere must have been extremely tense. The case seemed very unlikely to succeed and was in danger of being dropped at several stages. The evidence, however, revealed that the minister had a dubious reputation in his local neighbourhood. A police officer who had made inquiries found that 'he has been suspected of immorality for years'.[65] This may well have clinched the jury's sympathies, together with Clarke Hall's rigorous cross-examination of the defendant. This case demonstrates that the NSPCC did not restrict its court actions to those cases which it thought it could win easily. Its relatively successful track record in the courts must also be attributed to the merits of its legal representatives.

The NSPCC defended itself indefatigably against the criticisms of high court judge Mr Justice Grantham who, in 1895, stated that it was the duty of the police not the NSPCC to prosecute cases of unlawful sex under the Criminal Law Amendment Act.[66] The Society argued that its special expertise in children's cases made it more suited to the task, having prosecuted some 4,000 cases of sexual assault on children, within the previous ten years. It stated that:

> If ... the prosecutions were left to the Police, they would in general be presented to the court without legal assistance, the Police-Constable would not be permitted to make an opening statement, and he would not be competent to cross-examine the accused persons if they tendered themselves as witnesses.[67]

It was better, argued the NSPCC, that prosecution should be conducted by an expert solicitor who had a solid background in dealing with crimes against children and was able to deal with child witnesses with sensitivity. Other judges praised the Society for discretion, tact, fairness and force and Lord Herschell's investigation into the role of the society in 1897 could not fault its role in prosecution. The London police magistrates consulted by Herschell gave evidence to the effect that the solicitor to the Society 'had discharged his duties admirably'.[68]

The continued efficiency of the NSPCC's legal department becomes even more apparent when compared to the experiences of smaller societies who, with fewer resources, were unable to employ a regular, loyal, solicitor. The National Vigilance Association experienced severe problems in finding appropriate legal representation, partly because it was unfortunate in its choice of lawyers but also because of its reluctance to offer employment on a permanent full-time basis. One solicitor went on strike in 1886, refusing to represent the society because it was not adequately covering his expenses, and he threatened to resign a year later unless his salary was raised.[69] In 1888 a new solicitor was employed part-time but the executive committee soon became dissatisfied with him: for proceeding with cases without consultation, for failing to turn up at court hearings and, finally, for taking on the defence of a man accused of indecently assaulting a child.[70] This certainly did not tally with the NVA's priorities of protecting 'women, minors and children'.[71]

Although the police tended to pass cases involving girls over 16 to the NVA or the Jewish Association, London police and magistrates viewed the NSPCC as the main point of referral in cases of criminal and indecent assault of children.[72] Both the NVA and the Jewish Association, although ostensibly aiming to provide a legal service for wronged women and children, were never really able to establish themselves as thorough and systematic prosecuting agencies, mainly a result of their failure to ensure proper legal representation in the courts. Of the six cases of child sexual abuse which the NVA prosecuted in the London courts in 1890, only three ended in conviction. In 1900 they won two and lost one.

Were more cases reported/prosecuted as a result of the foundation of the NSPCC? Did the publicity surrounding the Society and its work in the courts act as a deterrent to offenders? The NSPCC itself argued that the policy of offering confidentiality to informers and the approachable demeanour of its inspectors made it more likely that information should be given.[73] It also maintained that the dropping off in the number of reported cases in the 1900s was a sign of its success: abusers had been frightened off by its campaigning work and the high profile of its inspectors.[74] Yet other interpretations of the figures are possible. The increase in the number of prosecutions after 1885 could be as much a result of W. T. Stead's mass publicity campaign and of the sudden change in the law which, by raising the age of consent from 13 to 16 in 1885, suddenly rendered illegal a whole group of previously licit sexual liaisons, as of a sudden willingness to trust NSPCC inspectors. The fall in prosecutions after 1900 could mean that knowledge of the new law had at last spread.

Many people had been happy to inform the police of sexual abuse incidents before 1884; with the appearance of the NSPCC, there was now simply a choice over whom to turn to for help. None of the depositions analysed in the previous chapter describe the involvement of NSPCC inspectors. Courtroom narratives continued to follow a similar pattern before and after

1884: detection and apprehension of abusers by neighbours, friends and family who then went to the police to make a complaint. Any NSPCC involvement appears to have been in the latter stages, after a complaint had been made to the police. While a substantial number of cases – approximately half of the sexual abuse cases which came before the Central Criminal Court between 1890 and 1910 – were NSPCC prosecutions, many of these might well have ended up in court anyway, as police or private prosecutions.

Finally, it is important to stress that cases of sexual abuse formed only a small percentage of NSPCC business as a whole. In 1890, for example 'cruel immoralities' (as the statistical reports referred to it) formed only 4 per cent of national business.[75] Less than 2 per cent of cases reported to the West Riding branches in the 1890s and early 1900s involved sexual abuse.[76] Cases of this nature did, however, have a higher profile in the metropolis, forming 7 per cent of the Society's London business in 1890 and 11 per cent of cases investigated by the East End branch in that year.[77] Contemporaries might have interpreted this as a sign of greater 'immorality' amongst the metropolitan poor. It is more plausible, however, that this high figure was the result of intensive philanthropic activity in the East End, which, through increased family surveillance, meant that the most secret of abuses were more likely to be reported. Higher figures in London could also be linked to the Society's special relationship with the Metropolitan Police and magistracy which meant that cases were referred routinely to the NSPCC rather than to other philanthropic organisations.[78]

The number of sexual abuse cases referred to the NSPCC was low nationally because of the alternatives offered by other societies. As this chapter will demonstrate next, local rescue and philanthropic societies, Poor Law officials and magistrates, in conjunction with a range of children's homes, found and provided residential accommodation for abused children as well as or instead of pursuing prosecution.

The issue of custody

In 1925 a special investigating board – the Departmental Committee on Sexual Offences against Young Children – reported its findings to parliament.[79] The committee, which included women JPs Clara Martineau and Clara Rackham as well as NSPCC director Robert Parr, was alarmed at the number of child victims removed from parental custody even when the offender was not a family member. The committee found 'instances in which children, who had good homes of their own, have been sent away to a special institution for many years, because the parents have been induced to believe that such action is necessary where a sexual offence has been committed against a child'.[80] The committee had interviewed representatives of a wide range of rescue and welfare organisations, including the Church Army, the Manchester Diocesan Association for Preventive and Rescue Work, the Jewish Association for the Protection of Women and Girls and the

Committee for the Moral Reform of Children in Islington and Finsbury, finding a broad consensus:

> Many witnesses have urged that the gossip of the neighbourhood, the strain on the child, and, in some cases, the bad habits acquired as a result of the offence have such an effect that the child should be sent away in every case to a special institution to receive experienced care and training.[81]

All female sexual abuse victims, not merely those in parental danger, should be removed from their home environments and placed in industrial schools or training homes. The evidence demonstrated the continued operation of the social purity viewpoint that 'fallen' women and girls required reformation and retraining.

Even within the NSPCC under both Waugh and Parr, there was some ambivalence about the issue of custody. Just as it stressed that it was not a 'prosecuting agency', so too the Society emphasised its reluctance to remove children from their parental home:

> The Society does not seek to 'rescue' children from cruel parents. It seeks to make parents behave properly to their children, and to abolish the need for rescue. ... It does not seek to break up families, but to make them worthy of their name and of the land they are in.[82]

Indeed, on the whole, it was true to its word. Behlmer has estimated that less than 1 per cent of all children involved in NSPCC cases were removed from their parents.[83] Once again, however, sexual abuse cases provided the exception to the rule. Cases of incest were clearly 'emergency' cases where the removal of the child from parental custody was an absolute requirement. Yet even where abuse had taken place outside of the home, custody was often a contested issue.

Changes in child custody law had given philanthropic institutions increasing authority during the last third of the nineteenth century to remove children from their parents and to send them to training homes. The Industrial Schools Act of 1866 legislated for the committal of children to certified industrial schools if they were found begging, wandering without home or proper guardianship, destitute (including orphans and those with one surviving parent in prison) or frequenting the company of thieves.[84] The 1880 Industrial Schools Amendment Act, popularly known as Ellice Hopkins's Act, added to this list children who were found living 'in immoral surroundings', with common prostitutes or frequenting their company.[85] The 1885 Criminal Law Amendment Act allowed parents or guardians to be divested of custodial authority if it appeared, during court trial, that they had caused or encouraged the seduction or prostitution of their child.[86] Finally, the 1891 Custody of Children Act gave judges the power of discretion to reject applications for *habeas corpus* writs where parents had neglected or ill-treated their children.[87] This series of acts transformed the role of children's homes in the nineteenth century; the orphanage of the 1830s, which aimed to feed and clothe the destitute and parentless, was replaced with the training home of the 1880s which was supposed to remedy the effects of 'bad' parenting, and to retrain its child inmates morally, physically and industrially, in order to take on their roles as efficient citizens.

The survival of case records for specialist homes set up to take 'fallen' girl children makes it possible to evaluate further the attitudes of the NSPCC and other rescue organisations towards the issue of child custody. The Church of England Waifs and Strays Society, founded in 1881 and later known as the Children's Society, supervised a string of industrial schools and reformatories throughout the country, including homes at Leytonstone (1865–97) and The Mumbles (1885–1901) which were set up particularly to take 'fallen' girl children.[88] In 1901 the Salvation Army set up a new home, the Nest, at Clapton, North London, which soon came to be associated with the worst abuse cases.[89] The work of the children's homes and industrial schools will be discussed in detail in chapter 7; their records will be used, here, to show that reform of the child as much as punishment of the offender was a central priority in sexual abuse cases.

The case records for the children's homes show that the NSPCC was just one among a large number of philanthropic organisations and individuals seeking homes for 'fallen' children. Between 1902 and 1914 a total of twenty-two girls were sent to the Nest, from all areas of the country, after experiencing sexual abuse. Nine of these were NSPCC referrals but the others were forwarded by Salvation Army officers, lady philanthropists,[90] magistrates, and local rescue groups such as the Bath Vigilance Association. In eight of the Waifs and Strays cases, explicit reference was made to sexual assault; only one of these cases was referred by the NSPCC, the remainder forwarded by local clergy or lady philanthropists, the Reform and Refuge Union, Oxford Association for Friendless Girls, and the Leeds Rescue Committee. Even where the NSPCC had played a dominant role in court proceedings, it might have little say over what happened next. Any number of philanthropic bodies could arrange for the child to be sent away, either through the formal mechanism of the magistrates' court using child protection and custody legislation, or through more informal methods of persuasion.

Certainly child victims of incest were more likely to be sent to an institution than those who had been assaulted by strangers. Nearly half of the sexually abused girls at the Nest were victims of incest, over a third having been assaulted by their fathers. Prosecution had only taken place in 40 per cent of sexual abuse cases, clear evidence that most never came to court. In incest cases, the NSPCC and other rescue organisations used a whole range of strategies to remove children from parental care. If there was not sufficient evidence to prosecute for sexual assault, charges of neglect or cruelty might be applied, as in the case of 14-year-old Ena, introduced at the beginning of the chapter. In 1913 the lady philanthropists of the Thanet Rescue Society, Kent, were determined to remove 11-year-old Beatrice from the clutches of her invalid father who, it was alleged, had sexually assaulted his daughter repeatedly while her mother was out at work.[91] Although there was 'not sufficient evidence to justify legal proceedings', the ladies developed a more roundabout approach to send her away to the Nest. Beatrice's case records state that 'the parents have been frightened into parting with the child' (perhaps by threat of prosecution). Custody, however, still lay with the parents and, when the Salvation Army decided that she needed to be sent to a home for 'mental defectives' in 1917, the parents refused and demanded her back.[92]

Despite these obvious 'emergency' cases, there were others that formed a greyer area. Some 50 per cent of the Nest's residents had been victims of extra-familial abuse rather than incest and strategies of removing these children from the custody of their parents appear more controversial. Similarly, half of the sexually abused children in the Waifs and Strays sample were not living with abusers when they were sent away. In 1895 the NSPCC, through its Rotherham branch, prosecuted the mother of 7-year-old Edith for neglect rather than the man who had criminally assaulted her (the assault had taken place over a year previously and it was felt there was insufficient evidence).[93] The woman's failure to obtain adequate medical treatment for her daughter's resultant syphilitic condition provided the means for poor law officials, working closely with the NSPCC, to remove her from parental custody. The mother's moral reputation was also held to be dubious since she lived (unmarried) with a 'coloured man' in a succession of lodgings or, when times were especially hard, workhouses.[94] The girl was eventually sent to the Waifs and Strays Industrial School for Girls at Far Headingley, Leeds.

The NSPCC was deeply aware of the controversy surrounding the issue of child custody. Central headquarters made it clear, from the turn of the century onwards, that local inspectors could only remove children from parental custody if this had been approved by the London directorate. The *Inspector's directory* of 1904 instructed that:

> Where, from the hopeless character of an offender, it seems necessary in its interests to remove a child from a parent's custody, a full Report must be sent to the central office, which alone determines whether an application should be made for such change of custody. The Society will not accept the custody of a child when an application to the court has not been previously authorised by Central Office.[95]

The 1910 edition added 'the *fact that a child is in grave moral danger*' (emphasis in original) to the criteria necessitating removal from parental custody.[96] The tone of the custody statement was an adamant one, suggesting that problems may have arisen in the past because inspectors had acted independently or official instructions had not been complied with. 'Immoral surroundings' and 'grave moral danger' were highly arbitrary and subjective categories.

One unusual case hints at irregularities and, indeed, disagreement within the ranks of the NSPCC as to whether a child should remain at home or be taken into care. In Wallsend in Northumberland in 1908 a man was arrested and charged with the rape of two sisters. The local NSPCC inspector investigating the matter decided to charge the mother, said to be a prostitute, with neglect, although the father (who was not involved in the assaults) was described as a 'respectable, steady, good man, a labourer'.[97] The inspector wrote to Florence Booth and she immediately offered the children places at the Nest. The matter was already settled before Mrs Booth was informed that Robert Parr had refused help and 'would not allow his inspector at Wallsend to do anything more in the case'.[98] The case records do not go into details about the nature of the disagreement but it is clear that the issue was one of the propriety of removing children from their natural parents. The removal of these children was clearly controversial; if not necessarily a 'happy' home, few grounds of complaint could be found against either her father or indeed, one suspects, her mother. Although Parr attempted to step in, the children were already on their way to the Nest, and they were not returned to their parents.

In other cases where the NSPCC refused to accept custody, other individuals or organisations tended to intervene. In 1910 Margaret, aged 11, became the victim of the prejudice of her schoolmates and their parents after a man accused of her rape was cleared by a court in Lincoln on the grounds of insufficient evidence.[99] She was ill for three months after the attack and was then refused readmission to her local school by the managers since 'some of the parents of the other children threatened to withdraw their children' if she was allowed to attend. This case uniquely highlights a wider popular confusion over the moral status of the abused child. The Lincoln parents saw Margaret as an immoral and threatening influence on their own children. It is impossible to gauge whether they would have been more sympathetic if the man had been convicted. Either way – liar and blackmailer, or victim contaminated by abuse – she was perceived by them to be sexually precocious. The NSPCC inspected the child's home, finding it to be 'bad and dirty', and, in line with policy guidelines, administered a warning. The lady philanthropists of a local Children's Aid Committee were not prepared to leave the matter at that. They were intent on sending the child away, even thought her father adamantly refused. After a succession of visits from committee members and Salvation Army officials, he finally gave in 'after seeing postcards of the Nest' and being told he could visit the child in the Home.[100]

The desire to institutionalise girls who had been sexually abused arose as much from fears about their moral status as corrupted children as from concerns to protect them from defendants. This attitude was shared by a wide range of protection agencies and carers. A Northampton girl, Mary, had been taken in by Salvationists as a baby when her mother died and her father absconded.[101] When, as a 13-year-old, she was sexually assaulted by a man (no details are given about him), her carers put her in the workhouse pending court proceedings. They seem to have abandoned Mary, no longer wanting her in their house and busily arranging for her to live elsewhere. After the man had been sentenced to 6 months' imprisonment, Mary was sent down to London to live at the Nest.[102]

Finally, the case of 12-year-old Alice demonstrates the stigma of sexual abuse, the panic about moral corruption, the worry it could spread to others and the judgements made about the sexual behaviour of impoverished mothers.[103] When she was three, Alice's father, a sailor, had abandoned his wife, taking the child with him. In 1889 he was sentenced to 15 years' penal servitude for sexually abusing Alice, by then aged 11, and for two offences of bigamy. Alice returned to live with her mother and grandfather in West Hartlepool; although 'wild at first', her behaviour improved on attending school. A local rescue committee continued to keep her under observation and the school board where they lived, 'took the greatest care to have the child watched at school so that she might   not do harm among her companions'. Although Alice had good reports from the school it seems the rescue committee were keen to get her away to a training home, finally applying to the Waifs and Strays Society when it was found that her mother, who had tried hard to discipline her daughter's initial wildness, was immoral: 'Another reason for removing the child was found out by the School Board people, her mother goes home sometimes with a policeman who partly maintains her.' This was the final straw and Alice was rushed into an industrial school. Michelle Cale has demonstrated that child savers often used the argument that a mother was 'immoral' and therefore unfit to take care of her children as grounds for removing girls from parental care.[104] In Alice's case, the evidence against her mother simply provided the opportunity, under the 1880 Industrial Schools Amendment Act, to gain custody of a child whom they regarded as 'corrupted' and in need of reform.

It was under the directorate of Robert Parr that steps were taken to establish a standardised custody policy in cases of sexual abuse. Parr had been involved in the campaign for the 1908 Punishment of Incest Act, making incestuous abuse a secular rather than a clerical matter, and was a main mover behind the 1907 Probation of Offenders Act, which aimed to keep minor offenders together with their children.[105] By the time he was appointed to sit on the Departmental Committee on Sexual Offences against Young Persons in 1925, he had clearly rejected the social purity rationale which argued that all sexual abuse victims, as polluted and contaminated, must be removed from their homes. It is probable that Parr, as an appointed 'expert' on child welfare, played an important part in shaping the opinion of the committee. The report recommended that 'it is a *grave step* to remove a child from its parents, and this should not be done unless the necessity for this action is clearly established'.[106] NSPCC custody policy was, however, an area of contestation in the late Victorian/Edwardian period. The rhetoric of innocence/corruption had shaped NSPCC constructions of sexual abuse during the 1880s and 1890s and ideas about what constituted 'immoral surroundings' or 'grave moral danger' were not necessarily clear cut, as the case of Edith has demonstrated. Decisions were often based on the moral expectations of middle-class philanthropists and officials rather than the social standards and material conditions of the urban poor. The cases investigated here show that child savers often attempted to remove children from their parents on fairly spurious grounds – such as 'immoral surroundings' – suggested by custody legislation; when this failed, they sometimes resorted to persuasion and even threats. Despite Parr's attempts to change attitudes towards custody in sexual abuse cases, his views were not met by the proliferation of rescue societies and philanthropic individuals who were actively weeding out 'fallen' children for training and rehabilitation well into the 1920s.

This chapter has examined the strategies and procedures of the child welfare and rescue societies involved in the prosecution of sexual abuse in the courts. The next two chapters will focus on a different aspect of court procedure: the giving of evidence and the evaluation of witness statements. Two contrasting sets of voices will be examined in turn: those of the medical experts, called to give forensic testimony as to the signs of abuse on the child's body and, secondly, those of the child victims themselves, who were required to describe their version of events. The dualistic concept of the 'fallen' as victim/threat permeated the construction and reception of these forms of evidence.

4 Signs on the body
The medical profession

Introduction

In his published lectures of 1852 Charles West, co-founder of the Hospital for Sick Children at Great Ormond Street in London, warned doctors that they needed to learn a different 'language of signs' or 'semeiology' if they were to understand the illnesses of childhood.[1] The young child might scream, cry or throw a tantrum at the approach of a total stranger. It was likely there would be problems with verbal communication. 'You cannot question your patient,' wrote West 'or, if old enough to speak, still, through fear, or from comprehending you but imperfectly, he will probably give you an incorrect reply.'[2] How was the doctor to locate and identify pain or illness in the child? The answer lay in a language that was based not merely on the voluntary sounds and gesticulations of the child patient, but on bodily signs; the child's body required both detailed observation and careful interpretation if its full physiological meaning was to be understood. When allegations of sexual abuse arose, the detection and interpretation of these bodily signs – the semiology of the body – led the doctor out of the surgery and into the courtroom.[3] According to statute law, a child's testimony was not in itself sufficient to convict a defendant of sexual assault; forensic or other circumstantial evidence was necessary in order to prove that an offence had been committed. The medical doctor was an essential witness in cases of child sexual abuse.[4]

During the Cleveland affair of the late 1980s, the forms of medical evidence which were used to diagnose sexual abuse became a point of controversy as Dr Marietta Higgs argued for the reliability of the 'anal dilation' test.[5] Such controversy was by no means new. The signs of abuse and how to read them formed a crucial area of debate in British medico-legal circles throughout the nineteenth century, intensifying from the 1840s onwards. This debate centred on two issues: the identification of penetration and, secondly, the significance of vaginal discharges. It is important to emphasise that the debate referred, almost exclusively, to the bodies of girl children. Although French forensic physicians Adolphe Toulmouche and Ambrose Tardieu were investigating the signs of sexual abuse on male children during the 1850s, English texts tended to restrict the debate to girls.[6]

Police surgeons and general practitioners could turn to two sets of medical texts for advice on interpreting signs of abuse on a girl child's body. The most influential sources were probably the texts of medical jurisprudence produced by leading experts in forensic medicine and continually updated in response to legal changes. These included Thomas Percival's *Medical ethics* (first published in 1803), Michael Ryan's *A handbook of medical jurisprudence* (1831), and the *Elements of medical jurisprudence* by American physicians T. R. and J. B. Beck which became well known in British medical circles during the 1820s. During the second half of the century, Alfred Swaine Taylor's *Elements of medical jurisprudence* became the established authority on forensic medicine as it ran to twelve editions between 1844 and 1891. All these texts included detailed discussions of the use of forensic evidence in court cases of rape and unlawful carnal knowledge.

Towards the end of the century a second source of information became available to doctors who were aware of the growing literature on the diseases of childhood. While the study of paediatric medicine is usually said to have originated in France at the end of the eighteenth century, British doctors were slow to enter the field. While Dr West's lectures were reprinted from the 1850s onwards, providing a unique example of British paediatric medical research, it was not until the 1880s that a new set of paediatric works, which included translations of foreign-language texts and collaborations between British and American doctors, began to emerge. These included the works of British doctors Eustace Smith (1884), J. F. Goodhart and G. F. Still (1905), translations of the lectures of Dr Henoch of Berlin (1889), the work of American physician L. Emmett Holt (1897), and the transatlantic production of the *Encyclopaedia of the diseases of children* (1891–1901).[7] From a British perspective, the literature concerning diseases of childhood could, in 1890, be said to be 'of essentially modern growth'.[8] However, like established texts dealing with the adult body, the new paediatric literature was ordered in terms of anatomy, describing the organs of the body one by one, their disease and breakdown. Within this structure (which automatically precluded discussion of psychological or mental development) the sexual abuse of young girls was presented as part of the discussion of genito-urinary illnesses and, in particular, vaginal discharges.

It is necessary to ask, however, whether any general conclusions about nineteenth-century medical opinion and practice can be drawn from the medico-legal and paediatric texts. While they may be considered as representative of the views of medical specialists, it is unclear to what extent their arguments either influenced or reflected the minds of the vast rank of general practitioners. It is extremely likely that those specifically employed as police surgeons owned a well-thumbed copy of Taylor's *Medical jurisprudence*, but it is also possible that less 'expert' doctors, summoned as a matter of emergency to attend police court cases, had little idea of prescribed practice and procedure. In order to build up a picture of the extent of forensic knowledge and its interpretation on a daily basis, it is necessary to turn to the evidence given by medical practitioners in court cases of sexual assault. As well as analysing the specialist medical text, therefore, this chapter will also move on to consider the testimonies of doctors that were recorded in the depositions prepared for criminal trials between 1830 and 1914. How did doctors view the child's body? How did they search for and measure sexual abuse? What importance was attached, in court, to medical evidence? What about cases which never came to court?

The legal depositions are testimony to the male dominance of the medical profession in the period up to the First World War. Although women were allowed to qualify as physicians from 1865, their admission to the profession was slow, and indeed all doctors called to give expert evidence in the Middlesex and West Riding samples were men.[9] Occasional references can be found to the employment of 'female searchers' who were brought into local police stations to examine girl-children for signs of sexual abuse in the presence of doctors.[10] Women doctors made occasional appearances in the provinces. In 1904 Marion Elford acted as medical witness in a case of criminal assault tried at the Lincoln Assizes; she commented on the incongruous procedure whereby all women (except herself as expert witness) were asked to leave the court to protect them from the shocking details of the case.[11] It was not until 1927 that Nesta Wells took up her position as the first woman police surgeon in Britain, employed by the City of Manchester Police.[12] Other authorities were slow to follow, and the Medical Women's Federation continued to campaign for the employment of women doctors by local constabularies throughout the 1930s and 40s, arguing that it was essential for women and children who complained of sexual assault to be examined by a female doctor.[13]

Given the exclusive position of the middle-class male doctor, this chapter will set out to examine the ways in which notions of gender and class, intersecting with medico-moral epistemologies of both childhood and sexuality, affected interpretations of bodily signs in cases of sexual abuse. A widespread and often institutionalised hostility to women within the male medical profession was revealed in misogynist descriptions of child victims and their mothers, but also in a tendency to make judgements that went against female complainants. Doctors were extremely reluctant to recognise and diagnose sexual abuse and a whole battery of alternative explanations was found for suggestive signs including physiological disease, physical dirt, forgery and precocious imagination. Where signs were incontrovertible, doctors' reticence or lack of up-to-date knowledge meant they would only substantiate less serious charges. Doctors, like philanthropists, were confused about the moral status of the child victim – as on the one hand innocent and, on the other eminently corruptible – and their views were coloured by class as well as gender prejudices. As they focused on the bodies of working-class females, possible signs of abuse were read within a wider symbolic framework that was based on the cultural meanings of disease, dirt, pollution and the transgression of bodily boundaries. The analysis will begin by focusing on the debates in specialist medical texts, outlining the ways in which expert doctors refused to acknowledge that sexual abuse might be all too common.

Crime and anatomy

Evidence of rape

In the first half of the nineteenth century debates centred on the degree of penetration judged necessary for an offence to constitute statutory rape or unlawful carnal knowledge. The judgement of Rex v. Russell in 1777 had established that, although some degree of penetration must be proved, the hymen could still be intact.[14] A different precedent, however, was set in the case of Rex v. Gammon in 1832 where the judge, Baron Gurney, observed: 'I think that if the hymen is not ruptured, there is not a sufficient penetration to constitute this offence.'[15] The problem was compounded because the absence or presence of the hymen could not really be regarded as conclusive proof either of rape or virginity respectively. Some girl children, it was acknowledged, were born with a congenital lack of a hymen or with a hymen which was extremely elastic. Some specialists argued that it was, effectively, impossible to rape a child who had not yet reached puberty (the age of 10 was sometimes given) since she was not sufficiently developed to allow full penetration;[16] only in India, it was argued, where sex with children was condoned through child marriage, were such brutalities likely to take place, with mortal consequences.[17]

The doctor in court was caught up in the controversy. A letter to the *Lancet* from Dr John Adams, called to the Old Bailey in 1843 to act as medical witness in a case of alleged father–daughter rape, demonstrates the confusion facing the general practitioner.[18] Adams examined the girl and found no signs of penetration (the girl had an unruptured hymen), although two other 'highly respected medical witnesses', who were called in later, claimed she had been raped. Adams was concerned about the 'present, imperfect legal definition of rape' and he asked the *Lancet's* readers for advice:

> In what does the crime consist? ... If penetration implies merely the introduction of the male organ as far as the vulva, and does not demand of its completion the introduction of the organ into the vagina, then I am free to admit that in the case under consideration the offence was fully proved; but if the latter condition be requisite, then I positively deny – this *not* having been accomplished – the commission of the offence.[19]

Taylor responded in his 1844 edition of *Medical jurisprudence*, stating that statute law simply required proof of penetration and did not mention rupture of the hymen. He acknowledged that this was still open to interpretation and that 'we shall blatantly find different judges taking different views'.[20] By 1852 Taylor was able to quote case law which clearly established that: 'it is now ... an admitted principle that a sufficient degree of penetration to constitute rape in law may take place without necessarily rupturing the hymen'.[21] Although the degree of physical injury might differ, the moral damage was, he argued, the same.

By the 1850s, therefore, experts had agreed that penetration of the vulva alone needed to be proved in order to establish that rape or unlawful carnal knowledge had been committed; the lifting of the death penalty for crimes of rape in 1841 must have rendered this view more acceptable.[22] Taylor argued that some degree of penetration on children would, if force was used, lead to severe injury.[23] If the assault had taken place in a less forceful fashion it could be indicated by any combination of inflammation and abrasion, discharge, blood clots, a lacerated hymen, painful urination, pain in walking, and vaginal dilation. Problems arose, however, in determining the aetiology of these symptoms; while they were all potential signs of abuse, some might arise from physiological disease and others could be faked on the child's body.

Venereal disease

English medical writers demonstrated an astonishing refusal to attribute discharges in children to sexual abuse; they argued, instead, that they were most commonly caused by catarrhal infection or infantile leucorrhoea. Vaginal discharges in children were, indeed, commonly and popularly read as a sign of abuse by mothers and other child-carers who interpreted them as sexually transmitted diseases. Many experts, however, took great pains to deny this assumption. In an 1859 lecture on vulvitis, Dr J. Y. Simpson noted that: 'Very often, especially when it occurs in patients of the lower orders, the disease is improperly imagined, by the relatives and friends ... to be the result of venereal infection.'[24] The matter was controversial because knowledge of sexually transmitted diseases and, in particular, their identification, was limited. As a result of medical research, syphilitic discharges were identified by the mid-nineteenth century, but gonorrhoea was not isolated until 1879; some doctors were unable to distinguish gonorrhoea from non-venereal infections even after the turn of the century.[25] While transmission of gonorrhoea was an obvious sign of sexual abuse, vaginitis and vulvitis could also result from mechanical irritation or manipulation.[26] In 1910 Taylor noted, for the first time, ground-breaking research on the causes of vaginal discharges which had taken place since the discovery of the gonoccocus, directly linking them to sexual abuse: 'accurate biological examination ... has tended to show that, after all, a large proportion, something like 75 per cent, of them are gonorrhoeal'.[27] Throughout the nineteenth century and, indeed, well after 1900, medics had been arguing exactly the opposite. They had refused to believe the amateur diagnoses of female carers and had, instead, argued that most vaginal discharges were produced as a result of common childhood disease, exacerbated by lack of personal hygiene.

The representation of the lower classes as ignorant and/or dirty in the nineteenth-century medical text was often coupled with a scathing attack on the integrity of plebeian mothers. In 1831, Michael Ryan used the following lampoon to explain how he believed charges of sexual abuse were formulated. The central character, the mother, takes her daughter to the doctor, suffering from some dubious-looking discharge:

> She goes to a medical man, who may unfortunately not be aware of the nature of the complaint I am speaking of, and he says, 'Good God! Your child has got a clap!' ... I can assure you a multitude of persons have been hanged by such a mistake. I will tell you what takes place in such cases; the mother goes home, and says to the child, 'Who is it that has been playing with you? Who has taken you on his knee lately?' The child innocently replies 'No-one mother; nobody has, I declare to you.' The mother then says, 'Oh, don't tell me such stories; I will flog you if you do.' And thus the child is driven to confess what never happened, in order to save herself from being chastised: at last she says 'Such a one has taken me on his lap.'[28]

This crude reference to a Victorian version of 'false memory syndrome' was repeated and elaborated during the course of the century. In 1859 Simpson commented that: 'An excitable mother will, by threats and by suggestive and leading questions, get the frightened child to own to some absurd and groundless tale, in confirmation of her own maternal theory of the origin of the malady.'[29] Thirty years later Eustace Smith, physician to the East London Children's Hospital, wrote: 'Vulvitis is a very common derangement amongst the children of the poor ... we must be on our guard against accepting any suggestion (such as some mothers are very ready to make) that their child has been tampered with by a person of the opposite sex.'[30] Once again the children of the poor were represented as dirty and contaminated; their mothers as ignorant and overzealous in their accusations.

False accusations

Even what appeared to be brutal lacerations and severe syphilitic afflictions could be ascribed to purely medical causes. As Karen Taylor has shown, British and American physicians were extremely reluctant to attribute the transmission of syphilis to sexual contact when it afflicted children.[31] Where it was considered, medical writers tended to suggest acquired syphilis had been contracted through means other than sexual transmission; these included breast-feeding, use of dirty towels, and vaccination with contaminated needles or serums.[32] During the 1850s Dublin doctor William R. Wilde (whose son, Oscar, was later to gain greater notoriety) was involved in a series of medical controversies surrounding the interpretation of signs of rape on girl children. In 1853 he maintained that 'innocent persons' were exposed to 'great danger' from false charges arising from the misinterpretation of infantile leucorrhoea as a sign of abuse.[33] He also argued that greater attention should be given to the malignant disease, noma pudendi, associated with bad hygiene, which involved the inflammation and mortification of the genital organs, resulting, sometimes rapidly, in death. In 1858 he went on to argue that a defendant, Amos Greenwood, who had been tried at the Liverpool Sessions for the manslaughter of a 9-year-old girl, who had died after she had allegedly contracted syphilis from him, had been wrongfully convicted.[34] Wilde maintained that, although she had shared a bed with the man, she could not have been assaulted as her parents, who were asleep in the same room, did not hear her cry out; she had died as a result of noma pudendi. He consulted twelve leading figures in the field of forensic medicine – including Taylor – who failed to agree and came to a variety of conclusions. Dr W. B. Kesteven argued vehemently against Wilde, maintaining that 'the child's death was attributable to attempted intercourse resulting in syphilitic inoculation, the disease having assumed the most virulent form'.[35] Here, then, was one lone doctor making associations between syphilis and sexual abuse.

In all editions of *Medical jurisprudence*, Taylor introduced his discussion of rape by arguing that medical evidence was particularly valuable given the prevalence of false accusations, quoting from one author who suggested that only one real rape was tried at the assizes for every twelve 'pretended cases'.[36] He argued that 'false charges of rape on children are now not unfrequently made'.[37] Purulent discharges were wrongly attributed to sexual abuse out of ignorance or they were used for malicious purposes: 'children thus affected have been tutored to lay imputations against innocent persons for the purposes of extorting money'.[38] Medical and forensic experts also suggested that injuries could be forged or faked on the child's body (usually by mothers) to back up false claims, for purposes of revenge and blackmail or to get a certificate of divorce.[39] Taylor wrote that: 'cases are recorded in which such injuries have been purposely produced on young children by women, as a foundation for false charge against persons with a view of extorting money'.[40] The possible stereotyping of the incestuous father was overwritten with that of the duplicitous mother, abusing her position as child's carer and confidante. The relationship of mother and child was, in the most extreme cases, portrayed as sinister and abusive. This effected a shift of blame away from the male assailant; it was the mother who was constructed as the figure of blame.

This, then, was the advice offered by medical experts to doctors and police surgeons called to examine children's bodies in relation to charges of sexual abuse. To what extent did they read and heed this advice? How 'expert' was the general practitioner called to give police evidence? Dr Wilde's investigations into the Amos Greenwood case evoked hostile responses from Liverpool doctors, who felt he was casting aspersions on their skills. One Liverpool surgeon, Dr Brown, wrote that: 'The characters of noma pudendi, vaginitis, blennorrhoea, etc., are well-known to any reading first year's student, and we have learned nothing new from the papers recently published.'[41] His anger at the posturing of so-called 'experts' is apparent. His comments about medical training suggest that police surgeons and perhaps even general practitioners, were highly aware of the debates surrounding the interpretation of signs of sexual assault. Should Dr Brown of Liverpool be seen as representative of the general medical profession or as a somewhat unusual example?

Doctors in court

From the early days of the Metropolitan Police Force, each London division had employed its own surgeon to attend to the medical needs of its officers; a second role swiftly developed as police surgeons were summoned to examine victims or offenders for evidence of an allegation.[42] This practice of employing police surgeons spread from London to Birmingham and Manchester, while police in other districts (including the West Riding and rural areas of Middlesex) continued to call out local doctors on a more *ad hoc* basis. The evidence in this section is drawn from depositions prepared for child sexual abuse trials at the Middlesex and West Riding Quarter Sessions which contain the witness statements of police surgeons, hospital consultants and GPs in private practice.[43] The statements suggest that doctors were at least conversant with the debates on the signs of abuse contained in the pages of the medico-legal advice manuals but that their knowledge was sometimes far from up to date. Moreover, these doctors, like the medical experts, were extremely reticent about the proofs of rape and unlawful carnal knowledge and tended to argue for lesser charges of indecent or common assault.

Lesser charges

The medical testimonies reveal significant inconsistencies in procedure surrounding the summoning of doctors and the framing of charges. Until the 1860s, when police surgeons were regularly consulted, the responsibility lay with complainants themselves to go in search of a doctor. Even when the police were more systematically involved in the later period, there was often a substantial delay. Although the Middlesex depositions show that some surgeons were summoned to the police station within hours of the offence, other doctors deposed that they examined the child three or four days afterwards. Delays of a week or ten days, which had severe consequences in terms of medical evidence, were not unknown.[44]

Furthermore, it is apparent that comparatively minor charges of indecent assault were often lodged in relation to brutal attacks which appear to have been tantamount to rape. Despite Taylor's 1852 assertion that damage to the hymen was not necessary for an offence to constitute statutory rape, medics were extremely reluctant to argue this point in court.[45] In September 1870 London police surgeon, George Bagster Phillips, was called to the Stepney station to examine a 7-year-old girl and the man accused of her assault. He diagnosed both as suffering from gonorrhoea and said that a vaginal rupture indicated 'violence of some kind'.[46] Despite the strong nature of the medical evidence it was an indecent assault charge which was prosecuted and convicted although the brutality of this offence could have justified charging the man on a more serious count.

It could well be that doctors were using out-of-date textbooks which they had purchased when they first trained. In a case involving a 10-year-old girl which came before the West Riding Quarter Sessions in June 1865 a local doctor, who practised in Holmfirth on the outskirts of Huddersfield, told the court that, although there was swelling and redness, no penetration could have taken place since the hymen was entire. He continued: 'I am ... of the opinion that it is next to impossible without great violence ... for a child of the age of the – witness to be ravished.'[47] His comments seem more in line with earlier texts of the 1840s than with current expert opinion; they were certainly out of step with Taylor's 1852 publication. As late as 1895, a surgeon from the Yorkshire mill-town of Hipperholme examined a 10-year-old girl and found her sore and swollen with a 'partial rupture of the hymen'. He commented that she must have been in great pain but did not state that this was evidence of rape.[48] The defendant was tried for indecent assault and was sentenced to two years' imprisonment for an extremely brutal act. Thus it seems that a number of violent cases, which could have been interpreted as statutory rape or its attempt, were going through the courts as indecent assault charges. Perhaps it was assumed that juries were more likely to convict on a lesser charge given the controversy surrounding medical evidence of this nature. Indeed police, doctors and lawyers involved in plea-bargaining should be viewed as equally complicitous.

Faking signs

Doctors in court were clearly acquainted with the debates about false accusations and the interpretation of disease which were recycled in medical texts throughout the century. In line with the recommendations of the majority of these texts, they often refused to read discharges as signs of sexual abuse. In July 1870 a Middlesex mother accused her lodger of assaulting her 6-year-old daughter after she found that her 'private parts were inflamed and there was a discharge'.[49] Surgeon George Wright argued that it 'must have been the result of a cold or from contact with a man suffering with gonorrhoea'. He was not prepared to produce a conclusive statement and the case was acquitted when it came to trial. In cases involving children of the lowest classes, doctors might comment on the presence of dirt and filth as an accessory to disease. In April 1880 Frederick William Spurgin, police surgeon for the Marylebone division, examined an 8-year-old child, daughter of a sweep, who lived with her family in one room in Barnet's Court. There was inflammation and the child was suffering from a discharge that might have resulted from the fact that 'the parts were very dirty and unwashed'.[50] He argued that the signs could be interpreted either way: 'the child's condition was such as might have resulted from natural discharge or from slight violence to the private parts'. By 1900, however, surgeons had developed more sophisticated techniques of determining gonorrhoea which meant that discharges could now be analysed to establish causation. In an unusual London case, involving the alleged indecent assault of a 9-year-old boy by a woman lodger, samples were sent to the department of bacteriology at Guy's Hospital. The gonococcus micro-organism was found in the samples.[51] Procedures such as these revolutionised the interpretation of medical evidence which, until at least the 1890s, must have resulted in the dismissal of a large number of well-founded accusations.

Physical injuries, like disease, were attributed to causes other than sexual abuse. Highgate surgeon Dr Wetherell suggested in 1865 that irritation might have been 'produced by other causes ... such as over exertion or strain'.[52] The forging of signs on the child's body seems to have formed a key area of controversy when medical witnesses were cross-examined in court. Once again, it was almost always mothers who were identified as suspects in faking signs. In April 1880 three surgeons – George Etheridge (GP), Richard Thomas Wallace Smith (GP) and Thomas Bond, who was lecturer in forensic medicine at the Westminster Hospital – were called to give evidence at Lambeth Police Court in a case involving a man accused of raping his 7-year-old daughter.[53] All three were questioned in court by the defendant, who claimed that the injuries had been faked on the child's body. Etheridge was adamant that the child had been raped: 'I do not think that such appearances could have been produced by the mother tampering with the child through spite – in my opinion such appearances were caused by an assault by a male person.'[54] Smith took a similar line, but Bond was less clear: 'I cannot swear that it was done by a woman's finger but I should think it improbable ... violent pressure from the mother might have caused these injuries.'[55] The case was convicted when it came for trial at the Old Bailey but it clearly demonstrates the subjective nature of medical opinion as to the interpretation of signs. A similar case that had come before the Middlesex Sessions in 1870 concluded very differently. Hackney surgeon William Fowles, examining the infant victim, had found abrasions and swelling to the genitals as well as bloodstains on her linen, suggesting violence had been used.[56] He did not, however, indicate the origin of this violence. The child was too young to give evidence in court but her mother claimed she had been assaulted by her father. The jury interpreted the medical evidence as suggesting that the mother had inflicted wounds on the child's body. The local newspaper reported that 'it was supposed she was anxious to be revenged upon him'.[57]

The issue of false charges, like the concept of disease and dirt, was clearly related to notions of class as well as age and gender. In October 1870 an 11-year-old servant girl accused her master of assaulting her at his house in Whitechapel. The contrast between the social class and status of the victim and her alleged assailant was significant. The master owned a tailor's business and employed a number of people. The child's parents were clearly very poor: she described her father as a 'bird dealer' and the child was herself making a contribution to the family economy through the 1s 6d she earned each week. Police surgeon George Bagster Phillips told the magistrates at Thames Police Court that there was inflammation and swelling of the vaginal tract and that the hymen was wanting.[58] He was then cross-examined in court in an attempt to prove that the signs of abuse had been faked on the child's body: 'the appearances might be caused by mechanical violence. ... The child's own finger might have done it.' The defendant, whose reputation was guaranteed by a selection of character witnesses, was acquitted at the Middlesex Sessions when the case came for trial. In cases involving younger children, fake signs were assumed to be the work of mothers. Where older girls were involved (like this independent 11-year-old) attempts were made to demonstrate that that they themselves were responsible for inventing the allegations.

Medical misogyny?

The medical profession was extremely concerned that one-to-one appointments with female patients could result in false accusations of sexual assault against 'respectable' physicians. A number of prosecutions served to feed this anxiety. In 1870, a young woman accused a 32-year-old surgeon of administering chloroform with intent to criminally assault her. The case was acquitted, but the Old Bailey judge advised the defendant not to 'examine female patients in future without having some other person present'.[59] In 1890 the issue was once again brought to the attention of doctors when a 14-year-old girl alleged that she had been raped by a medical student while she waited in a room at the London Hospital. She attended an identity parade but failed to pick out her assailant whom, it was subsequently deduced, had already absconded. The *Illustrated Police News* reported that: 'as the girl was leaving the hospital a large number of students, who had heard of the affair, groaned and hooted her'.[60] The mass hostility of what was to be the new generation of physicians must have been a disturbing sight. The newspaper later commented that: 'the possibility of both charges being "got up" by a couple of corrupt little girls is not to be ignored'.[61] The best solution, it argued, was to introduce a rule that dispensers and hospital-dressers should not 'have anything to do with little-girl patients except in the presence of a nurse'. Any reading of the medical depositions and the debates over false charges must be contextualised in relation to the panic over the allegations of female patients and in relation to elements of an institutionalised misogyny within the medical profession. The hooting and shouting of the London medical students resonates with the protesting voices of those involved in the Edinburgh riot against the admittance of female medical students including Sophia Jex-Blake in 1870.[62]

It must be emphasised that an analysis of medical opinion which focuses on the material contained in court depositions is necessarily flawed. Depositions provide information about those cases that actually went to trial; they do not tell us much about those which were dismissed at the earliest stages, either at the police station or the police court. Given that medical evidence was an essential consideration in the decision to commit for trial, it is hardly surprising that, in 60 per cent of the deposition samples which featured doctors, medical statements were given which specifically confirmed the charges against defendants. In 25 per cent of cases neutral evidence, which presented a number of possibilities to the jury, was given; in a further 15 per cent of cases, medics refuted the allegations but the case was tried because there were other forms of evidence to be considered. Juries usually convicted in line with the medical evidence. These figures do, however, gloss over the circumstances of trials. Only qualitative analysis of the depositions can suggest the involvement of doctors in reducing and softening charges. Doctors were reluctant to press for charges of rape and unlawful carnal knowledge, preferring instead, where medical evidence was incontrovertible, to opt for relatively minor charges of indecent or common assault.

It is extremely probable that a large number of cases never came to trial because the medical evidence was deemed insufficient to prosecute from the outset. Two unusual articles provide information that can hint at the gaps in the sources and lead beyond supposition. In 1886 American doctor Jerome Walker, employed as physician to the Brooklyn Society for the Prevention of Cruelty to Children (USA), published an article in the *Archives of Pediatrics* in which he analysed twenty-one cases of sexual assault involving children that had come to his attention in the previous four years.[63] He had produced medical evidence corroborating the allegations in nine cases and contradicting them in another nine; in two cases he had given neutral evidence. Walker argued, throughout the article, that sexual abuse was not an imaginary problem but a real one that must be taken seriously. In 1894 Lawson Tait, gynaecologist and police surgeon to the Birmingham constabulary, published a far cruder article in the *Provincial Medical Journal*, in which he described how he had recommended prosecution in only 5 per cent of the seventy cases which the police had referred to him between 1886 and 1893.[64] He argued that allegations of sexual abuse resulted from attempts at blackmail and extortion. Both articles are unusual, firstly in content (doctors did not generally choose to write in such a forthright way about cases of sexual assault) but also because of their respective positions and reputations. Walker, in his work for the Brooklyn SPCC, was clearly a specialist on the medical evaluation of child abuse. Tait was, by this time, an extremely controversial figure in British medicine as a result of his use of ovariotomy to treat 'menstrual epileptic mania' and his rejection of antiseptics. His reputation remains to this day that of an extremist with an uncompromising hostility to women, although it must be acknowledged that he had a profound practical influence on police practice in Birmingham.[65] Neither can, therefore, be seen as representative of the average doctor. However, given that they demonstrate views that are in many ways at odds, they can be usefully seen as opinion markers within the medical establishment. Most doctors probably fitted into the hazy morass of opinion somewhere in between.

'Little minx' or 'little victim'?

In 1894 Lawson Tait argued that most cases of sexual abuse reported to the police were 'trumped up charges' made by 'vile conspirators and black-mailers', usually mothers and girl children, to extort money or destroy the reputation of their alleged male assailants.[66] While in all other spheres, the law worked to the disadvantage of women, when it came to sexual crime, women were, he argued, in much the better legal position. The gendered double standard of sexual and moral values actually operated in their favour.[67] Tait maintained that 'women clearly have the best of it, and chiefly because the real truth about them cannot be proclaimed on the house tops'.[68] The double standard, Tait argued, meant that women were a danger to men. He did not believe it was actually possible for a woman to be raped by a man: 'no sane man can believe that a woman of average health and strength, and not overcome by drugs, can be violated by one man'.[69] He stated that, until capital punishment for rape was repealed in 1841, 'thousands of innocent men must have been murdered'.

While Anna Clark and Judith Walkowitz have argued that 'narratives of sexual danger' were constructed in the nineteenth century with the effect of keeping women in fear of the street and the public domain,[70] Tait believed that what he called 'social custom and method of thought' served to put men in real danger from women. The danger for men, however, was based on private space rather than public. He argued that since male sexual behaviour was generally expected to be active and predatory, any allegation made against a man might be automatically believed. If, for whatever reason, a man found himself closeted and unchaperoned with a woman or young girl, he could not guarantee she would not make some allegation against him: 'However men may laugh and make jokes, they do not willingly travel with single unknown female companions in railway carriages'.[71]

Tait described the defendant in cases of child sexual abuse as a 'poor ignorant wretch' or 'unfortunate man'; in contrast, the girl children lodging the complaints were labeled as 'virulent little minxes', 'chits' and 'dirty little wretches' who lied and connived to produce an accusation of criminal assault. The process of victimisation was reversed; the alleged assailant should be identified as the 'victim', according to Tait, while the child was the evil, vile or malicious protagonist. Tait argued that those who told the worst lies were 'children of almost the lowest class of population';[72] poverty and social position were proportional in his eyes to corruption and sexual precocity. Levels of virtue or viciousness were related to class position; poverty and dirt created the corrupt liar. In one Birmingham case in which he was involved, two girls, aged 14 and 11, went to the police claiming that the younger had been indecently assaulted by her father.[73] Tait examined the younger child and concluded she was 'quite uninjured' but found that the elder child had been living as 'her own father's regular mistress' for over two years. He found it difficult to view her body as a child's body since it was no longer small and enclosed. Tait commented: 'the child's vagina was as large and lax as that of a married woman of mature experience'.[74] Tait suggested this girl or 'little wretch' was typical of girls making allegations of sexual abuse: '[She] was one of the most virulent little minxes I ever saw, and she made no secret of her reason for splitting on her father being the fact that she found him taking up with another girl. ... She does afford ... a perfect example of how the great bulk of these charges are brought about.'[75] Tait admitted that in a few cases he had uncovered what he saw as real and violent abuse, but even then, his lack of tact and sympathy produced a truly grotesque picture. He boasted how he had repaired the organs of a severely abused little girl – 'the celebrated case of complete and undoubted rape on a young child, the only case I have any knowledge of' – exhibiting her at a meeting of Birmingham doctors as a demonstration of his surgical skills.[76]

In 1886 Jerome Walker had published an article performing a similar task to Tait but revealing a different attitude. It would be fair to say that Walker was more prepared to see a child as a person and not merely as a case. He tried to describe children's mixed feelings and confusion with a degree of sensitivity. In the case of a 6-year-old girl who was abused by her uncle, he wrote: 'the child agreed to his proposition on account of his threat and because she trusted her uncle whom she seemed to be fond of'.[77] The man was found guilty of rape and imprisoned for twenty years. Of the rape of an 8-year-old, Walker wrote: 'This child seemed like an intelligent and well-bred girl. Her ready acquiescence in assuming the position the man desired her to can only be explained by a childish innocence and an implicit faith in the man.'[78] There is no mention of 'minxes' and 'dirty little wretches'; the language used is altogether different. Walker understood that abuses could occur because children trust adults and because adults have power over children. He did, nevertheless, demonstrate a clear class bias in his equation of social position and upbringing with the ability to tell the truth:

CASE XXI ... This case was not tried as there was no physical evidence of rape having been attempted. The statement of a girl of 14 years who has lived in public institutions, and as a menial in various families and has been cast about here and there, and is mainly conversant with low talk and vulgar actions, was also to be taken into account.[79]

The association of ignorance and duplicity with the lifestyles of the lowest classes echoes the medical texts discussed in previous sections.

Both Tait and Walker were called in to investigate cases of sexual abuse on young girls (one employed by an SPCC, one by the police), but each presented strikingly different conclusions. Forensic medicine aimed to establish an objective truth through scientific knowledge, but its application was extremely arbitrary, often resting entirely on individual interpretation and on the attitude of the doctor towards the alleged victim. Despite their radically different conclusions, Tait and Walker did, nevertheless, have something in common. Both inherited a perception of the child's body, in terms of morphology, pathology and bodily pollution – a perception bound up with the class and gender position of the male professional – which can be traced in medical discourses throughout the nineteenth century.

Pollution, transgression and morality

Medical readings of the child's body and its boundaries were directly related to knowledges of gender and sexuality and of the transformation from childhood to adulthood. The discussion of child sexual abuse formed a focal point for these different knowledges. Doctors revealed clear sets of expectations in the way they described the abused child's body. Lawson Tait, as already indicated, had not expected to see a child with a 'large and lax' vagina. Jerome Walker also recorded his surprise in examining the body of a 9 year girl and finding that 'the vagina gaped open as it would do in a woman who had had children' even though, so he stated, 'there is no reason to believe that the child had been tampered with'.[80] The child's body was supposed to be closed and contained. The bodily transformation from girl child to adult woman was read in terms of opening, disclosure and discharge; and it was intrinsically bound up with sexual and reproductive function. The case of the male child was of course quite different: in terms of topology, the male's body remained the same. The body of the adult man might be dirty and corrupting, but was again closed. Only when the male was penetrated through sodomy could the male body open and become feminised. In his 1873 edition of *Medical jurisprudence*, Taylor detailed one example of (what he called) pederasty, a case which he had examined in 1833: that of the actress Eliza Edwards.[81] Eliza's dead body was brought to Guy's Hospital unclaimed, and, after disrobing, was found to be male. The reproductive organs had been strapped up and 'there was strong evidence that he had been for many years addicted to unnatural habits'. Taylor noted that 'the anus was much wider and larger than natural' and that the folds of skin had been worn away 'so that this part resembled the labia of the female organs'. Taylor's reading of the sodomist's signature in terms of the male actress's feminised body was echoed in other works.[82]

The child's body was supposed to be pure, closed, intact and hence unmarked by other bodies; it was also supposed to be clean. The child's body, if healthy, should be free from any trace of sexuality. In 1831 Ryan commented that a child under the age of 10 'cannot have desire'.[83] In 1856 William Acton wrote that: 'in a state of health no sexual idea should enter a child's mind'.[84] Children should be kept clean, he urged, and, if irritation arose in the sexual parts, they should be carefully washed to ensure moral purity and prevent the development of sexual precocity. Dirt was inextricably linked with sexuality, cleanliness with purity.[85] Michel Foucault has suggested that the great nineteenth-century panic about masturbation, to which Acton made a major contribution, indicated that the Victorians had 'discovered' infantile sexuality.[86] For Victorians, however, the issue was described not in terms of child 'sexuality' but in terms of child 'precocity'; the difference of construction is an important one. The notion of precocity suggested abnormal and premature development; it indicated not that all children were sexual but that the harmful acquisition of sexual knowledge could impede natural development and growth. Victorians feared the precocious child because they so desperately wanted to cling on to the idea of the innocent one. While they had, indeed, unwittingly 'discovered' child sexuality, they preferred to confine, restrain, and label it as 'abnormality' rather than to face up to the facts of its existence.

The body of the adult woman stood in absolute contrast to that of the child, with very different body boundaries. Firstly the adult woman's body was read as open or 'gaping' (through menstruation, pregnancy and intercourse). The invention of the speculum and its use, in particular, to survey the internal bodies of alleged prostitutes under the Contagious Diseases Acts of 1864, 1866 and 1869, served to claim the woman's body as a public terrain, open to the view of public officials.[87] Secondly she was represented as dirty, polluted (by the invasion or colonisation of the male body) and polluting (because of the fluid condition of her body). The woman's body produced a mass of discharges, menstrual and vaginal, which had to be controlled or regulated. Sally Shuttleworth has highlighted the 'common obsession with female secretions' that can be gleaned from both popular medical advertisements and the writings of Victorian medical experts.[88] Shuttleworth links discussions of feminine discharges with concerns about effluvia and excrement as polluting elements in the physical environment:

> Women with their concealed inner recesses and harbouring of polluted blood, contained naturally within them the sewers that so preoccupied the sanitary reformers of the mid century. ... One physician described the uterus as 'the sewer of all the excrements existing in the body'.[89]

The notion of women's discharges as polluting was most evident in the operation of the Contagious Diseases Acts which identified women rather than men as responsible for the spread of contagious diseases.

It is extremely significant, therefore, that the consideration of child sexual abuse in all the handbooks of child medicine should be located within the discussion of vaginal discharges in childhood. Discharges from the child's body, particularly the sexual parts, were problematic to the Victorian observer. They did not tally with accepted notions of the child's bodily boundaries as fixed and closed (not fluid like the adult woman's). Discharges were associated with dirt, excretion and pollution and were incompatible with the attempts of middle-class reformers to reclaim the child as pure and uncorrupted. This contradiction suffused the pages of the paediatric medical text.

It is important to point out that it was essentially poor city children about whom the 'expert' physicians were writing. Medical specialists, based in the large free hospitals of Berlin (Henoch), New York (Holt and Walker), Birmingham (Tait), and London (Eustace Smith in the East End) all, as authors, cited their life's work as the experience on which their comments were founded. It was experience gleaned from dealings with the poor children of city slums and tenements who were their daily patients. Frank Mort has analysed the way in which nineteenth-century middle-class commentators on the urban poor constructed notions of sexuality in terms of a set of central polarities: 'physical health/non-health, virtue/vice, cleanliness/filth, morality/depravity, civilisation/animality'.[90] These polarities were firmly wedded to class positionings; the bourgeoisie constructed the labouring poor and lumpenproletariat of the slums as associated with disease, vice, dirt and immorality. Elizabeth Wilson has written that:

> Morality was inextricably entwined with cleanliness, disorder with filth. For the Victorians excrement became a metaphor and a symbol for moral filth, perhaps even for the working class itself, and when they spoke and wrote of the cleansing of the city of filth, they may really have longed to rid the cities of the labouring poor altogether.[91]

These discourses spilled over into the medical text, where they were pinned on the anatomical bodies of the children who claimed they had been abused.

The meanings ascribed to vaginal discharge, penetration and to the shifting body boundaries of girls appear to have been linked to notions of dirt, sexual pollution, class and behaviour. A girl's sexual innocence/precocity, her personal integrity or capacity to lie, was related to her class and to the moral environment in which she was raised. Tait's use of the terms 'dirty little wretch' and 'virulent minx' immediately identified poor children as contaminated, corrupted and therefore liars; he elucidated the connections between poverty and corruption later in his text where he stated that the worst liars were the children of almost 'the lowest class'.[92] The same categorisation was apparent in Walker's comments on the case of the 14-year-old orphan, who was not believed because she was 'conversant with low talk and vulgar actions'.[93] The environment that had shaped her character was identified as morally contaminating or contagious; she had already become soiled or corrupted in some way and her word was not to be believed. Dr Walker's conclusions reflected a belief in some form of 'moral miasma', a term originally coined by Michael Ryan to describe the way immorality was emitted from brothels and houses of ill-repute. Wilson has discussed this construction:

> The idea of the 'moral miasma' must have terrified the Victorians. According to the miasma theory of the spread of disease, you could catch an illness by breathing in the noxious smell of sewage. Could you not also then become literally infected with depravity merely by coming close to the 'contagion' itself?[94]

Walker's attitude was noticeably different in another case, that involving a more respectable patient. The victim was given credibility as a witness because she was an 'intelligent and well-bred girl'.[95] He was, similarly, reluctant to accept that abuse could happen in respectable middle-class circles. Although a medical friend had reported his surprise in finding a gaping vagina in a young girl patient, Walker commented that, since she was 'of good family', there was 'no reason to believe that the child had ever been tampered with'.[96] Poverty and dirt, indeed, often the whole lifestyle of the lower classes, could be seen as corrupting and immoral.

This discussion of pollution and dirt can be placed in a wider symbolic context. Anthropologist Mary Douglas, in her influential work *Purity and danger*, has argued that since 'dirt' is essentially matter which is out of place, attempts to regulate excretion from the external boundaries of the human body must be seen in terms of social ordering:

> All margins are dangerous. If they are pulled this way or that the shape of fundamental experience is altered. Any structure of ideas is vulnerable at the margins. We should expect the orifices of the body to symbolise its specially vulnerable points. Matter issuing from them is marginal stuff of the most obvious kind. Spittle, blood, milk, urine, faeces or tears by simply issuing forth have traversed the boundary of the body. ... The mistake is to treat bodily margins in isolation from all other margins.[97]

Douglas suggested that anxieties about the body boundaries of the individual reproduce concerns about threats to the boundaries of the social body. Hence the medical obsession with the regulation and containment of women's and children's bodily discharges can be related to wider concerns about sexual and moral disorder in society, and to a resultant need to define and contain childhood and womanhood in order to achieve this.

The child could be contaminated by the dirt of her surroundings but also by the actual process of sexual assault. Her body, once molested or penetrated, was seen in a different light. She, too, would lose her natural modesty and bodily inhibitions and begin to demonstrate attributes associated with corruption as a result of contamination by her assailant. Walker wrote:

> While it is true that, in general, children that are innocent dread an examination, and that those, especially over ten years old, who have been assaulted take an examination as a matter of course, still some of the latter class, like a certain proportion of female prostitutes, honestly dread an examination.[98]

The assaulted child was associated with the prostitute and, therefore, with all the notions of moral fall, depravity and sexual promiscuity which had been attached to the prostitute.

While the protection of the innocent child was seen as an absolute requirement in terms of moral economy, the 'truth' of an allegation of sexual abuse depended on an assessment of the moral status of the complainant. Was the child innocent before the assault or had she been corrupted by her own filthy environment? Should she herself be seen as a contaminating influence within society? The issue of who was victim and who the seducer was invariably confused. It was not just Tait who drew attention to the figure of the 'corrupted' child in the narrative of sexual abuse. French physician Dr Moreau of Charlerôi suggested doctors should question the child and her companions carefully about their dirty habits and commented that: 'it was surprising how vicious, how skilful and learned in vice, these little children proved to be'.[99] Dr Lacassagne agreed that 'many of the children were thoroughly corrupt and vicious, and were seeking to obtain money by exaggerated or false accusations'.[100] Even the *Illustrated Police News*, as we have seen, perpetuated the stereotype of the 'corrupt little girl'.

Thus the semiology of the body was positioned within a wider symbolic framework. The medical debates on signs of abuse were clearly related to the Victorian problematisation of childhood and sexuality and to attempts to define and contain the bodies of both women and children. They were constructed in relation to a wider cultural anxiety about social and bodily pollution; pollution as, interchangeably, physical filth, disease and moral contamination. Pollution was a significant vector of transformation. It could, most significantly, transform the girl child into an adult woman and the sexual innocent into the depraved or fallen. Once corrupted, she herself became a polluting element in society as she connived, seduced, lied and cheated. To Victorian doctors the working-class girl child was as much the source as the victim of physical/moral pollution. How her testimony was treated in the courtroom is the subject of the next chapter.

5 'Witnesses of truth'?
Children in the courtroom

Introduction

In August 1905 a Brixton pastor was brought to trial at the County of London Sessions for the indecent assault of three girl children, all under the age of 12. As the grand jury prepared to deliberate the case, judge Mr Loveland 'advised them to have each child before them, because they would be able to judge by their demeanour and the way they gave their evidence whether they were witnesses of truth or not'.[1] While medical evidence could be gleaned from the child's body, it was vital to ascertain the credibility, reputation and character of the child witness in order to evaluate oral testimony. The child's word was essential in determining how and by whom an act had been committed. This chapter sets out to examine how children's statements as witnesses were constructed and interpreted in the courtroom, in relation to ideas about age, gender, class and status. What 'demeanour' was associated with truth and what with 'falsehood'? Were boys and girls judged differently?

It is clear that children were treated more sympathetically than adult victims of sexual assault. In the present study sample of jury trials only 45 per cent of cases known to have involved adult victims ended in conviction compared to 69 per cent of cases involving child victims. Yet child sexual abuse cases were by no means guaranteed successes for the prosecution. In addition to the 31 per cent that were acquitted or thrown out by the grand jury, a large number were probably dismissed by magistrates at petty sessions. The survival of magistrates' courts' records is patchy for the earlier part of the century, but an examination of child sexual abuse cases which came before Thames Police Court 1870–1914 shows that less than half of all reported incidents resulted in conviction.[2] Both this chapter, which focuses on child victims, and the next, which examines attitudes towards defendants, demonstrate that the relative class and reputation of the two parties, interpreted with regard to age and gender, were significant factors that influenced the decisions of magistrates, judges and juries.

In her study of the Kentish courts 1859–80, Carolyn Conley has demonstrated very persuasively that a fundamental consideration in reaching a

verdict was 'the perceived character of the victim versus the perceived character of the accused'.[3] Conley's emphasis on the importance of reputation in
the courtroom, as well as on the ways in which the reputations of women
were evaluated differently from those of men, is a significant insight on the
workings of the Victorian criminal justice system. Indeed, reputation or
'respectability' was a key line of inquiry in the Middlesex and Yorkshire
courts from 1830 to 1914 in relation to both child and adult victims; but
what did the child's reputation depend upon?

Neither social class nor age nor gender are alone sufficient to explain
courtroom decisions in child sexual abuse cases. Rough data that can be
abstracted suggests that, firstly, children of a higher class location were more
likely to be believed in court.[4] Secondly, cases involving children under the
age of 9 were more likely to end in conviction than children aged 9–16 once
the case came to trial.[5] Thirdly, boy victims under 12 were dealt with more
sympathetically at trial than girls of a similar age.[6] Fourthly, although
notions of age of consent were clearly important in the reception of evidence,
they fail to explain differences vis-à-vis class and gender. Thus the data indicate a complex set of variables that were clearly related but cannot show how
they fit together. Detailed analysis of qualitative evidence will be used to
demonstrate that the key to the evaluation of children's reputation,
respectability and therefore their testimony in the Victorian period lies in
the gendered conception of, on the one hand, childhood innocence and, on
the other, juvenile delinquency.

Testimony and suggestibility

Children as young as 6 or 7 appeared in London's packed and bustling police
courts to give information which was transcribed, by a court clerk, as a
formal written deposition when the case was committed for trial. In rural
areas, children's evidence might be given in the calmer surroundings of their
own homes or a magistrate's residence. On 1 June 1865, 10-year-old Eliza
Cartwright produced the following sworn statement in front of magistrate
Mr Mansfield at Marylebone Police Court:

> I live with my grandmother at no. 8 Little Park Street. The prisoner is
> my father. My mother is dead. I have been sleeping of late at no. 2 Little
> Park Street in the first floor front room with my father – and my two
> little brothers. One is seven years old, the other is four years – Last
> Friday morning I was sleeping next to my father. He pulled up my
> chemise then he lay on top of me and put his privates into mine – he
> did not hurt me very much – Before that he said you are not asleep,
> come over and sleep with me or I'll give you a good hiding. I then
> kicked him and bit him – He hurt me on my privates and nowhere else.
> He then got up and went to work – after that I got up and went to my
> grandmother and had some breakfast. My father has done the same

thing before five times altogether. On a Saturday night previous he did
the same thing to me – I cried on that occasion for an hour or two. ...
Last Sunday night week I went over and slept with my grandmother – I
slept four nights there – On Monday night my father would not let me
sleep with my grandmother – We have only got one bed.[7]

The formal and slightly stilted language, the confused sequencing of events
and the chronological and thematic fragmentation that results as the narrative jumps backwards and forwards across time and space mean that it is
important to ask whether it really is Eliza who is speaking. In short, the
narrative sounds very unlike the tale of a 10-year-old child. The pauses and
breaks indicate that the deposition was framed in response to questioning by
the magistrate, possibly along the following lines: Where do you live? What
happened on Friday morning? Did he hurt you? Why were you sleeping
next to your father? Did you resist? Where did he hurt you? Has he done it
before? The statement was a collaborative effort, put together by child,
police, magistrate, neighbours and grandmother. It was designed to give
information appropriate to the courtroom setting rather than an account of
the child's views, thoughts or feelings on the matter (except in so far as they
might be used to demonstrate resistance). The narrative was constructed
within the very specific and formulaic genre of the courtroom testimony, a
genre which adult witnesses might well have been acquainted with but
which a child witness had to learn for the first time.[8] This is not to gloss
over the child's role in the production of the testimony, nor to detract from
very particular and personal experiences that clearly formed the basis of the
narrative. The deposition does, indeed, give a very rich and detailed picture
of the circumstances of one little girl's life in 1865, of power and authority
in the home, of family duties and responsibilities. It is important to stress,
however, that children's depositions, like those of adults, were carefully
constructed legal documents. In the case of children, however, the act of
construction itself became a focus of courtroom inquiry because of doubts
surrounding an infant's understanding of truth.

The problem of authorial voice was a focus when Eliza was cross-examined, as her responses indicate:

My grandmother is not friendly with my father. They have had several
disputes and don't speak to each other. She has never said to my father
that she would serve him out. She has called the prisoner a rogue and a
scoundrel but I have never heard her say she would have him punished.
My grandmother taught me the word privates on the last occasion. My
two brothers were asleep. I did not scream, I cried because my head
ached. ... My grandmother saw me crying and questioned me – She did
not put many questions. ... I have been living with my grandmother
since that time – My grandmother told me I was to tell the truth to the
court. No-one else except my father did the same to me. I never play

about with boys on the street. ... I sweep up the room and do all that is required. I then go to play – my grandmother has not been friends with my father ever since my mother's death.[9]

Once again the questions themselves were not transcribed but it is possible to deduce their nature. It is clear that Eliza was subject to a rigorous cross-examination in court about the origins of her statement, her truthfulness, her malleability or suggestibility in the hands of others and her sexual reputation. She was required to demonstrate the credibility of her testimony. Such an experience in court was not unusual for a child witness and, whereas Eliza was questioned by the magistrate, others were questioned by the defendant or alleged assailant himself.

Since Eliza was 10, she was able to give her evidence on oath. For younger children, inability to understand the meaning of the oath and to distinguish between truth and perjury could provide an impediment to their appearance in court. In 1773, legal expert William Blackstone followed Sir Matthew Hale in arguing that, in cases of rape, girl victims ought to give information because such cases were so often committed in secret. He wrote: 'it seems now to be settled, that in these cases infants of any age are to be heard, and if they have any idea of an oath, to be also sworn: it being found by experience that infants of very tender years often give the clearest and truest testimony'.[10] Legal advice manuals and indeed statute law stressed that defendants could not be convicted on a child's testimony alone (whether on oath or not); there had to be other supporting evidence.[11]

Concerns about the truthfulness of a child's statement led to a set of elaborate procedures in and outside of the courtroom to establish whether the child could distinguish the real from the imaginary and whether she possessed the rationality to describe what had happened to her. Children were frequently questioned by police, magistrates, lawyers, judges and even doctors about their understanding of truth and lies. In December 1879, for example, a surgeon who had examined a 6-year-old girl deposed that 'I asked her what would happen if she told lies and she said she would go to hell', a response which was, within a Christian eschatological framework, deemed the correct one.[12] Medical jurists Beck and Beck remarked in 1838 that a child could be heard if she was 'sensible to the wickedness of telling a deliberate lie'.[13]

Yet, despite Blackstone's confident remarks about the sincerity of small children, it seems that many judges and magistrates were unwilling to hear the evidence of children who could not demonstrate this basic knowledge of the sin of perjury. From its foundation in 1884, the NSPCC continued to argue that cases involving children fell through the legal net because their evidence was deemed inadmissible in the courts on a daily basis.[14] It is clear that problems with the evidence of very young children meant that many cases involving children under 7 or 8 were dismissed at the earliest stages of prosecution. Only those considered sound or watertight cases advanced beyond police, magistrate or grand jury for trial on indictment.

As well as the issue of rationality – the ability to remember events accurately and to distinguish truth from falsehood – the courts were also concerned with the issue of suggestibility: the way in which adults in authority (often mothers, although, in Eliza's case, her grandmother) could influence a child's statement. In cases involving children of all age groups, whether under 8 or over, victims were frequently questioned about the origins of their statements. The *Weekly Dispatch* reported a court hearing involving a 10-year-old girl who had gone to live with her next-door neighbour after incest charges were pressed against her father in June 1835: 'She had lived some while with the woman … the wife of a policeman, and it came out in the accident of examination that every morning she had told her "what to say" and gave her a penny.'[15]

The notion of the malleable child, whose words could be influenced and shaped by adults, was a constant point of reference in medico-legal texts which discussed the interpretation of oral as well as forensic evidence in sexual assault cases:

> In numerous cases I myself have seen little but wide-awake children with the utmost unconstraint or impudence drawl out a full description of the commission of the deed to the most minute particulars so that little sagacity was required to recognise it as a lesson dictated and learnt by heart.[16]

These particular comments implied that the adult who tutored the child rather than the adult who assaulted the child was responsible for her moral corruption by feeding her inappropriate knowledge.

As prosecuting agencies recognised, the theatre of the court could be such an intimidating environment for children that it was probably necessary to reassure them about their evidence before they entered the courtroom. At one 1890 trial, the defence alleged that a NSPCC officer had read the girl's statement over to her after committal proceedings, asking her whether it was right, and telling her to 'stick to her story'.[17] Such a practice, probably common when prosecuting lawyers represented adult witnesses, was seen as sinister in relation to children because of the issue of suggestibility.

Child witnesses in sexual assault cases presented a particular dilemma for the courts. The explicit nature of the charge required children to describe the physical assault but, because sexual knowledge was associated with adulthood, it was assumed that children's vocabulary would limit what they could say. The use of 'adult' vocabulary would immediately raise the question of suggestibility. Children like Eliza who used formal words like 'privates' or 'person' to refer to genitalia in court were questioned as to where they had learnt them. Seven-year-old William told the magistrates at Wood Green in 1910 that he had been told the word 'penis' by the police:

I first heard that man [the detective sergeant] say penis. I know what it means because my mother told me what the word meant. My mother told me what to say about it yesterday. She spoke to me about it this morning & told me not to make a mistake.[18]

Parents and officials involved in the prosecution had a clear sense of what sort of language was appropriate in the courtroom. The Yorkshire depositions do record colloquial slang or children's words – 'neddy', 'robin', 'pigeon' and 'dicky bird'[19] – but most referred to 'person', 'private parts' or even the evasive 'that below the belly'.[20]

For boy children and girl children of all ages, questions of language, vocabulary and the ability to tell the truth were a central focus of cross-examination. Children who had attained an age where they could make rational judgements might nevertheless be questioned to see if they had developed dishonest habits. Eight-year-old Tabitha was questioned about parental discipline in 1865: 'Mother beats me sometimes for being so long on errands. Sometimes she beats me for telling stories.'[21] *The Times* reported on an Old Bailey acquittal in October 1860: 'The little girl candidly admitted ... that she had told several stories in reference to her conduct on the day the occurrence took place, and that she had also been punished by her mother for telling falsehoods.'[22] A defendant faced with allegations of assault by his 13-year-old servant girl in April 1860 accused her of lying and stealing groceries from his house.[23]

Romantic child/delinquent child

Recent scholarship in sociology, literary studies and history has demonstrated that 'childhood' is a social and imaginative construct and that the notion of 'childhood' as a state of innocence was a Victorian middle-class ideal or fantasy.[24] Peter Coveney and Hugh Cunningham have both shown how, from the Enlightenment onwards, the older Calvinist view of the child as contaminated by original sin, evil by nature and in need of rigorous discipline and supervision, was replaced by the romantic notion of childhood as a prelapsarian state of virtue.[25] But what of the child who failed to fit this mould, who was clearly not 'innocent'?

The term 'delinquency' emerged, from the beginning of the nineteenth century, to describe both juvenile offenders and those children usually of the poorest sections of society, street-wise and semi-criminal, whom the middle classes found it impossible to define as 'innocent'.[26] Even if children were born in a natural state of innocence, this innocence was clearly open to corruption: by peers, parents or environment. Although transformation to the 'knowing' state of adulthood could begin at any age, it was most likely to happen as children moved out of infancy and began to approach puberty or what we now term 'adolescence'.[27] Amongst the labouring classes, children over the age of 8 often went out to work, had childcare responsibilities and socialised with adults on a regular basis. This was a pattern that persisted for much of the century despite the attempts of middle-class reformers to restrict children's labour and to introduce compulsory education. Even after the 1870 Education Act which made school attendance compulsory for the first time, girl children in particular were often absent on a regular basis because of family responsibilities.[28] Reformers were concerned about the developmental impact of entering the adult world too soon, of gaining premature knowledge that might lead to moral corruption, and of the way knowledge/corruption spread amongst friends and acquaintances.

Juvenile delinquents were seen as social threats who needed to be reformed and re-educated; the concept of the reformatory school, originally formulated as an alternative to prison for child offenders, was soon expanded into the plan for a wide-ranging system of training and industrial schools to take all sorts of 'problem' children.[29] Delinquency, however, had different manifestations that were dependent on gender. As recent studies by Michelle Cale and Pamela Cox have pointed out, control of female sexuality was the central aim of industrial and reformatory schools for girls.[30] Linda Mahood and Barbara Littlewood have, similarly, demonstrated that delinquency in boys tended to be associated with the criminal activity of thieving while delinquency in girls was associated with sexual precocity, wandering the streets and living in 'immoral surroundings'.[31] The reputation or respectability of male youth was dependent on honesty and truthfulness with regards to money. For girls, reputation was based on sexual respectability.

The remainder of this chapter will demonstrate that this gendered model of delinquency was applied to all children involved in the criminal justice system once they had moved beyond the 'tender years' of infancy, whether they appeared as defendants accused of a crime or as witnesses in another case. Children of 8 or 9 had to prove their integrity as 'witnesses of truth' (and therefore demonstrate they were not delinquent) in response to cross-examination by a defence lawyer who would submit questions based on the gendered delinquency model. The confusion as to whether abused children were victims or threats, morally innocent or guilty of delinquency, affected the way they were dealt with in the witness box.

The abuse of girls

Ten-year-old Eliza Cartwright was asked in 1865 whether she had played with boys in the street or had sexual relations with other males.[32] The intent behind the questioning was to ascertain her moral reputation; to find out whether she had been innocent or precocious before the assault took place. She was asked whether she had resisted the assault because, in 1865, carnal knowledge of a girl aged 10–12 was a misdemeanour only (and less severely punished) if consent could be demonstrated.[33] While the questioning about her sexual reputation might have been related to an attempt to prove consent, it also performed another function: it was an attack on her moral integrity as a witness. Girl children as young as 9, who were under the age of consent throughout the period, were regularly questioned about their morality. It was believed that those who were depraved, corrupted or precocious, would make up stories, inspired by over-vivid sexual imaginations, which could then be used to trap and blackmail innocent male parties.

'Moral' corruption

In March 1835 Charles Gardener was sentenced to death at the Old Bailey for the rape of 9-year-old Mary Pugh. The girl was an orphan, who had lived in a series of lodgings with a Mr and Mrs Hardman, who had performed the role of guardians. After the trial, petitions of appeal were presented by a number of parties who attempted to cast aspersions on both the medical evidence and the testimony of the child. Witnesses accused the woman and girl of immorality and blackmail. A former landlord claimed that Mary Pugh and Mrs Hardman had made similar allegations about him and that they were 'immoral and depraved so much so that he forbade his children from associating or holding any conversation with them'.[34] He alleged that he had once seen Mary Pugh sitting on the privy, with the door wide open, 'indulging in a disgusting practice'. The governors of the school that Mary had attended decided to pursue the charges of immorality. Two of them, a minister and a 'lady' parishioner, visited the girl in the Victoria Asylum at Chiswick, a home for 'fallen' women, to question her in more detail about her evidence. The minister sent a report of their interview to the Home Secretary, writing that: 'Having heard insinuation of the artfulness and corruption of [Mary Pugh] ... I thought it desireable to see this child with the view and hope of ascertaining the real state of mind.'[35]

The interrogation of Mary Pugh in the asylum was an attempt to find out if she was a witness of truth or not:

> We spoke pointedly on the importance of Truth ... and endeavoured to impress upon her mind that passage of scripture 'be sure your sins will find you out'. ... We read also the account contained in Acts V of Annanias of Sapphira being struck dead on the spot for falsehood. The child coloured up highly and we said to her 'now, dear child, consider those things and tell the truth: do not be afraid'.[36]

Mary finally succumbed to the barrage of religious dogma, 'confessing' that she had lied:

> We then said 'What, who, could put it into your head to tell such awful lies about him?' She replied 'My mother [meaning Mrs Hardman] never told me to tell stories about him'. 'Who then? Somebody must have

done it?' She put down her head, & paused, and said it was her own self. We then renewed our entreaty that she would tell the truth without fear of anybody. ... It is evident to me that the woman [Hardman] by whom [she] has been brought up since her mother died, possessed a wonderful power over her.[37]

Despite this confession the judge upheld the conviction on the grounds of conclusive medical evidence, although the death sentence was commuted to transportation. The case is interesting, however, because it provides detailed information about the ways in which attempts were made to undermine the evidence of female children and to cloud their reputation.

Girls of the poorer classes, even when they were clearly under the age of consent like Mary Pugh, were depicted as corrupted, depraved and delinquent throughout the nineteenth century, as a brief survey of cases demonstrates. In May 1850, Bow Street magistrate Mr Henry heard a case involving the indecent assault of a 10-year-old beggar child by a 74-year-old man. *The Times* reported that 'the examination of the child by Mr Henry disclosed a state of ignorance and early depravity perfectly revolting'. The magistrate sentenced the man to two months' imprisonment for common assault because 'the depraved nature and conflicting statements of the girl made it useless to send such a case for trial'.[38] In October 1855, a 39-year-old shoemaker was acquitted at the Middlesex Sessions of indecently assaulting two 12-year-old girls, one of them a former servant of his. *The Times* reported that 'they were very bad girls; two of them had been in the habit of staying out at night, and one had decoyed another girl of her own age from her home'. The assistant judge commented on the 'depraved testimony' which the girls had produced: 'it was really shocking to see girls of that character making such a charge'.[39] Although the depositions for this case indicated that one of the girls stayed out because she was afraid of beatings by her father, this was used against her. As Mahood and Littlewood have demonstrated, since the street was seen as a locus of sexual danger for girls, it was assumed that girls who wandered at night must be vicious, corrupted and 'fallen'.[40]

Girl children were often described in court as 'wretched little husseys'[41] and, indeed, as 'delinquent'. In November 1850 a Polish count, who ran a china shop in Holborn, was accused of sexually abusing a poor orphan girl with whom he had cohabited since she was 11 years of age. The count argued that 'she was addicted to the vilest habits and had the most corrupt desires' and *The Times* described the girl as 'without any apparent sense of shame, or a consciousness of her moral delinquency'.[42] The case was dismissed by the Middlesex grand jury, who threw the indictment out.

Some defendants argued that the girl victim herself was responsible for what had happened, that she was, very clearly, neither innocent nor respectable. A Bradford man, accused of assaulting a 9-year-old girl in May 1865 remarked: 'I seed she was a brazen lass and I was trying to get her away.'[43] An 11-year-old Wakefield girl, facing severe cross-examination about her behaviour by the defence, told the West Riding court: 'I did not ask him to sweetheart me. I did not lie down of my own accord.'[44] In some cases defendants pleaded guilty but argued that the girl concerned was precocious in order to reduce the charge from felony to misdemeanour or to argue for a mitigated sentence. In 1895 a 19-year-old youth charged with unlawfully knowing his 13-year-old cousin, appeared at the West London Police Court for committal proceedings. It was difficult for him to deny the allegations since she was pregnant; he argued, however, that she had consented to the relationship and that 'she was not a pure girl when he first knew her'. The magistrate, Mr Rose, accordingly released him on bail pending the trial and stated 'that he did not wish to keep him in custody for an hour longer than necessary'.[45] In June 1910 a 32-year-old man was tried at the Old Bailey for unlawful carnal knowledge of his 15-year-old niece which had, once again, resulted in her pregnancy. According to the *Illustrated Police News* the man told the court: 'I was drunk at the time. She led me on.'[46]

The paradox of innocence

There was an essential paradox associated with the evidence of the girl child victim of sexual assault. A girl who really was innocent and virtuous should be ignorant of the language and meaning of sexual acts and would, therefore, be unable to articulate what had happened to her. Responses of 'yes' or 'no' could not be believed since she was unable to understand the nature of the questioning. If, however, she possessed the language to describe sexual acts, it was a clear sign that she was depraved and therefore untrustworthy. In 1835 physician John Leeson used this conflicting argument to assert that the evidence of children should never be relied upon: 'You must well know that when females are young *and presumed to be innocent and virtuous*, how little they must know of what constitutes carnal knowledge, therefore how liable they must be to swear *under false impression*.'[47]

The fainting or sobbing girl child provided a spectacular and melodramatic focal point for newspaper reports. If the vicious child gave her evidence in a cool and calculated manner associated with brazen indifference, the girl who displayed shame and trauma often elicited substantial sympathy from the courtroom crowds:

> The little girl, who had been evidently terrified at the whole scene, appeared scarcely able to stand when the learned counsel put questions to her, for the purpose of invalidating her evidence. ... Although Mr Phillips addressed her with the utmost gentleness, the poor child was unable to sustain herself any longer, but sobbed aloud and pressed her hand upon her heart, as if to prevent it from bursting. She was an object of deepest compassion to all in the court, and would have dropped upon the ground if an officer had not caught her in his arms.[48]

The NSPCC went on to argue in 1913 that the situation was distasteful and torturous; but, during the nineteenth century, the performance and display of the child victim in court was a crucial aspect of trial proceedings, essential to the jury's assessment of demeanour.[49]

Fainting and sobbing – as extreme demonstrations of modesty – did not, however, necessarily signify 'innocence'. As Mary Poovey has pointed out in her discussion of 'the proper lady', the modest condition, although idealised as a sign of feminine chastity, was an untenable position.[50] Discussing the heroine of Fanny Burney's novel *Evelina*, Poovey has written: 'When she blushes, she unwittingly signals not only her modesty but also her consciousness of her innocence.'[51] The act of blushing, while signifying embarrassment in 'compromising circumstances', also indicated an awareness of knowledge which 'denotes experience and hence potential, if not actual, corruption'. Modesty could, therefore, be seen as 'knowledge disguised'.[52] Thus even the child who blushed and pointed at bodily parts rather than naming them outright was indicating shame and therefore knowledge of their function. Poovey's 'paradox of modesty' was, throughout the nineteenth century, influential in both drawing room and courtroom.[53] The 'ideal' girl victim gave her evidence in a clear but uncontrived and ingenuous manner, without specifically naming body parts or demonstrating awareness of the significance of the assault.

The abuse of boys

In the 1990s, media exposure of cases involving the sexual abuse of boy children by adult men has led to the identification of male rape as the 'last taboo'.[54] Only recently have male victims begun to articulate their experience and to seek the help of support agencies and courts of law. In Victorian England, male rape was surrounded by whole sets of silences. Firstly, while the 'seduction' and 'prostitution' of young girls was constructed as a social problem requiring the attention and intervention of philanthropists and social commentators, the sexual abuse of boys was almost never discussed. Secondly, very few cases involving abuse of boy children ever reached the public sphere of the courts. Of the study sample of child sexual abuse cases tried in Middlesex and Yorkshire 1830–1914, only 7 per cent involved boy victims. Thirdly, many male victims may have lacked the knowledge or vocabulary to describe what had happened to them. In one rare 1840 testimony a 16-year-old apprentice hairdresser, whose master summoned him to his bed every night, revealed the depths of his ignorance: 'I did not know the nature of the thing and did not tell my father.'[55] Another 14-year-old apprentice, abused by the same man, told the magistrate: 'The reason I did not tell father before was I did not know what a crime it was.'[56] Yet the silence must not be over-exaggerated. The presence of the 7 per cent of court cases is sufficient to demonstrate the existence of both relevant legislation and certain shared understandings about the abuse of boys by men. How, then, did these understandings influence court trials? How were boys evaluated as witnesses? Furthermore, if the abuse of boys was recognised and articulated, why was it so frequently side-stepped and concealed?

Although the eighteenth-century Societies for the Reformation of Manners had made a series of attempts to close molly houses (male brothels) in London, the clamp-down on sex between males gained momentum from the 1780s onwards.[57] Constables of the Metropolitan Police (founded in 1829) were given the duty of patrolling notorious haunts such as Hyde Park in plain clothes in order to arrest men seeking sex with males.[58] During the 1830s and 1840s the London courts were packed with cases involving men accused of 'inciting each other to commit unnatural acts' or 'indecently assaulting each other'.[59] As Tim Hitchcock has pointed out, such measures went hand in hand with a refiguring of attitudes towards sex between males. Where sodomy and associated acts had previously been delineated as sins in the eyes of the Church (along with pride and avarice), they were recast through the language of the Enlightenment as 'abnormal', 'unnatural', or contrary to the biological laws of the 'natural' world.[60] Where sodomy had been viewed as an act committed by married and unmarried men alike, the eighteenth century saw a growing emphasis on heterosexuality as the 'norm' and on other propensities as characteristics of a deviant subculture. If, as Jeffrey Weeks has suggested, the 1880s and 1890s saw the labelling and construction of the 'homosexual' as a full-blown stereotype, such a project was, in fact, prefigured by developments much earlier in the century.[61] The Labouchère amendment to the Criminal Law Amendment Act of 1885 outlawed the committing and procuring of acts of 'gross indecency', and of any attempt to do so.[62] It was, however, an extension of previous policing aims rather than a sudden innovation. The trial of Oscar Wilde in 1895 might well have crystallised the codes and meanings associated with 'homosexuality';[63] but the fact that the trials were reported in a language of euphemism that was popularly understood demonstrates that these codes were already a matter of common knowledge.

Although the regulation of sodomy and 'indecency' between males often involved the control of consensual acts, concerns about male rape and the abuse of boy children by men were acknowledged in case law and common law alike. Indecent assault legislation (as well as the laws on sodomy) was used to prosecute unwanted sexual assaults on adult males; like female rape, the *onus* was on the victim to demonstrate resistance. Although it has not commonly been recognised, nineteenth-century courts did acknowledge an age of consent for boy children.[64] Legal expert Alfred Swaine Taylor noted in 1846 that, if a case of sodomy involved a boy under 14, 'it is felony in the agent only' and was to be treated in the same way 'as for rape on girls under 12'.[65] Such an approach gave boys more protection than girls in legal theory. Two hearings at the Court of Appeal in 1872 set further precedents in establishing that boys of 'tender years' could not give their consent in relation to indecent assault and it is clear that many judges were following a similar policy even before these test cases.[66] In 1880 the Assault of Young Persons Act firmly fixed the age of consent for both boys and girls at 13, lowering it for boys and raising it for girls.

Boys' testimony

Depositions involving boy children reveal cultural interpretations of same-sex acts that were never touched upon in newspapers. Unlike the hairdresser's apprentices, other boys displayed a shocked recognition of abuse. One 1870 Middlesex deposition, which records the experience of 11-year-old Thomas Hall, hints at the absolute shame and humiliation associated with the notion of male rape. Thomas claimed that a lodger in his mother's house had asphyxiated him with chemicals to make him insensible and then, he believed, attempted sodomy (although that word does not appear to have been used in court). Thomas told the Marlborough Street magistrate: 'When I came to myself he was fastening his braces. He said "don't tell your mother, I'll give you some money." I got out of the room & felt faint & fell downstairs.'[67] His mother, a widow, took up the story:

> I ... found [him] lying across the front door & thought he was in a fit. He was pulling his hair & scratching himself. I said 'what have you done?' He said 'don't ask me. I have done nothing wrong it is not my fault. He did it the devil, I can't tell you, I'll cut my throat.'[68]

This 11-year-old boy identified almost at once what had happened although it is not clear how he would have labelled it. His extreme physical and psychological reaction – fainting, suicide – as an articulation of traumatic shame, humiliation, horror, rage and the disclaiming of personal guilt, suggests that male rape had a very forceful meaning, although never discussed in printed form. In 1905 a West Riding doctor examined a 9-year-old schoolboy, who had been subjected to a similar assault in Bradford, remarking that he was in 'an exceedingly nervous condition'. The boy's mother confirmed that he had been healthy and strong until the incident took place: 'since then he has been subject to fits and they have been getting worse'.[69] Thomas Hall's reaction also suggests another reason why male rape was perhaps under-reported: shame rather than ignorance.

Repugnance at male rape, particularly when it affected boy children, permeated the courtroom. All cases involving the sexual assault of boys under the age of 12 resulted in conviction in the Middlesex and Yorkshire samples: a 100 per cent conviction rate compared to 79 per cent for girls under 12. The assault of girl children was 'unnatural' because of the age of the victim. Within the Victorian moral order, sex between men was 'unnatural' because of their shared gender. Hence the assault of boy children was doubly 'unnatural' because of the combined stigma of gender and age. Although the sexual abuse of boys might be tried as sodomy or attempted sodomy (as well as indecent assault or gross indecency) adult witnesses rarely used the term 'sodomy' in the courts. 'Sodomy', after all, was identified as a crime in both active and passive partners and could involve consent as well as resistance.[70] In 1840 the father of the 16-year-old apprentice accused his son's boss of 'violating' and 'contaminating my child', positioning the assault within the non-consensual model of female rape as well as defining the boy as a vulnerable and innocent victim.[71]

Yet conviction rates began to slip when boys were older than 12 and the views of police, judges, lawyers and juries generally took on a different perspective; the courts were simply less likely to see youths as vulnerable victims. In the sample cases involving boys of 12 or 13, 75 per cent ended in a guilty verdict. In cases involving boys of 14, only 60 per cent of cases were convicted. Finally in cases involving boys of 15, who were well over the age of consent, an overwhelming majority – 67 per cent – were acquitted. Like girls in this age group, male 'youths' or 'juveniles' of the lower classes faced detailed questioning about their 'reputation' and credibility. For boys, however, the line of attack was different.

While the female delinquent was portrayed as sexually predatory, the male delinquent was depicted as financially scheming. I have demonstrated elsewhere that this stereotyping was pervasive in the courts of the late nineteenth century and that it was closely related to perceptions of social class.[72] When a gentleman of independent means was accused of assaulting a 14-year-old match-seller outside the Drury Lane Theatre in 1870, the lad was cross-examined about his sporadic schooling and his life on the streets. The boy was forced to admit that he had planned to extort money from the gentleman by promising sexual favours.[73] The intent behind such a cross-examination was to portray the matchboy as a delinquent street-wise youth trying to blackmail men. Such an approach was very different from the case involving 11-year-old Thomas Hall who lived with his mother, a 'respectable' widow, and was assaulted in their private home. Although fewer depositions exist for the earlier period, the gendered notion of corrupted and delinquent youth was still an important reference point. The hairdresser, accused of molesting his apprentices in 1840, cross-examined both boys in court accusing them of embezzling and stealing money from his business. In his address to the jury, he argued that the 14-year-old was 'a boy of bad character having cheated him of the 1½ [shillings] – and secondly, because if his story was true he would have told his father on the first occasion instead of waiting till Sunday'.[74] The testimony of boys over the age of 12 could be undermined if a previous reputation for thieving could be established.

The notion of precocity, delineated in relation to juvenile female sexuality and a focal point of investigation in court cases involving the sexual abuse of girl children, could not be deployed in cases involving boys. The term 'precocity' referred to the premature development or over-development of female sexual desire as a result of early stimulation. It was a sexual desire that was clearly heterosexual and was therefore (excepting the unusual opinions of doctors like William Acton) configured as 'natural'.[75] Since same-sex desire was constructed as 'unnatural' there could be no reference to innate or essential proclivities in boys. Thus boys were never questioned about their sexual reputations in court; they were, however, questioned about other issues connected to respectability, particularly about honesty and truthfulness with regard to money.

When, on rare occasions, the sexual abuse of boys was reported in the newspapers, it was explained in terms of the wickedness and corruption of older parties. Street boys might be depicted as blackmailers or tricksters but it was adult men rather than youths who were identified as sexually predatory. In 1860, a 56-year-old man and a youth of 15 appeared together at the Middlesex Sessions charged with 'unlawfully inciting each other to the committing of unnatural acts and practices' in Hyde Park, London. *The Times* described the boy, who was discharged, as 'the son of highly respectable parents' while the elder man, sentenced to two years' hard labour, was labelled a 'moral pestilence'.[76] In 1865 the *Leeds Mercury* reported a lengthy sentencing speech made by Justice Willes at the Yorkshire Assizes in Leeds Town Hall after the conviction of a Catholic priest (who was also a schoolmaster) for the indecent assault of a male pupil from a 'respectable' family. The judge opined that those acquainted with the ways of the world knew it was unlikely for 'a boy of his age and appearance ... to descend to the depth of degradation ... without having such a course suggested to him by an older and worse person'.[77] Rather than leading children into righteousness as his profession dictated, the priest had led them 'into paths which could only result in the degradation of their bodies and the destruction of their souls'. Justice Willes went on to speak of the 'detestation in which honest men' held such conduct.[78] Courtroom rhetoric was very different in cases involving boy victims compared to girls; it unfailingly identified adult men rather than male youths as figures of seduction. The silence that usually surrounded the abuse of boy children can be linked to the refusal to acknowledge that such acts were anything other than deviant aberrations, to the desire to protect homosocial cultures (single-sex schools, clubs, workplaces) and the need to enforce notions of 'normal', 'healthy', heterosexual masculinity.

Male prostitution

Yet cases involving 'adolescent' boys formed a grey area in terms of policing and prosecution because the police were clearly concerned about boys who earned money through prostitution but were unsure how to deal with them. Youths and men often appeared together in police courts charged with indecent behaviour in public (gross indecency after 1885), charges of indecent assault being added at later stages.[79]

When Howard Vincent, the Director of Criminal Investigations with the

Metropolitan Police, was called to give evidence before the 1881 Select Committee on the Protection of Young Girls, he called for measures to punish those who permitted their premises to be used for 'the commission of any act of fornication or immorality by any young person, whether male or female under the age of 18 years'.[80] He argued that 'there is a considerable amount of sodomy practised' and that it was an indisputable fact that 'there are boys and youths soliciting on the streets'.[81] Vincent also commented that, although sodomy, and indeed acting as an accessory to the act, were subject to the 'most severe punishment in Europe', there were problems connected with its enforcement: 'the difficulty, not to say the danger of obtaining evidence is very great indeed'.[82] It is unclear what he meant by 'danger'. He appears to have been referring to the difficulty of mustering sufficient evidence for a prosecution but he might also have been hinting at the involvement of men of high standing in such practices. Jeffrey Weeks has drawn attention to the efforts of the Metropolitan Police to cover up the Cleveland Street male brothel scandal of 1889 which involved the use of post office messenger boys as prostitutes and which implicated a series of eminent public figures including Lord Euston.[83] It was clearly felt that the exposure of such vices was more dangerous to 'public morality' than attempts at concealment.[84]

References to the seduction and prostitution of young men and boys were extremely rare in any official report; Vincent's evidence to the commission not only provides an indication of police concerns during the 1880s but also offers an important hint as to why 'gross indecency' was outlawed in 1885. Historians have suggested a whole string of motives for Henry Labouchère's amendment, including a desire to sabotage the whole Criminal Law Amendment Bill, which he thought 'absurd', by introducing a clause at a late key stage that he believed MPs would never agree to.[85] Five years after its enactment Labouchère offered another explanation for his motives, citing the influence of a report on male prostitution which was sent to him in 1885 by newspaper editor W. T. Stead.[86] He claimed that, having read the report, he drew up the amendment in an attempt to facilitate the securing of evidence in such cases. Stead's alleged report on male prostitution has proved untraceable and F. B. Smith has persuasively argued that it must have been a figment of Labouchère's imagination, inspired by professional rivalry as editors of competing sensationalist newspapers.[87]

If, however, the alternative assumption is made – that the report on male prostitution did exist – it is extremely likely that, given his profile in other reports on moral offences, Vincent was a key contributor. If Labouchère's comments about male prostitution are combined with Vincent's concern about male youth (evidenced in the Select Committee but undoubtedly more widely discussed in police, Home Office and parliamentary circles), it is possible to argue that the outlawing of gross indecency in 1885 must have been an attempt to deal with the perceived problem of boys aged 14–18 who were picked up by adult men, whether these boys were 'innocent' parties or openly pursuing business as male prostitutes. The 'gross inde-cency' clause, read purely as an attempt to stop consensual sex between men, is often seen as incongruous in a bill which otherwise aimed to 'protect young girls'. If, however, its central aim was the protection of young boys (whatever purposes it was actually put to), the clause fits neatly into place.

Sympathy and backlash

The nineteenth century clearly saw an intensification of concerns about the child – and about the need to protect childhood innocence – which led to the rise in the age of consent for girls and an increase in the number of cases of sexual abuse that came before the courts. This did not mean, however, that the child witness was always viewed sympathetically by the courts; rather, children faced rigorous cross-examinations to ascertain whether they were 'witnesses of truth' who really had been innocent before the assault. The increase in prosecutions for child abuse and the moral panic about juve-nile prostitution were paralleled by the development of the issue of juvenile delinquency which led to the scrutiny, surveillance and attempt to regulate the behaviour of the children of the poor. Indeed, concerns about delinquent youth came to such a head that the 1890s saw something of a backlash against the child protection movement. Conviction rates for child sexual abuse cases sent to the Old Bailey plummeted from 72 per cent in 1890 to 44 per cent in 1895 and, to the Yorkshire Assizes, from 87 per cent in 1890 to 45 per cent in 1895, suggesting that judges and juries were running out of sympathy for girl victims. As Harry Hendrick has argued, children of the labouring classes were seen, interchangeably, as threats as well as victims. Many members of the Old Bailey jury would have agreed with the comments of lawyer Mr Geoghegan, defending a client against the allega-tions of a 'precocious' 15-year-old girl in November 1885, that 'there would soon have to be a society for the protection of men and boys, and not of women and girls'.[88]

The story of these children will be resumed in chapter 7, which examines the institutional homes set up for 'fallen' girls. In the meantime, it is neces-sary to turn attentions to the defendant, to explain attitudes towards the abuser in court, as well as verdict and sentencing, within the context of wider debates about gender, masculinity and sexuality in this period.

6 Masculinity, 'respectability' and the child abuser

Introduction

In 1907 Old Bailey judge Justice Darling sentenced a 50-year-old man to ten years' penal servitude for raping his 11-year-old daughter. Addressing the defendant, he remarked: 'The story told here today by the girl and your wife represents you as a perfectly idle, vicious man. You are a person of whom I am afraid there are numbers in London, who do not work, who do not want to work, but who want to drink and who are immoral.'[1] Darling linked incestuous abuse to a debased lifestyle that he associated with unemployment, idleness, drunkenness and criminality. He identified abusive behaviour as typical of men of the underclass, residuum or, as Charles Booth described them in 1889, the 'vicious classes'.[2] This behavioural model was the antithesis of the ideal of masculine respectability – the 'manly' man – established by a proliferation of middle-class texts during the nineteenth century. Samuel Smiles's *Self-help* of 1859, one of the most famous and popular renditions of this theme, provided a detailed prescription for male virtue, based on action and industry, self-respect, self-reliance and self-control.[3] Although the concept of manliness underwent several transformations during the course of the century, Smiles's central message still resonates through Darling's statement. Morality, industry and virtue were closely related; economic failure was both a result and a sign of idleness and moral deficiency.

Darling was clearly disgusted at the man's action, as were most commentators faced with the appalling brutality of child abuse and incest. Yet this horror does not appear to have led to increased severity in the courts: 31 per cent (nearly a third) of all defendants who were tried for sexually assaulting children were, in fact, acquitted.[4] This chapter examines how this could have been possible. By analysing, in turn, the viewpoints of child savers, defendants and judges, it shows that the sex abuser was commonly evaluated as 'deviant' in relation to notions of 'respectable' masculinity in the Victorian and Edwardian judicial systems. The 'normal' father and breadwinner who protected and provided for his family remained beyond reproach.

Carolyn Conley has argued, in her study of rape cases in Kent 1859–80, that the decisions of judges and juries was based on an evaluation of the reputation of the defendant in relation to that of the victim.[5] Whereas feminine virtue was a matter of moral or sexual reputation, the 'respectability' of adult male defendants was based on hard work and family duties. The evidence from the Middlesex, London and Yorkshire courts supports this emphasis on 'respectability'; for men, fatherhood and a permanent job were signifiers of social status which carried great weight in the courtroom.

Conley, however, tends to underplay the importance of perceptions of class in the construction of 'respectability'. It will be argued here that a more nuanced interpretation of Victorian codes of 'respectability' is called for, which allows for the interplay of class, status (and sometimes also race and religion) as well as age and gender. Statistics suggest that the likelihood of conviction was inversely proportional to the social class of the defendant. The concept of manly virtue constructed men of the 'vicious classes' as child abusers and, frequently, privileged the 'respectability' of the professional and middle classes, placing them beyond behavioural criticism and censure.

Lucia Zedner has argued that, throughout the nineteenth century, female criminality was seen as especially deviant because it involved the rejection of character traits – including passivity, selflessness, and moral virtue – which were associated with the 'natural' or 'normal' condition of womanhood.[6] Male criminals, she has suggested, were perceived to present less of a social threat because their aggressive or acquisitive behaviour was an extension of rather than a deviation from the initiative, mendacity and competitiveness expected in the 'normal' man. Zedner's thesis, however, fails to provide an adequate explanation for the way sex abusers were treated in the English courts. There are, certainly, references to men as sexually predatory by nature. One judge, sentencing a 67-year-old Barnsley man to death for child rape at the Yorkshire Assizes in July 1840, told him: 'you have arrived at that period of life at which you cannot plead the excuse of violent passions'.[7] Yet references to men as essentially aggressive were disappearing fast as they were replaced in the courtroom with a racialised discourse of class/respectability. Sexual abuse was increasingly delineated as a heinous offence committed by 'brutes' and 'savages' – in other words, social deviants – rather than by 'normal' men.[8] This construction firmly placed the male abuser in the category of male 'otherness'; the abuser was the vicious, idle slum-dweller who represented the antithesis of the 'normal', respectable, breadwinner.

Sexual abuse – gender specific?

According to the statistical data gathered for this study it was almost always men who were accused of rape or sexual abuse: 99 per cent of the cases sampled involved male defendants. Only 14 defendants, out of a total of 1,590, were women. Six of these women were charged in conjunction with other male defendants on what could be termed accessory charges: administering drugs to enable rape, abduction, aiding and abetting unlawful carnal knowledge, procuring, and encouraging the seduction of another female.[9] The two women implicated in W. T. Stead's 1885 attempt to buy a 13-year-old girl on the streets of London – former procuress Rebecca Jarrett and French midwife Louise Mourez – are included in these figures.[10] In another case, cook Jane Tate was prosecuted, with parlourmaid Maria Smith, on a joint charge of causing the prostitution of Tate's 13-year-old daughter, Florence; Tate and Smith were each sentenced to 18 months' hard labour and the girl removed from parental custody.[11] Those found guilty of aiding and abetting rape tended to receive similar sentences to male defendants found guilty of rape with whom they appeared in court.

Women who facilitated the rape of their own children were seen by judges as especially brutal, as this 1905 case, reported in the *Child's Guardian*, attests:

> At the Leeds Assizes Mr Justice Jelf heard what he described as the most shocking case that had ever come before him. It was a charge brought against a man for criminally assaulting a girl of eleven years, and against the girl's mother for not only consenting to, but actually aiding and abetting in the assault. ... The judge sentenced both prisoners to five years' penal servitude, and said of the woman, that of all the mothers that he had come across, she was the most cruel and the most wicked.[12]

These comments must be related to Victorian/Edwardian ideals of both femininity and parenthood. First, as Zedner has demonstrated, women were generally construed as unselfish by nature, while motherhood was supposed to foster altruism and compassion.[13] Women's brutality towards their children was considered especially monstrous as a direct contradiction of the nurturing and caring role considered 'normal' and 'natural' in mothers. It is inadequate, however, to leave the analysis at that. As John Tosh has pointed out, fatherhood was also associated, in both middle-class and radical working-class circles, with responsibility for the moral supervision and training of children.[14] The crime that Justice Jelf referred to with such repugnance was gauged in terms of both deviant womanhood and also deviant parenting. The father who sexually abused his children could expect a similar reaction.

Only one woman was accused of abusing a child to satisfy her own sexual needs rather than those of others. In March 1900 Mary James was tried at the Old Bailey for indecently assaulting a 9-year-old boy, the son of her landlady. The court was told how the boy usually slept on a sofa bed in the parlour but that James, who looked after him when his mother was out, invited him into her own bed one evening.[15] The boy's mother pressed charges when she found her son suffering from gonorrhoea. In court, defendant and prosecutrix attempted to slur each other's moral reputations; each accused the other of promiscuity, prostitution, drunkenness, and of suffering from venereal disease. James was convicted and Justice Ridley sent her to prison for six weeks.

Why did Mary James abuse? Did others like her slip through the net because they were not 'usual suspects'?[16] Given the tenuous nature of the historical evidence it is difficult to find answers to these important questions. The recent high profile case of Rosemary West has highlighted the fact that women do carry out acts of sexual abuse on children.[17] Psychotherapist Estella Welldon has suggested that female abusers tend to target what she calls their 'sexual perversions' against either 'themselves or ... their own creation ... that is, their babies'.[18] It is worth noting in the light of Welldon's comments that the case of Mary James involved a woman's alleged abuse of her position as carer. Single and childless, James had built up a close relationship with a boy whose mother was often out; she was frequently called upon to act in place of his mother. He, perhaps, was the child she never had. It would be extremely problematic, however, to impose arguments drawn from psychological observations of present-day female abusers on historical subjects; care must be taken to present cases such as that of Mary James within their historical context.

Greater levels of physical intimacy were clearly deemed acceptable between women and children; this intimacy transcended even the familial or the neighbourly relationship.[19] Ellen Ross has demonstrated how working-class women performed an important role as primary carers not only of their own children but also of the children of friends, relatives and neighbours.[20] The intimacy and close proximity of women's and children's bodies through childbirth, breastfeeding, and the daily physicality of childcare are vital factors whose historical significance has received scant attention.[21] Mothers were the first to spot the signs of sexual abuse on their children's bodies, noticed at bath-time or in dressing and undressing. It could be argued that the intimacy of women and children, accepted and expected, might provide the vital concealment for abusive relationships.

On the other hand, it is possible that such intimacy renders abuse less likely. Sociologist Jeff Hearn has suggested that men in present-day society would be less likely to abuse if they played a more significant role in child-care practice.[22] There is no evidence of women assaulting unknown children in streets or parks; while it is possible that such cases were concealed because they were never suspected, it is probable that complaints would have been made if women behaved in an especially predatory manner. The statistical evidence that 99 per cent of defendants in the case study were male, coupled with research on present-day societies which suggests that sexual abuse is still very much a male specific crime, suggests that explanations for abuse must lie in the constructions of masculinity and male sexuality in this period.[23]

Despite the low involvement of women in court cases of sexual abuse, stereotypes of the 'wicked mother' and the 'evil procuress' flourished in the 'seduction' narratives – including the 'Maiden tribute' – that appeared in the popular press during the 1880s.[24] In 1909 references were still being made to the belief that impoverished mothers were ready and willing to sell their own children: 'It is a fairly common practice among the mothers of quite young girls in the terribly over-crowded slums to force their daughters to sleep with men lodgers; and that women similarly situated, and perhaps a shade more degraded compel their little girls to go on the streets soliciting.'[25] The delineation of the complicitous mother, pre-empted in medico-legal texts, attempted to draw attention away from the male assailant and the gender specificity of sexual abuse, blaming bad mothering as much as male viciousness for the prevalence of 'juvenile prostitution' and 'child seduction'. However, as Lucy Bland has demonstrated, Victorian and Edwardian feminists sought to highlight the issue of gender specificity, and to fix responsibility on predatory male sexuality.[26] Despite attempts to blame women for sexual abuse, male social purity and child welfare campaigners were forced to address the problem of the 'beast in man'.

'Manliness' and the child-saving movement

As gender-specific crimes, the way in which rape and indecent assault were treated in the courts (by male judges, juries and lawyers) was closely bound up with ideas about masculinity and male sexuality, ideas which shifted and changed during the course of the nineteenth century. Anna Clark has described how 'in the late eighteenth-century a libertine discourse permeated slang and masculine popular culture, glorifying rape as a source of amusement … as a way of proving … masculinity to other men'.[27] This discourse associated sexual conquest with virility and defined male sexuality as predatory by nature; its influence, she has argued, was reflected in the reluctance of judges and juries to try cases of rape in assize courts.[28] Zedner's suggestion that male criminality was an extension of the aggressive attributes considered 'normal' in men does, indeed, fit with this 'libertine' formulation of rape.[29] Clark has demonstrated, however, that, from the early nineteenth century onwards, the association of masculinity with libertinism was replaced in newspapers, court rooms, public lectures and prescriptive literature, by the emerging concept of Christian 'manliness' based on chivalry, moral purity and self-discipline. The development of the 'cult of manliness' and its role in the construction of middle-class self identity has been well charted.[30] As a concept 'manliness' itself underwent a transformation between the 1840s and 1880s – from an evangelically-inspired quest for spiritual perfection which emphasised selflessness, hard work and family duties in the early Victorian period – to a robust stoicism, perfected through athleticism, team sports and militaristic discipline in the late Victorian period.[31] It will be argued, here, that middle-class codes of manliness, which emphasised social and moral purity, were closely related to the confrontation of child sexual abuse by the late nineteenth century. The figure of the chivalric hero was constructed in opposition to, on one hand, the 'savage' child abuser, and, on the other, the vulnerable child victim. While the abuser represented the deviant 'other', the child victim was configured as the desired 'other'.

John Tosh has suggested that 'the dominant masculinity is constructed in opposition to a number of subordinate masculinities whose crime is that they undermine patriarchy from within or discredit it in the eyes of women'.[32] Tosh has cited the demonisation of the homosexual and campaigns against wife-beating as prime examples. At various points in the nineteenth century the figure of the child sexual abuser became a similar target, construed in relation to class identities and oppositions. The *Pall Mall Gazette*'s aristocratic 'monster', despoiling the daughters of the poor, appealed to both long-established middle-class notions of moral superiority over a decadent and corrupt aristocracy and to working-class notions of 'respectability' in the face of exploitation by the ruling classes.[33] The second construction of the sexual abuser had very different class connotations. The idea that incest resulted from overcrowding amongst the lowest orders was established by the 1840s, as newspaper reports attest.[34] The notion of an 'immoral' residuum was often contrasted with another category, the 'respectable poor', which consisted of law-abiding, hardworking families. The notion of 'respectability' became an important aspect of class identification, uniting the bourgeoisie and upper-working classes against the aristocracy on one hand and the 'vicious poor' on the other.

The spectre of sexual abuse was, by the 1880s, a clear case in point of a form of masculine behaviour which could potentially discredit 'patriarchy'. Josephine Butler's campaigns to repeal the Contagious Diseases Acts during the 1870s had exposed the sexual double standard, involved women in the discussion of sexual politics in the public arena and blamed men for prostitution; publicity material gave prominence to stories of the seduction of young girls at a very early age.[35] Middle-class ideals of virtuous masculinity were deployed by male and female social purity workers during the 1880s in relation to the issue of 'juvenile prostitution' and child abuse. Sexual assault was constructed as the worst form of brutality, the mindless excess of the 'unmanly' man in opposition to the chivalrous actions of the 'manly' man. Ellice Hopkins used the issue to rally male support for the Church of England's organisation for social purity men, the White Cross Army, in 1883: 'the wonder is that the chivalrous, deep-hearted men of England, have not united in some organization long ago to defend women from dishonour, on the face of the fearfully debased manhood that degradation of mere children bears witness to'.[36]

While the early Victorian rhetoric of manliness had stressed the role of the father as moral protector of his own private family, social purity campaigners of the 1880s called on 'true manhood' to defend women and children generally as a duty connected with patriotic loyalty. The concept of the family man was mixed with the new heroism; the spiritual quest, previously private and introspective, was to be turned outward and directed towards the moral salvation of the nation and, vitally, of the nation's children. The imperial hero was to fight against savagery at home as well as abroad. Describing his own personal investigation into London's 'white slave trade', W. T. Stead drew on a wide range of literary references from Dante to gothic melodrama. The bravado and spirit of exploration conjured up in the boys' adventure stories of the 1880s was also an important feature:[37] 'For four weeks, aided by two or three coadjutors of whose devotion and self-sacrifice, combined with a rare instinct for investigation and a singular personal fearlessness, I cannot speak too highly, I have been exploring the London Inferno.'[38] Rider Haggard's own talents were to be harnessed by the NSPCC as a speaker at local meetings, further reinforcing the links between the action hero and the child saver.

In 1885 NSPCC director Benjamin Waugh produced a eulogy to Stead which provided a powerful delineation of the kind of masculinity which the child savers hoped to nurture.[39] Waugh traced Stead's desire to protect girls back to his boyhood in Howdon-on-Tyne where he 'felled to the ground a boy companion who had gone to look at a girl who had turned aside to tie up her garter'. Waugh described Stead in chivalric terms as 'the young Howdon knight' who understood that 'to champion chastity was right'. Stead's involvement in the campaign to raise the age of consent was defined as a crusade inspired by a 'manly cleanliness of heart'. Stead's moral commitment, his emotional response to child suffering (he was depicted as weeping when he met sexually brutalised children at the NSPCC's London shelter) was portrayed by Waugh as combined with hard work and strong family ties. His heroism was demonstrated in his willingness to go 'into the hells where manhood was destroyed, and woman damned'. Waugh concluded the praise of his friend by arguing that: 'the age of chivalry is ever with us. ... The soul of man may sleep for a season; but at any moment, starting from its lethargy, it may display a vigorous vitality, a heroic rescue, a chivalrous determination equal to that of the most famous ages of antiquity.[40]

The question remains as to what extent this 'reconstructed' masculinity was dominant or influential. As Frank Mort has pointed out, MPs and Home Office officials, who repeatedly blocked attempts to outlaw incest or raise the age of consent, saw social purity and feminist leaders as 'faddists and fanatics'.[41] As Tosh has indicated, there was still an obvious and indeed sizeable market for female prostitutes despite the activities of the purity campaigners.[42] On the other hand, social purity campaigns seemed to have had a significant groundswell of support from the masses: over a quarter of a million Londoners attended the demonstration in Hyde Park in support of the Criminal Law Amendment Bill in July 1885.[43] The town hall in Leeds was described as packed for a similar meeting.[44] William Booth's Salvation Army, which aimed for both spiritual conversion and moral rejuvenation from its foundation in 1865, developed successful populist strategies for recruiting working-class members, linking in with other currents in socialism and trade unionism which sought to reform masculinity.[45] Pamela Walker has shown, however, that men who forfeited the pugilism, gambling and drinking associated with certain traditions of working-class masculinity, became subject to ridicule and attack.[46] The pub still provided an essential social focus for men, and, to a lesser extent, women in poorer areas.[47] Working-class communities developed their own moral guidelines and forms of self-regulation separate from the attempts of philanthropists to impose a prefigured morality upon them. The terms 'honesty' and 'respectability' were widely used but this did not mean they were always understood in exactly the same way.

Eroticising innocence

According to statute law the pre-pubescent body of the 12-year-old girl was an entirely legitimate object of male sexual desire before 1885.[48] Child-savers attempted to expose the desire of so-called aristocratic rakes for young virgins; they aimed to draw attention to the monetary value that was placed on innocence as a sexual commodity. In idealising the condition of innocence, however, they were perpetuating and, indeed, developing, the same erotic discourse which positioned the body of the underdeveloped girl child as 'other'. The vulnerable girl child and her chivalric male protector were constructed as binary opposites in an inherited and already fetishised language of innocence/experience. 'Littleness' and 'innocence' were sexualized in similar ways in both social purity writings and in texts whose intentions were more explicitly erotic.

In his survey of 'child-loving', attempting to span some 200 years of cultural history, James Kincaid has traced the roots of modern concerns about child abuse and paedophilia to nineteenth-century notions of children as sexual innocents. He has suggested that 'by insisting so loudly on the innocence, purity and asexuality of the child, we have created a subversive echo: experience, corruption, eroticism'.[49] The child, conceived of as 'other' within a discourse of sexuality, becomes an object of erotic desire. For Kincaid the figure of 'the paedophile' is constructed out of the projection and denial of 'our' desires concerning the child. One of the central problems with Kincaid's thesis is his failure to establish exactly who 'we' are. He ignores any suggestion that subjectivity and sexual desire may be gendered, failing to engage with the large body of feminist-influenced studies which have sought to analyse sexuality and sexual violence in relation to structures of power and authority. Nevertheless Kincaid does make points which become more useful when related to specific contexts, thereby escaping the 'we' problem. The concept of sexual innocence, which was elevated in the Victorian 'cult of the little girl', was clearly dependent on its opposite: the lurking shadow of experience and adult corruption. Furthermore, social purity writers of the 1880s, in buying into this idealisation of innocence, further commodified and, indeed, fetishised it.

Stead's 'Maiden tribute' articles, in exposing the tension between sexual innocence and sexual knowledge, clearly resonated with more pornographic genres:

> At one villa in the north of London I found ... a lovely child between fourteen and fifteen, tall for her age, but singularly attractive in her childish innocence. ... There was another girl in the house – a brazen faced harlot, whose flaunting vice served as a foil to set off the childlike, spirituelle beauty of the other's baby face. It was cruel to see the poor wee features, not much larger than those of a doll, of the delicately nurtured girl, as she came into the room with her fur mantle wrapped closely around her, and timidly asked me if I would take some wine. ... It seemed a profanation to touch her, she was so young and so baby-like. There she was, turned over to the first comer that would pay, but still to all appearances so modest, the maiden bloom not altogether having faded off her childish cheeks, and her pathetic eyes, where still lingered the timid glance of a frightened fawn. ... 'She saw old gentlemen', she said, 'almost exclusively. Sometimes it was rather bad, but she liked the life.'[50]

The construction of the innocent girl child victim in texts such as Stead's further eroticised the child as an exotic 'other'. Baby-faced innocence was, here, contrasted with brazen-faced harlotry; but appearances concealed the fact that the moral condition of the two girls was pretty much the same. Both were of, we presume, a similar age, both lived in a brothel, both were, in fact, already working as prostitutes. The innocent appearance of the 'lovely child' concealed her already fallen condition; she actually admitted that she 'liked the life'. Soon, the passage suggested, she too would become brazen faced. At present, however, her 'maiden bloom' had not yet quite faded. Her docility and vulnerability are emphasised in the description of her 'pathetic eyes' as those of a 'frightened fawn'. This innocence is juxtaposed with the threat of its 'profanation' and destruction; the metaphorical significance of 'innocence' is dependent on the sense that it is about to be ruined or lost.

If innocence is ephemeral, then the text which discusses it is always one of postponement. The most efficient and permanent postponements could be achieved through death, hence the popularity among nineteenth-century authors of 'killing off' the virtuous children in their stories. Carol Mavor has described how, in Lewis Carroll's photographs, the perfect beauty and innocence of the child is frozen forever as a *memento mori* in an attempt to evade both the maturity and decay associated with the ageing process.[51] As Kincaid has established, however, the flipside of perfection was destruction; of innocence, corruption. In his 'Maiden tribute' articles Stead revelled in the significance and 'value' of virginity; the seduction of the virgin was described in terms of ruination and despoilation. Stead's emphasis on virginity as a valued condition or commodity was of course nothing new. The long western philosophical tradition based on the concept of binary polarity ensured that praise of virginity/purity was automatically positioned in relation to the threat of its corruption/contamination. During the nineteenth century, however, the concept of virginity was interpreted in relation to new ideas about the child and childhood; ideas which involved a whole series of emotional and personal investments. What was particularly new about Stead's articles in 1885 was his candid articulation of all those anxieties about childhood and sexuality which had previously dogged nineteenth-century minds. Once and for all, he clearly exposed the child as a sexually desirable object although his purpose, in doing so, was to contain these desires as morally out of bounds. He explicitly recognised another premature closure or resolution for innocence, the resolution which was told in the courts on a daily basis: rape and sexual assault.

During the 1880s, therefore, notions of social purity and threatened innocence served to fashion the child as an object of desire (although, after 1885, an unattainable one). As Clark has also demonstrated, the concept of male chivalry might have constructed rape as 'unmanly' but, in its dependence on female virtue and passivity, cast women and girls as potential victims, in need of male protection.[52] Furthermore, in positioning them as vulnerable and passive in opposition to the active strength of the 'manly man', it maintained their position as 'other'.

If chivalrous masculinity was constructed in opposition to the vulnerability, innocence and defencelessness of the girl victim, the question is, essentially, at what cost? It is, of course, impossible to tell whether the incidence of sexual abuse increased in response to these developments (although Kincaid has hinted that child pornography began to develop around this time).[53] It is also extremely difficult to gauge how these constructions might have interacted with the desires and psyches of defendants who appeared in court charged with child assault. A few cases offer vague hints. Most defendants offered explanations that were scripted in terms of respectability and responsibility.

The defence

Defendants from all social backgrounds appeared before the courts on sexual abuse charges, but the majority came from the vast ranks of the working classes, whether artisan, semi-skilled or unskilled labourers.[54] This does not mean that the middle classes were less likely to abuse children; rather, they were less likely to be charged with doing so. The thoughts and opinions of individual defendants must always evade us: the explanations of events that they gave the courts were of course, to a large degree, a simple reflection of what they or their lawyer thought that the court wanted to hear. Yet the defences and responses of those accused of sexual abuse, as reported in newspapers and depositions, do tell us a great deal about understandings of masculinity and male sexuality, family, childhood and adulthood amongst working men.

Although there are clear references in eighteenth-century criminal trials to the belief that sex with a virgin could cure venereal disease, this myth did not crop up as an explanation of defendants' behaviour in the nineteenth-century cases sampled.[55] Many defendants, unsurprisingly, denied that any act of sexual abuse had been perpetrated: 'It is all a tissue of lies. There is not one particle of truth in it ... they questioned her and put these ideas into her head.'[56] One defendant, perhaps intentionally or perhaps unwittingly, played on ideas of guilt/innocence, power/vulnerability and adulthood/child-hood by declaring himself 'as innocent as a new-born babe'.[57] As chapter 5 has demonstrated, methods of cross-examination were used in court to cast doubt on the moral status and reputation of the child victim, thereby under-mining the credibility of the child's evidence in court. Defendants frequently suggested that allegations had been contrived by girl victims or their mothers out of malice or for purposes of blackmail, exploiting the idea of masculine vulnerability in the face of feminine guile.[58]

It is also important to consider the male assumption that sex was a commodity that could be secured by buying a woman's services. Defendants often offered money to children or their parents either prior to or following a sexual assault, believing this would settle the matter.[59] The notion of male sexual desire as impulsive was combined with the excuse of after-payment for services rendered and a shifting of responsibility towards the victim. A girl of 12 or more who was thought to be 'immodest' was seen as a legiti-mate object of attack, hence the defence that 'she was not a pure girl' who had 'led me on'.[60]

'Drunk or mad'

Other defences were commonly used which, similarly, enabled accused men to abdicate personal responsibility for their actions. The most popular excuse was alcohol:

[His] conduct had been unintentional, and was probably owing to his having taken a little drink, which had produced great effect upon him (1855).

All I did was playing [sic] with her but I was the worse for drink at the time (1860).

If he had not been drinking he should not have acted with such folly ... and had been more foolish than criminal (1865).

I was very tipsy – I do not recollect anything that occurred (1870).

> He had been drinking all day, and, going into a warm room, the fire had upset him and made him not know what he was doing ... he had a very good character before (1875).

> It's all through the blasted drink. I admit being in the closet three quarters of an hour with the boy. I don't know what made me do it (1880).

> I ... had one drink. I came over silly. ... I admit taking a liberty with her. I am sorry for what I have done (1910).[61]

Drink could be relied on as a mitigating factor because it suggested that the act was unpremeditated. Alcohol had caused the defendant to lose control of his 'normal' faculties of restraint. Where possible, it was alleged that the defendant was usually of a sober and respectable disposition and that this particular incident had been a freak occurrence. The drink excuse bridged the gap between libertine and stoic notions of masculinity since it depicted sexual conquest as an uncontrollable impulse that was unleashed in men through intoxication. Given the centrality of public house and beer shop in many working neighbourhoods, it would seem that drinking and sexual libertinism were still, throughout the century, constituents of certain working-class archetypes of manliness.

By the last quarter of the century, defendants were also arguing that they suffered from a specific medical condition, often acquired abroad, which meant that alcohol had an unusual effect: 'while abroad he had had a sunstroke, since which time any indulgence in liquor produced an effect upon him rendering him almost irresponsible'.[62] Another man was reported to have told his arresting officer in 1895: 'Yes I must have been either drunk or mad. I had a sunstroke when I was abroad and when I get drunk I don't know what I am doing.'[63] The wife of a 40-year-old carpenter accused of behaving indecently on Hampstead Heath in the presence of 'several little girls' told the magistrate 'that her husband who had been in Egypt was not accountable for his actions when he had taken a drop to drink'.[64]

Medical experts, throughout this period, described tropical climates as having a debilitating effect, both physically and morally, on British visitors. Strong warnings were given concerning heat stroke which could have 'serious effects on the brain and nervous system'.[65] Childcare manuals argued that western children were especially vulnerable to climate and should be brought home from the colonies before the heat weakened their constitution and affected the nervous system; hot climates could lead to early sexual development and, in girls, an earlier age for the onset of menarche.[66] The permanent damage which, it was thought, would result if children stayed in the tropics was also a point of reference in court. A Huddersfield mother explained that her 17-year-old son, accused of tampering with a 3-year-old girl, 'was born in India ... he was always a poorly lad. He had sunstroke in India when he was about 6 or 7 years old. He has had fits. He cannot speak properly. He is not right in the brain.'[67]

The defences offered in the courts suggest that expert medical opinion was reflected, at the popular level, in the opinion that hot climates disturbed the mind and the passions, disrupting a man's normal rational control over his body. If, as Joanna de Groot has demonstrated, colonial expansion was delineated, through discourses of race and gender, as male penetration of lands and territories positioned as feminine through their exoticism and otherness, it was ultimately the feminine 'other' who was responsible for seducing the male visitor, for 'unmanning' him of his 'manly' restraint, and for spreading the disease of promiscuity.[68] The indigenous peoples of India and other colonies were frequently portrayed as sexually aberrant or primitive as well as mentally backward or unstable.[69] The popular rhetoric of the sickness induced by the foreign suggested that femininity and savagery had contaminated the normal sturdy and moral British male. Such a defence or plea for mitigation was far removed from an insanity plea since it suggested that a man was subject to disruption on rare occasions which could, in the future, be controlled. The defence also appealed to romantic notions of conquest and exploration, grounded as they were in notions of masculine strength and virtue. The defendant was, indirectly, positioned as a 'manly' man, who, as a colonist or soldier had played his part in the imperialist project.[70]

Physical intimacy

In indecent assault cases which involved touching and stroking, the question of what sort of physical relationship was appropriate between an adult man and a child was often raised. Many defendants denied that 'indecency' had taken place; they stated that they had kissed or touched a child out of love and affection (rather than, we would presume, sexual arousal or desire). A Yorkshire quarryman told magistrates. 'I never behaved indecently towards the child. She came and took hold of my coat. I just had my arms around her and put her on her back ... I never touched the child indecently.'[71] In September 1888 an elderly man accused of indecently assaulting two girls on a bench at Hampstead, told magistrates that he had 'only played innocently with the children'. The *Hampstead and Highgate Express* reported that 'for years he had been known as Father Christmas and had acted in that character. It was his practice when he met nice little boys and girls, to give them a halfpenny or fruit or sweets.'[72] In the courts defendants often referred to the father–child relationship as an ideal model for the definition of 'normal' physical contact between adults and children. A 50-year-old watchman said 'he put his arm round the children and kissed them as though they might be his own children'.[73] A marble polisher, accused of indecently assaulting a child he met in the park, said: 'I am the father of a family & have three children – I took this child in my arms as I would do my own.'[74] Within working-class male cultures, entry into waged labour, marriage and setting up home (as head of household) were significant rites of passage marking maturity and responsibility. Fatherhood was a signifier of social status and respectability which crossed the boundaries of class; defendants and defence solicitors made reference to wives and offspring whenever possible.

It is also clear, however, that the affection of men for children other than their own was viewed as increasingly problematic as a result of the publicity given to abuse. One defendant, arrested for assaulting a girl as she looked in a shop window, told the police constable 'I put my arms round the girl's neck, but I thought it was my next-door neighbour's child.' The magistrate at Thames Police court, Mr Saunders, discharged the case in August 1885 but advised the man 'to be careful about accosting or interfering with young children'.[75] The negotiation of the boundaries of physical familiarity depended on gender as well as on the degree of social relationship. The physical intimacy between women and children clearly transcended the familial or neighbourly relationship. It was acceptable for men to kiss, hug and touch children in a playful manner if they were the children of family and friends; it was deemed inappropriate, on the other hand, if they were strangers.

Fatherhood

The model of the 'loving father', idealised in the rhetoric of the courtroom by judges, lawyers and defendants alike, was a pertinent reference point in cases of sexual abuse. The authority and responsibility associated with fatherhood, which was usually discussed in relation to duties of protection and nurture, could also become the power to abuse and terrorise. Although acts of brutality by parents became the subject of surveillance in the later nineteenth century and although changes in custody law created opportunities for State and philanthropic intervention, the case for the 'policing of the family' should not be overstated.[76] The rape of married women by their husbands was not criminalised until 1991 and incest, although a sin in the eyes of the Church, was not made illegal until 1908.[77] Sexual abuse of children was legally regulated through age-of-consent legislation which meant that girls aged 13–16 could be seen as legitimate objects of their father's sexual affection until 1885. It was often difficult to prove a child's age if there had been no official register of her birth. Even after the 1908 Incest Act, cases were still unlikely to come to court. Some fathers may well have assumed that marital rights over wives extended to children as well. As Linda Gordon and James Hammerton have argued, the family must still be considered as a private, patriarchal domain in which force and aggression might well hold sway.[78]

If social workers and government legislation had yet to make their mark, there were nevertheless contradictions between the traditional legal notion of a father's authority and the conditions that were attached to it by family and neighbourhood. As Hammerton has pointed out, some men may have felt uncomfortable with the increased emphasis on respectability.[79] The relationships of parents and children, mothers and fathers, older and younger brothers and sisters were intricately complex and subject to continual negotiation. Claims to authority could meet with disagreement, refusal, resistance and conflict. It is clear that, in many working families, violence was an everyday experience as a form of parental discipline. Indeed, many of the children who appeared in court in cases of sexual abuse involving strangers or neighbours spoke of an initial reluctance to tell their parents through fear of corporal punishment. Mary Ann Taylor, aged 12, was badly assaulted by a man in a lane between Seacroft and Leeds when she was out with her sister and a friend. She later admitted to magistrates that: 'I did not tell my father because I was frightened he would flog us.'[80] Mary Ann's sister told her mother and violence was subsequently used as a threat to get the full story out of the girls: 'I told my husband and he said to [Mary] that if she did not tell he would strip her and flog her.' Despite the possible presence or threat of violence in the home, it is nevertheless clear that mothers and neighbours made a distinction between everyday violence and sexual assault or abuse.

Defendants involved in incest cases, on the other hand, demonstrated a blurring of these distinctions and it is clear that they attempted to use the power, authority and force associated with fatherhood to get what they wanted out of their children. This usually consisted of positive affirmations ('he said he was doing nothing wrong & he would not hurt me') as well as threats to punish.[81] Elsa Hammond, age 15, told Wakefield magistrates of her father's threats in 1885: 'He said "Have you told your mother anything?" ... "By God you bugger if ever you do I'll murder you".'[82] At the same time it was their awareness of neighbourhood codes of condemnation that made these threats necessary in order to keep the matter silent and secret. While parliamentary reports condemned the one-room system as likely to lead to incest and immorality, overcrowding often limited the opportunities for abuse. Where families did live in one room, fathers (if not widowed) waited for their wives to go out to work to attain the privacy they needed to molest their children.[83] Some defendants behaved with arrogance when caught, confident in the knowledge that cases were difficult to prove. When Thomas Cartwright was arrested for the incestuous assault of his 10-year-old daughter in June 1865, he was said to have told the police officer: 'They can't give me but seven years and they must prove it.'[84]

Most defendants were aware of the exposure, shame, cowardliness and humiliation associated with incest; hence the denials and refusals to accept responsibility. Some even attempted to take their lives. In 1905 James Chubb's wife and stepdaughter, age 11, approached the police for assistance when they felt they could no longer tolerate his violence and sexual abuse. When a police constable from Baildon police station near Bradford arrived to make the arrest, Chubb, somewhat the worse for drink, broke down. As his wife told the court, '[He] said nothing but sat in the corner & commenced to cry. He then picked up a knife from the table and tried to cut his throat.'[85] Yet abusers were clearly not too ashamed to commit these offences in the first place or to assert their authority to silence and subjugate their children. As I have demonstrated more fully elsewhere, notions of masculinity that privileged the authority of father over wife and children created an important structure of power, resting on a notion of paternal authority and subservient obedience, which, although challenged, could all too easily be abused by Victorian fathers.[86]

'The cult of the little girl'

Finally, it is necessary to consider whether men accused of abusing girl children were influenced by the eroticisation of innocence and 'littleness' that permeated textual discussions of childhood towards the end of the period. Very few defendants spoke of their desires in court – most tended to deny the offence or to blame something or someone else – but occasionally we have the odd glimpse. When Jane Tate and Maria Smith appeared at the Old Bailey in 1910 charged with attempting to prostitute 14-year-old Florence Tate, a police inspector told the court how he had watched the two older women parading the girl around the West End, 'speaking to gentlemen'.[87] Florence, her hair in curls, was usually dressed in a white dress and a big black hat. When the Tates' flat, which was allegedly paid for by a variety of gentlemen, was searched, police found letters from a particular admirer:

> My dear little one – I have not forgotten our ride home in the taxi, and I hope you have not. I have thought much about you and wondered if you are settling down in the flat. I hope to see you tomorrow, and will come up about three. But perhaps you will think it best not to see me again. Perhaps you will not care for a new papa. Well, we will talk it over. ... With love and a kiss till to-morrow.[88]

The *Illustrated Police News* drew attention to the incongruity of the ages of the parties involved with the heading 'Old Man's letters to a mere girl'. In a second letter her 'littleness' was again a point of attention and a term of endearment: 'My dear little one – I have not forgotten you, and am longing to see you again. ... Now keep a good little darling, and love me as your dear old dad.'[89] The affection of the parent and the role of father were portrayed in terms which were clearly erotic. Perhaps the 'gentleman' was using the role of 'loving' father to try to get Florence's trust; perhaps it was an attempt to assuage his own sense of guilt at being what Kincaid would call a 'child-lover'. In his letters, fatherhood had become an excuse for touching and kissing; it is not clear where the parameters of intimacy would be set, if at all.

The 'cult of the little girl' is also apparent in an 1885 case, involving a

London barrister, who was charged at the Middlesex Sessions with indecent exposure and with indecently assaulting an 11-year-old girl. When the police searched the man, they found a pocketbook which contained the following love note:

> What a beautiful little girl you are
> I love your sweet beauty –
> If you will let me love you, I will
> Make you such lovely presents.[90]

The child was depicted in terms of littleness as well as sweetness (which suggests innocence, passivity and kindness). In his desire to shower her with gifts the barrister saw himself as patron and benefactor if not as father. Both men, barrister and secret admirer, revealed the desire to possess the child; the first wanted to be father, the second to buy the child's love with presents. It is significant that both men were extremely well-to-do and that both chose to idealise little girls with whom they were previously unconnected, probably to evade the observation of family or friends. As a result of the cultural upbringing associated with their class these two men articulated their desires through the rhetoric of the 'cult of the little girl', their actions rather than their words giving it a twist which was explicitly sexual.

Thus fatherhood emerged as a crucial focal point in courtroom discussions of masculinity. Male respectability was personified and idealised in the figure of the father. Defendants and their lawyers, in both incest and other sexual abuse charges, used this figure to assert innocence. On the flip-side, however, the father's responsibility to protect and discipline could provide the ideal guise through which to perpetrate and conceal abuse. Depositions reveal that men involved in incest charges expected to have authority over their families and became violent and angry if this authority was questioned. At the same time they were aware of the shame and humiliation – the 'cowardliness' – associated with putting this authority to wrong uses. Notions of 'manly' respectability, which implied family duty and responsibility, conflicted with older beliefs in absolute male authority in the home. The way in which judges and juries evaluated fatherhood and male 'respectability' will form the next area of consideration.

The judicial bench

The old-style eighteenth-century judge, portrayed by Vic Gatrell as a bad-tempered, bigoted 'mediocrity', was becoming gradually although not universally outmoded.[91] Daniel Duman has argued that the professionalisation of the bar from the 1830s onwards served to transform the judicial bench by the mid-nineteenth century.[92] He has suggested that the judges appointed towards the end of the century owed more to skill than patronage, had undergone an intensive legal training and selection process, and were intent on maintaining high professional standards. During the course of the nineteenth century the sons of professionals and business proprietors replaced the landed gentry who had dominated the eighteenth-century bench.[93] It is important not to over-emphasise the effects of these changes. It is clear that judicial ineptitude and, indeed, buffoonery were still present. Commissioner Kerr was described as 'invariably rude to council'; while Judge Rentoul 'never put the case for the defence to the jury' with the result that a large number of his cases ended up in the Court of Criminal Appeal.[94] It is also clear that a number of judges were appointed because of their political affiliations rather than legal knowledge. In 1897 *The Times* suggested that Judge Darling had been promoted purely on political grounds since 'he had no sign of legal eminence'.[95] It is probably fair to say, however, that this sort of comment was becoming more the exception rather than the rule.

Despite these moves to professionalisation, nineteenth-century observers described the decisions of judges in sexual abuse cases as random and inconsistent. In 1894 a Home Office investigation into court cases involving the rape of girls under 16 concluded that there was a 'wide divergence of views amongst judges' which produced a great disparity in sentencing even within the same court.[96] At the Old Bailey in May 1890 Justice Hawkins sentenced a 29-year-old man, who had raped his wife's young niece on repeated occasions, to five years' penal servitude. This contrasted with the sentence of life penal servitude that Baron Cleasby had imposed in May 1876 on a 38-year-old defendant for kicking and raping his 15-year-old daughter.[97] Judges also held wildly varying opinions on the use of flogging to punish sexual assault.[98] While the Home Office emphasised the inconsistency of sentencing in sex abuse cases, NSPCC and feminist campaigners drew attention to judgements that seemed incredibly lenient. In 1914 the NSPCC reported on the 'ridiculously light sentences' passed by Judge Atherley Jones. A lodger who admitted raping his landlord's daughter while threatening her with a pistol was bound over, while a man who raped his 13-year-old stepdaughter was sentenced to three months' imprisonment.[99]

Contemporaries failed to find a consistent pattern because they focused on the wrong factor – the charges which defendants faced – as a point of comparison. If, however, the focus is shifted elsewhere – onto both the socioeconomic class, and the status or 'respectability' of defendants – a clearer and more systematic pattern emerges. Carolyn Conley suggests, in her study of criminal justice in Victorian Kent, that social status was more important than class in measuring the criminality of an offence: 'though socioeconomic class played a significant part in judicial decisions, explanations, when offered, were usually conducted in terms of respectability and community'.[100] As a result, Conley's study of rape trials offers an analysis of the notion of 'respectability' which, although prioritising age and gender, makes very little reference to perceptions of class. It will be argued, here, that notions of 'respectability' were located within a wider discursive field that centred on the construction of identities. Age, religion, race, gender, and also social class were all significant aspects in the formulation of ideas about 'respectability'. Since the previous chapter has concentrated on gendered perceptions of age in the courtroom, the focus, here, is on the interaction of class and status.

Social class and 'respectability'

A crude analysis of conviction rates for different occupational categories of defendants suggests that socio-economic class requires some detailed consideration. Where sufficient information is available about the occupation of the defendant and age of victim in the study sample, it seems that working-class men were more likely to be convicted of child sexual abuse than men of the middle classes; indeed, the higher the class, the lower the conviction rate. Conviction rates dropped from 77 per cent in cases involving the unskilled (general labourers, hawkers, scavengers), to 71 per cent in cases involving labour that was semi-skilled or skilled (baker, shoemaker, carpenter, mason), to 60 per cent in cases involving small-scale employers and the lesser professions (shopkeepers, publicans, clerks, schoolmasters) and, finally, to 33 per cent in cases involving top professionals and men of property (accountants, clergy, physicians, barristers). This did not mean that more 'innocent' middle-class men were accused of sexual assaults on children, but, rather, that they were less likely to be convicted when their case came for trial. Although the use of occupation as an indicator of socio-economic class is problematic (there is a clear difference between a 'builder' who hires himself out as casual labour and one who owns a large business enterprise), these figures do, nevertheless, provide a useful indicator of trends.[101] They suggest there was some correlation between occupational category and perceptions of class in the courtroom. They do not indicate how these perceptions operated nor why it was that, across class categories, some defendants were convicted while others were not. Answers to these questions can be pursued by examining the interaction of class, status and ideas about 'manliness' in the courtroom.

The status of 'respectability' involved a great deal more than occupation or position within systems of production. It involved appearances (what a man looked like, where his family lived), marital situation and qualities of character. Martin Wiener has argued that, during the course of the nineteenth century, reformers and judges together participated in 'a common discourse of moralization' which depicted the building and shaping of character as an essential goal of the legal system.[102] Examining criminal policy rather than the day-to-day business of the courts, he has suggested that the qualities of self-discipline, industry and moral responsibility, which were associated with middle-class male respectability, were extended, via the courtroom and the judge, to the nation as a whole. Yet it would be misleading to view 'respectability' as a middle-class product. Defendants used the term 'respectability' liberally to imply that they were men of good character who supported their families through regular employment; their claims were frequently upheld by the courts. The value placed on respectability and the status accorded to it was a shared point of reference for both middle-class and working-class cultures as the century progressed. As Rohan McWilliam has commented, in his summary of recent scholarship on the historiography of radical culture, respectability 'emerged from within plebeian radicalism' rather than developing as a set of middle-class values and 'dripping down to the working class often as a form of social control'.[103] Yet, Wiener's account is still extremely useful. The emphasis on the discourse of respectability as shared should not detract from the significance of class in the negotiation of its meanings. In the opinion of judges, the middle classes were somehow *more* respectable by definition; professionals were identified as intrinsically morally superior and as a potential example to working people.

Although assize juries were the ultimate decision-makers, judges wielded considerable influence through their summing-up speeches and their control over proceedings. In some cases, judges sent juries away to deliberate again if they considered the verdict an inappropriate one.[104] Furthermore, many sexual abuse cases were dismissed or dealt with (as common assault) by magistrates at petty sessions where a jury was not required.[105] The profile of magistrates varied greatly: from the land-owning gentry, who acted as voluntary Justices of the Peace in rural areas, to the experienced lawyers employed on a regular basis by the London police courts. Yet it is fair to say that they were men of a higher social class than the majority of the defendants with whom they dealt on a daily basis. It is possible to detect, within the judicial bench and magistracy, shared attitudes as to what constituted respectable masculine behaviour, attitudes which, it can be assumed, were shaped by a wealthy background and public school education.

'Respectability' was, at a basic theoretical level, a word that was used to suggest certain valued characteristics that were attainable across class structures. When used in relation to men it meant honesty, self-restraint and hard work. A 'respectable man' was a dutiful husband and father, who took his role as provider and protector seriously in line with the Victorian domestic ideal. Judges and juries were of the opinion that sexual abuse by a father, whether of his own or another's children, was a particularly serious offence.[106] Yet fatherly duties also operated as a claim to responsibility; this meant that judges and juries found it very difficult to believe that a man who was a father could ever have committed acts of brutality. This inconsistency was apparent in a case tried by Justice Pattison at the Old Bailey in 1840. The judge sentenced a labourer to life transportation for the rape of a 14-year-old girl, remarking that the offence was 'considerably aggravated by the fact that he was a married man, and had several children'. Yet the sentence was not as severe as the judge made out. According to statute law, he could have been sentenced to death, but the jury recommended him to mercy on account of his 'previous good character'.[107] Across the spectrum of class, men who claimed the respectability associated with fatherhood and family provider were accorded the sympathy of the courts, as this court report from *The Times* attests:

> She was ... shown to be a girl of loose and demoralized habits by a numerous body of witnesses called for the defence, several of whom gave the prisoner (a married man and a father) the highest character for morality and general propriety of conduct.[108]

The man was acquitted without hesitation. This case fits very neatly with the model outlined by Carolyn Conley: that court decisions involved the weighing up of the 'perceived character of the victim versus the perceived character of the accused'.[109] The 'normal', hardworking father, who appeared to fulfil the duties expected of him, was seen as an unlikely child abuser.

The point that the qualities associated with 'respectability' could be achieved regardless of class position was clearly made during an exchange between defence attorney Mr Lewis and magistrate Sir Robert Carden when a case of indecent assault was heard at Mansion House police court in November 1860. The father of the victim, aged 13, had worked for the defendant who ran an engraving and copper-plate printing business. The relevance of the difference in their class positions was debated in court:

> Mr Lewis said his client was a man of the highest respectability, that he had only been recently married, and that he bore among his friends and acquaintances the highest moral character.
> Sir R. Carden said he was strongly impressed with the respectability of the father and mother of the child, and that every man was respectable if in the sphere in which he lived he acted an honest and upright part.[110]

Carden, on this occasion, refuted the notion that class and respectability were related, suggesting that respectability was entirely an issue of status. His comments were, however, unusual. Because of the serious nature of the charge, the case was sent to the Old Bailey for trial. The defence wheeled out a whole series of 'respectable witnesses, both male and female' who 'all described him as being a very moral, well-conducted young man'. It was also pointed out that he was recently married.[111] The jury acquitted after an hour's deliberation. This Old Bailey trial and, indeed, most newspaper accounts of nineteenth-century court hearings tended to reinforce some kind of connection between respectability and perceptions of social class.

The case of the American Indian chief

The nineteenth-century concept of respectability was constructed within a discourse of modernity and in relation to the notion of a debased and degenerate 'other'. To be respectable meant to espouse the values of a civilised, progressive, Christian society. Its antithesis was the savage, the uncivilised, the corrupted and the pagan. The racialised aspect of the concept of respectability, as well as the way in which attentions could shift from race, to status, to class, is carefully illustrated by an extremely unusual case that came before Union Hall Police Court, London, in February 1835. A 'North American Indian chief', who had been displaying his talents by shooting an apple from a man's hand in a performance at the Victoria Theatre, had been arrested on a charge of attempting to rape a girl of 10. The girl was the daughter of the landlord with whom the performers had been lodging in Lambeth. At the end of the first hearing, the magistrate, Mr Traill, commented that:

> Whatever might be the customs of that part of the continent of America from whence the prisoner came, if he was so uncivilized as not to know right from wrong, and perpetrated offences of a brutal character, he ought, while he remained in this country, to be looked after most attentively by the persons who brought him over, to check any evil propensity that he might have contracted in his native wilds.[112]

This stereotypical picture of the male savage as immoral and sexually predatory was completely overhauled when more information came to light about the chief's personal circumstances (which, it appears, were influential in his acquittal). An apology appeared in *The Times* a month later which aimed to 'correct various mistatements which have appeared injurious to the character of the Indian chief'.[113] It was revealed that the chief was involved in the sale of millions of acres of land to the British government, had supported the British during the war of independence, and had been tricked into coming to England by persons unknown to settle the land deal. He had taken to the stage to make ends meet when he found himself penniless as a result of the fraud. The press now depicted the chief's behaviour and demeanour in relation to a whole new set of value judgements. *The Times* emphasised his rank as a leader in his indigenous community, rather than the lowly status associated with the role of circus performer. His Christianity was stressed: 'the chief professes Christianity although his tribe are generally Pagans'. He was constructed as an honorary British citizen: 'by both past services and present domicile, he may be strictly regarded as coming within the range of British protection'. Finally, the emphasis on the extent of his land-ownership located him squarely within the class of propertied gentry, rather than identifying him as a mere lodger in somebody else's house.

Within the period of a month the Indian chief found his social position completely refigured in terms of nationality, status, religion and class. His re-evaluation through these four cultural categories was sufficient to refute the essentialist stereotyping of race; although one also anticipates a faint sigh of relief that the chief was at last homeward bound (would his position as well-to-do British citizen really have been sustainable over a longer period?). These four cultural categories were essential to interpretations of 'respectability' in court as well as outside it. The concept of 'respectability' cannot be seen as separate from ideas about class or status or nationality or religiosity; it was about all those things.

The lower orders

A whole trajectory of social commentators, philanthropists and journalists – Edwin Chadwick, Henry Mayhew, Andrew Mearns, William Booth – used a racialised language of class, to varying extents, to depict the urban poor as a savage tribal group.[114] They drew on the 'sciences' of phrenology, social Darwinism and, finally, eugenics to argue that poverty, immorality and a debased lifestyle were a result of bad hereditary stock; 'class' was identified, like 'race', as dependent on biological condition. Newspaper reports of court cases drew on this language, identifying savagery in the facial features of defendants. A labourer tried at the Old Bailey in 1850 was described in *The Times* as 'dirty, repulsive-looking', while 'the facts ... disclosed a case of the most revolting character, and clearly proved the wretched state of the dwellings of the poorer classes'.[115] Similarly, judges themselves were drawn to the view that immorality was more likely to occur amongst the lower classes. When sexual abuse was delineated as a sanitary or social disease, environmental and hereditary theories of contamination were often blurred. In April 1885 Justice Day was reported to have made the following comments at the Leeds Assizes following the trial of a 30-year-old man, who gave his trade as glassblower, for carnally knowing a 9-year-old girl: 'The offence . was far more frequent in the homes of the poor. The poor were compelled by their unfortunate circumstances to allow their children to be exposed to most grievous perils and dangers resulting from contamination with such men as the prisoner.'[116] He was found guilty and sentenced to 15 years' penal servitude.

Men of the middle classes were, in contrast, seen as suitably equipped to act as an example to the lower orders. In June 1845, a well-to-do master tailor was acquitted at the Old Bailey of the rape of a 15-year-old girl on the grounds that there was no evidence of her resistance. Baron Platt, nevertheless, went on to admonish the defendant for 'seducing' her:

> He had brought ruin upon and made a prostitute of the unhappy and wretched girl. ... His station in life and the rank in which the Court understood he moved ought to have induced him to teach propriety of conduct, and to have inculcated, by his example, morality amongst those in a lower grade than himself.[117]

The middle-classes were seen as possessing a moral and educative responsibility in relation to the potential criminality of the lower orders.

Newspaper reports suggest that, because a higher class position was closely associated with social status, gentility and moral respectability, cases involving men of the middling ranks were likely to be thrown out at petty sessions level. The following case, involving a vicar, was dismissed by magistrate Mr Mead at Thames Police Court in May 1895:

> Mr George Hay Younger, on behalf of the accused, spoke of the improbability of a clergyman committing such abominable acts, especially after having come from a funeral. ... The Prisoner had always taken notice of children and he was connected with the Waifs and Strays Society. ... He had a holiday home at Plympton where children were received. ... Mr Mead did not think a jury would convict, and therefore the prisoner would be discharged.[118]

The vicar's reputation, rather than a detailed investigation into the circumstances of the case, was the main consideration in the decision to discharge him. When cases involving men of the middling sort were tried and convicted, there is evidence that they were less likely to receive a custodial sentence and more likely to be fined. They were also more likely to be bailed before trial.

Mental illness

Judges and juries were sympathetic to pleas of drunkenness and mental illness but only if they provided a feasible explanation as to why a normally respectable man should lose control of his moral faculties.[119] As Judge W. H. Bodkin put it in 1870, there was a difference between a 'ruffianly attack ... dictated ... by mania' and one that arose out of 'brutal lust'.[120] Martin Wiener has demonstrated that the McNaughten rules, which governed pleas of insanity, were criticised for the narrowness of their scope and their medical inaccuracy.[121] Although only four defendants were detained as insane among the cases sampled between 1830 and 1914 (plus one for lunacy in 1905), pleas of mitigation involving fits or other mental illness were much more common and sometimes resulted in a reduction of sentence.

Issues of class and respectability were studied in relation to medical evidence of mental illness. In April 1880 a 70-year-old retired army major was found guilty of indecently assaulting a 9-year-old girl. The defence attorney told the judge he could not ask for an acquittal on the grounds of insanity because of the 'stringent proof' it required. He asked for 'merciful discretion' instead, based on the grounds that the major had sustained a serious head injury while stationed with the Madras Infantry in India. Over the previous few years the major had suffered 'two paralytic seizures' and was subject to such 'mental decay' that his address had to be written down for him on a piece of paper.[122] A letter of commendation from the battalion was read in court and a fellow officer said 'he had ever found him to be a most sober and one of the purest-minded of men'. Judge Mr Edlin bound him over in a sum of £300, commenting that 'he did not intend to send a poor gentleman who had so long served his country to prison'. The man's military background gave him status and respect which meant that, even on conviction for a rather sordid indecent assault, he was still evaluated as a 'gentleman'.

The same judge had taken a similar line in a case in 1875 involving a wealthy sharebroker who pleaded guilty to indecently assaulting two girls aged 11 and 12. The defence argued he was suffering from partial paralysis and cerebral disorder; it was also pointed out in court that 'he had for years been of an irreproachable character, and had risen to the position of secretary of the company in whose services he had been for 20 years'.[123] Although the prison surgeon was reported to have disagreed with the evidence given by the defendant's medical attendants, Mr Edlin was sympathetic, releasing the sharebroker into the security of his friends.

A central paradox with which this book is concerned is the apparent contradiction between the shock and horror that the notion of sexual abuse elicited and the readiness with which alleged abusers were acquitted or sentenced to fines and minor terms of imprisonment. The concept of respectability provides an explanation for the paradox. The notion of the 'manly' man as dutiful, hardworking and protective of women and children resonates through judges' comments in court-hearings involving sexual abuse. Sexual deviancy in men was clearly linked to notions of class, work and social status. Men of the lowest classes, particularly if they were unemployed, were seen as having the greatest tendency to abuse women and children; they were viewed as lazy, brutal and animalistic. Regular work, however, elevated the character and raised a man's moral disposition. Professionals were believed to have entered yet a higher moral plain. Class, therefore, was associated with both social status and morality. Although men of the middle classes were clearly convicted of sexual abuse, they were indicted in much smaller numbers. The sexual 'criminal' – the rapist or child abuser who was inspired by 'brutal lust' – was deemed to have little connection with the dutiful, hardworking, family man. The next chapter will examine alternative forms of provision to the family structure: the system of 'specialist' children's homes that aimed to rehabilitate and save from the harmful effects of moral corruption.

7 Specialist homes for 'fallen' girls

Introduction

In 1865 private benefactress Agnes Cotton set up the Good Shepherd Children's Home in Leytonstone, North London, to receive 'fallen' girls under the age of 13 who could not be accommodated elsewhere. Cotton described the inmates as 'poor little girls led into habits of impurity ... often too young and too childish to be received into Penitentiaries, too deeply tainted with evil to be admitted into ordinary Industrial Schools and Orphanages'.[1] These 'poor little girls' were children 'contaminated' by sexual knowledge, including victims of sexual assault. Agnes Cotton's home was one of the very few institutions willing to take girls with such a problematic personal history.[2]

This chapter examines the emergence and development of specialist homes for 'fallen' girls in the period 1830–1914, demonstrating that provision was sparse and piecemeal in the nineteenth century because of concerns about the corrupting influence of the precocious child and confusions about the boundary between childhood and adulthood. It was not until 1908 that a new set of residential specialist schools began to emerge as a result of collaborations between voluntary organisations and the Home Office. The chapter will also explore children's diverse experiences of welfare provision, which was largely in the hands of private philanthropic societies with very specific religious denominational affiliations.[3] The records of the homes run by the Church of England Waifs and Strays Society, the Salvation Army, and the Jewish Association for the Protection of Women and Children, can be mined to produce a comparative study of strategies for dealing with 'fallen' girls; strategies that were clearly informed by notions of gender, age, class and 'race'.

Residential provision for boys will not be examined in any detail because it made no distinction between sexual/moral categories. It is highly likely that many of the male inmates of boys' industrial schools had experienced sexual abuse, but it is extremely difficult to identify these cases. There are certainly indications of abuse within institutional homes, which may have been of a sexual nature. In 1894 boys at St Vincent's Industrial School,

Dartford, claimed two instructors had cruelly beaten and caned them.[4] In 1884 London School Board inspector T. M. Williams claimed that 'gross indecency' was being practised in the dormitories of boys' industrial schools and that 'those big boys must be corrupting the little boys'.[5] It was not until 1925, however, that provision for sexually abused boys was officially discussed and documented.[6]

In her recent study of industrial schools and children's homes in nineteenth-century Scotland, Linda Mahood has argued that welfare historians need to break away from a 'social control' paradigm, influenced by Foucault's work on the 'total institution', which focuses on impersonal technologies of discipline and surveillance.[7] As well as assessing the regulatory nature of welfare organisations, Mahood stresses issues of initiative, agency and resistance on the part of child clients and their parents. In this chapter I shall take Mahood's argument a step further, demonstrating that it is also important to consider the aims, motivations and daily experiences of workers and carers in girls' homes of this period. Welfare workers were more than simple cogs in a bourgeois mechanism that aimed to mould the lower orders into humble and obedient servants. As Michelle Cale has shown, many matrons and superintendents were in fact drawn from backgrounds of low social status.[8] In analysing and understanding children's homes, it is important to examine the relationships of carers and child residents, drawing attention to the intimate, the affective, the emotional, and the way in which these were intertwined with issues of authority and control.[9] It is not possible to explain the sheer variety in children's institutional experiences without this emphasis on the interpersonal.

'Sweet blossom of childhood'?

The development of specialist homes must be linked to the convergence of interests of a social purity movement concerned with 'fallen' women and an active child welfare lobby intent on saving ill-treated children. The London Society for the Protection of Young Females, founded in 1835, forwarded girl victims of 'seduction' to the metropolitan asylums for prostitutes in the first three years of its operations.[10] It soon decided, however, that this arrangement was unsatisfactory since most of the girls were under 15 and the disciplinary regime of the adult asylum was unsuitable. In 1838 the Society set up its own asylum at Lady Lake's Grove, Mile End, exclusively for girls under 15, 'in which they might be instructed in every religious, moral and domestic duty, and then fitted for useful service in future'.[11] They were, subsequently, sent into service with their maid's outfit, a Bible and a prayer book. Such an approach was unusual. It was not until the 1860s that the Rescue Society opened two homes for 'fallen' girls: at Woodford for those aged 8–12 and at Homerton for girls in the 12–16 category.[12] Both homes were small-scale, taking only fifteen residents, and operating on the 'family' system. The Rescue Society stressed that nothing was to 'distinguish them from ordinary homes'.[13] There were to be no uniforms, bolts or bars; hair could be kept long, food was to be generous, corporal punishment was not permitted, and visits from family and friends were to be allowed every two months. Younger children were taught to read and write, while older girls were instructed in housework, knitting, sewing and laundry. In 1865 Agnes Cotton used wealth inherited from her banker father to set up the Leytonstone venture, based on a different set of pedagogical criteria;[14] notions of a 'family' environment were combined with a more rigorous set of disciplinary strategies to deal with this special category of 'fallen' girls.

Thus the second half of the nineteenth century saw a rethinking of the categorisation of women and children. Where, previously, the needs of women and children had been identified as analogous, they were increasingly separated into distinct groups with their own specific medical, philanthropic, moral and social requirements. Roger Cooter has drawn attention to this process in the institution of the hospital where treatment of the diseases of women and children was split: 'as hospitals for women embodied distinctive ideologies of "femininity", so those for children implicitly embodied social and moral notions of childhood'.[15] Cooter's comments can be applied equally to the rescue home, although in this context, 'notions of childhood' were clearly gendered. The ideal of feminine purity affected the treatment of both adult prostitutes and 'fallen' girl children. Now, for the first time, girls were separated into different age cohorts, which were linked to gendered notions of mental/moral development.

From the mid-nineteenth century a wide variety of industrial schools and training homes developed as a result of the increasing identification of the child as the future of the nation. If it was not possible to transform life in the slums, if missionary zeal was not sufficient to convert and civilise dissolute adult elements of society, then the children themselves should be removed from the 'polluting environment' and retrained elsewhere. As Archdeacon Farar stated in 1886:

> If ... you take these poor children from such places, and surround them by bright, natural and healthy influences – if you keep them under the light and love beaming upon them from pure heaven of God, then you restore to them the natural simplicity and innocence of life ... you make them bright, industrious and profitable members of the commonwealth.[16]

Girls would be retrained in 'the sacredness of motherhood', boys to become 'vigorous colonists' within the empire; together, it was projected, they would make the nation strong.[17]

There was some disagreement amongst child savers as to whether character, behaviour and 'savagery' were hereditary. Miss Beckett Denison, the lady superintendent of the Doncaster Girls' Home, wrote in 1894 that: 'the more I see of girl life, the more difficult it seems to eradicate inborn evil natures inherited from parents'.[18] In 1901, however, the founder of the Waifs and Strays Society, Edward Rudolf, noted confidently that: 'if a child is rescued whilst it is young, environment will overcome heredity'.[19] The downward spiral of corruption and degeneration could be broken if the child was placed in a 'healthy' and carefully controlled setting. Changes in child custody law gradually gave philanthropic institutions the means to remove children from parents (see chapter 3). The new homes aimed to train children morally, physically and industrially, to take their role as efficient citizens within the context of empire.

What about children whose corruption had already been effected? Just as the rescue societies were increasingly differentiating between their clients in terms of childhood and adulthood, so homes for girl children were also categorising their child clientele: in terms of age but also in terms of sexual experience. As Michelle Cale and Pam Cox have demonstrated, the reformatory and industrial school system judged female juvenile delinquency in terms of sexual precocity.[20] Although the child prostitute required 'saving', she was also a danger to other children. It was seen as vital to separate the 'fallen' from the 'unfallen' lest the former contaminate or corrupt the latter. Hence the Rescue Society stated as policy that: 'those who have strayed from the path of virtue are not associated with other young girls. ... A proper classification of young women is one of the Society's most important principles.'[21] Sexually abused children were seen as threats as well as victims.

Most industrial schools and children's homes refused to take 'fallen' girls, and children of 12 or younger continued to be received into refuges and penitentiaries along with adult prostitutes. In 1880 Ellice Hopkins, who had campaigned to give magistrates authority to remove children from 'immoral surroundings', described the incongruity of the penitentiary child:

> I have myself had in my hands a child of seven, who was sold by her own mother, in the public den of infamy kept by her; who had passed through a public Lock Hospital, and whom I found in a public penitentiary, sitting up to a table among a number of abandoned women – as sweet a blossom of a child as you would wish to see – with her little thimble and needle and thread hemming a duster, the first use of which should have been to strangle the men who had degraded her.[22]

Despite her seedy surroundings, the child's redeeming qualities shone through in true romantic tradition. However, Hopkins made it clear that the 'sweet blossom' of childhood should not be detained in this inhospitable adult environment. Hopkins's call for specialist homes was partly met by the opening of a new residential school for 'fallen' girls at The Mumbles near Swansea in 1885. Like Agnes Cotton's Leytonstone home, which was certified as an industrial school in 1882, its application procedure was administered centrally by the Waifs and Strays Society and it admitted children from all over England and Wales.[23] A number of Anglican sisterhoods also provided homes for 'fallen' girls as young as 8 years of age.[24] However, the number of residential places was limited and demand for accommodation far outstripped supply.

The Waifs and Strays Society found it particularly difficult during the 1880s and 1890s to find homes for girls over 11 or 12 who were neither child nor woman. St Oswald's Home at Cullercoats, Newcastle, refused to admit 11-year-old Alice, sexually assaulted by her father, on the grounds that it did 'not take children from immoral surroundings'.[25] Two homes were already full and she was, at 11, judged too old for another. She was finally accepted by the Doncaster Girls Home the following year. In 1896 the Leeds Rescue Society asked the Waifs and Strays to help find a home for 12-year-old Caroline:

> The reason [Caroline] was not sent to an industrial school is that she is a fallen girl. She was passed into this home with a view that she should be received into a Penitentiary but she is under the age at which girls are admitted into these homes. She is small and childish looking for her age.[26]

She was briefly received into the Waifs and Strays Emigration Receiving house in Peckham but had to be removed, however, because her 'knowledge of evil' was considered too great for her to remain 'amongst comparatively innocent children'. Over the next year Caroline was sent to five homes in succession. Within a month of arriving at one training home in Bournemouth she was expelled 'for the sake of the other four girls', the matron having lost all patience with her: 'although I opened my little home for failure cases, there are exceptions to every rule. ... I am sorry for her, but after a girl has both struck the Lady at the head of the Home and also flatly refused to obey her she can never be allowed among the other girls again.'[27] She was finally sent to a Bournemouth Refuge for fallen women run by the Reformatory and Refuge Union.

On rare occasions, ordinary industrial schools seem to have been prepared to take younger victims of sexual abuse when placements were not available at Leytonstone or The Mumbles.[28] Girls of 6 or 7 were deemed more likely to forget, and more easily reformed. Older girls were, however, frequently shifted from one institution to the next far away from their original homes, often ending up in an adult-style penitentiary. The instability of these constant moves and the rigid discipline of the rescue homes often, it might be assumed, led to behavioural problems. While the period 1880–1900 saw philanthropists turn their sympathies towards the abused child, they were still unclear about the practical implications of their thinking.

From the turn of the century, however, a change in policy is detectable, once again the result of initiatives by religious interest groups. Firstly, a new home geared specifically towards child victims of assault – the Nest – was set up by the Salvation Army at Clapton, North London in 1901.[29] The

Salvation Army had been actively involved in the campaigns to raise the age of consent during the 1880s and became increasingly reluctant to admit children to its adult rescue homes. Secondly, in 1907 Secretary of the Church of England Penitentiary Society, George Cree, was shocked to discover that 508 child victims of criminal assault were living in the society's refuges and a further 354 children in its penitentiaries; over 80 per cent of these were girls of 14 or 15 years of age, but girls of 7 or 8 were clearly present.[30] As a result of these findings, which he communicated to the Home Office, a new group of industrial schools specifically designed to take girl victims of criminal assault was opened by the Church Penitentiary Society between 1908 and 1914: St Winifred's Home in Wolverhampton for girls aged 13–14, St Monica's in Croydon for girls aged 10–12, and St Mary's in Buxted for girls under 10.[31] In 1913 the Waifs and Strays Society opened an industrial school for 'fallen' girls aged 13–14, St Ursula's at Teddington; accommodation for criminally assaulted girls was also provided at the Princess Mary Village Homes, Addlestone.[32] The Home Office sent magistrates regular lists of the addresses of these specialist schools, encouraging them to commit girl victims who might benefit from the 'discipline and training'.[33] By 1914 industrial schools inspectors were moved to comment that: 'the schools in this class ... are steadily growing in number, and it is probable that no schools are rendering a more needed service to the community'.[34] But such a service was not always 'appropriate'. In 1925 the experts who formed the Departmental Committee on Sexual Offences against Young Children went on to conclude that the proliferation of special schools for 'fallen' girls had resulted in the unnecessary removal of children from perfectly happy home environments.[35]

Thus an overview of trends suggests a shift in policy after 1900, with a marked expansion of provision across denominations, which was facilitated and encouraged by the Home Office. It would be wrong to imagine, however, that child welfare and purity groups formed a homogeneous entity. Children's experience of life in these homes varied substantially. Experience depended on a girl's previous background, on her emotional and psychological make-up, on the age at which she was institutionalised, but most particularly on her relationships with the carers and with the other children in the home. In the rest of this chapter I shall examine the case histories of three girls who were referred to residential institutions in the late Victorian and Edwardian periods as a result of sexual abuse allegations. These studies will be used to explore the nuanced and differing responses of the Waifs and Strays homes, the Salvation Army and the Jewish Association, comparing and contrasting the policies, therapies and training methods that were in operation.

The Waifs and Strays Society: the case of Lily

In early 1895, the vicar of Downton, near Salisbury, Wiltshire, wrote to the Waifs and Strays Society, expressing his concerns about 11-year-old Lily and asking whether a place could be found for her in one of the Society's homes. Since the death of her mother when she was 2, Lily had been brought up by her grandmother 'in the midst of a family of big rough lads'.[36] When her father remarried she returned to live with him, but he became increasingly anxious about her 'whole moral character'. Not only was she caught telling lies and stealing from shops, neighbours and parents; there were worries that she had developed an 'immoral tendency'. Her case record suggests she had been sexually abused in her grandmother's household: 'she is curiously forward for a child of ten with men and boys; and there appears to be some reason for fearing that there has been a good deal of corrupt influence. Several acts of indecency have been detected.'[37] Her father had apparently tried all methods 'severe or kind' to control her behaviour but was finally persuaded that she needed to be removed from his care 'to be under stricter control'. The Waifs and Strays Society contacted Agnes Cotton and asked her to admit Lily to her Leytonstone home.

Cotton and her associates at the Good Shepherd Home argued that girls who had been morally corrupted developed particular behavioural traits that required special treatment:

> When it is remembered that these poor waifs are so degraded that they are considered too bad for admission to other Homes, and that in many cases their miserable childhood has left them savage and unmanageable, the perfect discipline under which they can now be brought, with the full sanction of the law, renders the work of their reclamation most hopeful and cheering, whilst those in charge have taken care at the same time to give to these little ones a home life marked by a reality of freedom and legitimate liberty.[38]

Thus Cotton aimed to balance 'perfect discipline' with sufficient space for individual development in order to cure and treat the 'savage' propensities that abuse had instilled. The physical condition of the girl residents would be improved by the healthy surroundings of the home; the building, described as 'bright, airy, compact', was situated on the border of Epping Forest and surrounded by four acres of land.[39] A seaside convalescent home was also set up for 'the most reformed little ones' who no longer required the strict regime of Leytonstone.[40] Their moral reclamation was a far harder task. The carefully controlled environment at the London home involved four hours' schooling a day for girls under 14, combined with training in laundry, domestic and needlework. This would equip them for domestic service when they left as well as encouraging self-control, restraint and respect for those in authority. The laundry enterprise, which in 1885 was recorded as making a net profit, was seen as a particularly valuable learning experience for the girls: 'the laundry is spacious and capitally fitted to enable young workers to do good work under elder superintendants – motherly women who, coming daily from their own homes, help to keep up the natural family character of the house'.[41] The notion of maternal authority as involving both intimacy, affection and careful discipline was taken as the ideal model for replication in the home.

Agnes Cotton argued, throughout her time as 'foundress and mother' of the home (the reference to maternal authority is again significant), that the difficult behaviour of the girls she received made recourse to corporal punishment a necessity. In 1894, the year before Lily arrived, she was forced to defend herself against allegations of 'undue punishment and unkind treatment', lodged with the London School Board, by three former residents and an ex-employee; the allegations included references to public canings and floggings with birch twigs.[42] The Home Office's Inspector of Industrial Schools was called in to conduct an inquiry into the complaints. Cotton herself objected to an investigation that was based on the accusations of three girls who were 'utterly untruthful' and the official report upheld her management, arguing that 'some of the charges should never have been brought against her'.[43] Her use of corporal punishment was supported since it was 'used but seldom and lightly and certainly never to such an extent as to amount to a charge of cruelty'.[44] It was also deemed acceptable to keep the girls' hair closely cropped on sanitary grounds although the inspector regretted that 'in some cases the cropping of the hair was treated as a punishment'.[45] The final report acknowledged that 'Miss Cotton had to deal with an exceptionally difficult class of girls; and in consequence, a somewhat stricter regime may be necessary'.[46] Although the London School Board resumed its policy of referral to her school, it is likely that this decision was a pragmatic response (there was nowhere else for these children to go) rather than a statement of positive approval for her regime.

When she received the application on Lily's behalf in March 1895, Agnes Cotton wrote back to Edward Rudolf, explaining the policy of the home: 'This case ... is not only urgent — but a thoroughly bad one. I must remind you that I feel the necessity & have the Secretary of State's permission to make use of the rod when need be. [Lily] is young and I hope to profit by it, if required.'[47] Lily was admitted to the home, but Cotton's approach was unsuccessful; the girl was, by her reckoning, far too wayward. In June 1897, she wrote to Rudolf once again:

> I am troubled by this child. Some months ago she seemed really improving, we tried to encourage her — now the evil influence of her rough brothers of which you warned me seems to be bearing much too far & her evident delight in evil associates — bad talk, bad ways, is sad to behold.[48]

The girl was returned to her father and stepmother on the grounds that she was beyond help after only a year's 'treatment'. Lily's case history and the Home Office inquiry into life at the Leytonstone home create an unswerving image of a disciplinary regime. Yet, it is likely that, after thirty years of provision, Agnes Cotton was deeply embittered and resentful of the scathing attack that had been launched against her. It is possible too that, in her older years, she was finding the vigorous resistance of the youthful residents a challenge she could no longer meet. The desired combination of motherly affection, guidance and authority was clearly slipping.

Correspondence relating to the Waifs and Strays home at The Mumbles demonstrates that the model of maternal authority was workable and successful elsewhere without the need to rely on the threat of corporal punishment. Miss Langley was described as 'so valuable a matron ... [who] takes so much trouble with the children'.[49] Former residents sent incredibly affectionate letters which have been retained in their case files. One girl directed an emotional missive to 'my dear Miss Langley', signing it 'from your loving child' and, at the same time, forwarding her love to the other children in The Mumbles home.[50] Pamela, who left when she was 16, covered a whole page of her letter with kisses for 'dear Miss Langley'.[51] As matron she clearly built up close personal relationships with the children. She was deeply moved when one girl died after being in the home a year, a result of spinal injuries which seem to have been inflicted by her parents' beatings: 'Miss Langley feels it very much, she is quite a mother to the little ones and this child was very good and obedient; her parents are both drunkards, and little [Bertha] has told how her mother beat and ill-used her.'[52] Such correspondence must of course be balanced against the 'failure' cases in which children and carers were involved in constant conflict, but they do shed a different light on the experiences of matrons, carers and superintendents. The daily work of caring for severely abused children was undoubtedly a difficult, upsetting and emotionally-draining occupation.

The Salvation Army: the case of Emma

In February 1908 10-year-old Emma was removed from her Leeds home 'in a terrible state of filth and neglect'.[53] Her father was serving three months' imprisonment, her mother was believed to be a prostitute, and there were concerns that Emma was in 'moral danger'. The NSPCC had found out that she had been involved in illegal and possibly abusive sexual activity but was 'unable to prosecute' the male parties concerned 'as they were only school boys'. Emma was 'rescued' by local Salvation Army officers who placed her in their Leeds women's hostel. In June she was transferred to the Nest, the Salvation Army's specialist children's home in Clapton.

When Emma arrived at the Nest in 1908 she joined children from a variety of unhappy backgrounds, many of whom had been sexually abused. Adventure writer Henry Rider Haggard, who visited the home two years later, reported that more than half of its sixty-two inmates had been the victims of 'horrible outrages too terrible to repeat, often enough at the hands of their own fathers!'[54] Two weighty ledgers, completed by the home's warden Brigadier Marianne Asdell and her fellow Army workers, record the background, progress in the home, and later career of each of the 193 children who passed through its doors between 1902 and 1914.[55] Inmates of the Nest were referred for a variety of different reasons, publicity material for the home tending to emphasise the most extreme. Uniquely amongst children's homes, Brigadier Asdell accepted both 'fallen' and 'unfallen' residents, although most were from backgrounds that would have been judged 'immoral' or 'degraded'. A quarter of all inmates were referred because of extreme poverty between 1902 and 1914: destitute mothers (often single women hoping to go into service) or widowed fathers were simply unable to look after their offspring. Of the inmates 14 per cent were orphans: one case, which has been absorbed into the latter category, was that of a small girl who had watched as her father brutally murdered her mother. Children who appeared to have severe behavioural difficulties – were 'unmanageable' or 'beyond the control of their parents' – formed 18 per cent of cases; 11 per cent had been rescued from conditions of 'moral danger', a category which included residing with prostitutes or with drunken/criminal parents.[56] A quarter of all children admitted between 1902 and 1914 were abuse victims; some 14 per cent had clearly been sexually abused, while 10 per cent of residents were the victims of cruelty and neglect. Throughout the period, the Nest remained most closely associated with the victims of sexual assault or brutality and it is clear that it developed a reputation for specialising in these sorts of cases.

At the Nest, Marianne Asdell and her staff aimed to rehabilitate children physically, emotionally and spiritually through a combination of exercise, play, work, discipline, love and affection. They aimed to save 'their souls, hearts, and minds as well as their bodies'.[57] The Salvation Army, like the Waifs and Strays Society, emphasised the importance of clean fresh air as a physical restorative that would counterbalance the harmful effects of overcrowded and filthy urban environments. The *Deliverer* described the home to its readers: 'indoors at the Nest is as breezy and sweet as big, open windows and spotless cleanliness can make a house ... out of doors in that wide, grassy, tree-surrounded garden is even more delightful'.[58] The garden acted as a 'health-valve for the many restless, feverish spirits that come to us'; as well as clearing the lungs, it was supposed to calm and restore an inner tranquillity.[59] Army homes were designed to foster 'the home-like spirit of love and kindness';[60] a supportive familial environment would teach emotionally neglected children how to love and care for others. Finally, in addition to schooling, girls were trained in domestic skills, although laundry work was rejected as too noisy and boisterous. Needlework was preferred because it helped develop self-control and had an important social function: 'laundry work has always been objected to ... we lose thereby the golden opportunity which the workroom life affords of personal and homely conversation with the lassies'.[61]

Marianne Asdell described Emma as a 'slight, fair, self-conscious child, often blushes' when she was first admitted.[62] Her musical talents were encouraged and she was taught to play the ocarina. Her case records also detail what were perceived to be problems of temper and obedience. In November 1910 she was described as 'still a very difficult child so sullen and disobedient' although it was later noted that 'she tries very hard to be good'.[63] Throughout 1912 and 1913 she exhibited 'outbursts of passion' followed by 'shame and sorrow'; she was described as having 'some difficulty in obeying, yet really trying'. In October 1913 we are told 'it is very uphill work for the child, but steady improvement is manifest'.[64] A month later Emma achieved full religious conversion and was sworn in as a Salvation Army soldier. In April 1914 she left the Nest to go into service.

It is impossible to tell whether Emma's moods were caused by the trauma of abuse and neglect, repressed memories, clinical depression, or frustration at the emphasis on humility, obedience and discipline in the home. The records are insufficient to sustain detailed psychological analysis; reading between these very brief lines could only produce an account that was flawed in its reductionism. They do, however, tell us a great deal about the attitudes of carers, their interpretation of emotional outbursts and their programme of treatment, therapy and cure. A large body of academic research has demonstrated that belief in an unconscious aspect to the mind was widespread by the 1880s.[65] The comments of Miss Beckett Denison, of Agnes Cotton and of Marianne Asdell suggest a shared opinion that heredity, immoral environment and abusive experiences could all create 'inborn [or acquired] evil natures' – corrupted inner selves – that had to be conquered, subdued and controlled through self-discipline. Asdell referred to Emma's 'outbursts', to an 'uphill' struggle and to shame and guilt when her passions burst out once more. For Cotton, the subjugation of 'evil influence' was based, ultimately, on the threat of physical punishment. For the Salvation Army, which condemned the use of corporal penalties, subjugation took the form of spiritual struggle. Notions of conscious and unconscious were positioned within a religious framework that viewed psychological disturbance in terms of a divided self where good battled against evil. Charlotte, admitted to the Nest in 1911 at the age of 12, was described as having 'severe struggles with herself', and as making 'good spiritual progress' which empowered her in 'conquering her evil habits'.[66] Asdell wrote in 1908 of Sarah, aged 13: 'her tendency is to be very good outwardly, but really has to fight against deceit within'.[67] Therapy and cure involved the conquest of inner passions through the development of a strong religious faith and strategies of self-control.

Inner thoughts and emotions were to be carefully disciplined. All children, both at the Nest and in the Waifs and Strays homes, were forbidden to talk of their former lives.[68] As journalist F. A. McKenzie explained, following his visit to the Nest in 1908:

> The one great rule insisted upon ... is that, from the moment the door is entered the tragedy is wiped out. No one ever speaks of it to them,

and they are never suffered to say a word about it. Then the merciful oblivion of time begins to do its work. There is always someone with them, helping them to play, helping them to work or teaching them. It need hardly be pointed out how necessary it is. A girl brought from evil surroundings might carry with her ways or speech that would act like poison among the others.[69]

A policy of silence was designed to protect other children but also to 'blot out memory' and 'help them forget'.[70] Any emotional remnant of memory was to be excised through prayer and the cultivation of a calm and tranquil disposition. This therapy of 'forgetting' might seem shocking in relation to an emphasis, during the 1980s and 90s, on recovering repressed memories of abuse as a necessary part of the healing process.[71] It is all too easy to adopt a Whiggish stance, to assume that social attitudes and methods of therapy have 'progressed' in both relative and absolute terms. Yet in 1900 'forgetting' was, arguably, the most useful alternative for the child victim of abuse. As Ellen Ross has demonstrated in *Love and toil*, working-class life was structured around the essential notion of survival; you simply had to 'get on with it'.[72] Whatever the possible deficiencies of the regime at the Nest or the value system it promoted, the tone of Marianne Asdell's comments about Emma is strikingly sympathetic and supportive. The workers in the home aimed to nurture and encourage child victims in their struggles against the effects of the worst abuse.

Emma, like many other former residents, continued to visit on a regular basis after she was sent out to work as a domestic servant in a local Clapton household. She changed situations a number of times in the first two years after leaving, given notice on one occasion on account of her 'lazy habits' and on another for staying out all night. Her contact with the home seems to have broken down when her work took her further afield. The entries in her case history end with a last report that she was 'doing well'.[73] Emma was amongst the list of residents who would probably have been deemed a 'success' by the Salvationists. Others fell rather shorter of the mark. A quarter of the girls admitted between 1902 and 1914 were deemed unsatisfactory; four of them, on reaching 15, were sent on to rescue homes for older girls as they were deemed too corrupting an influence on the younger children. Although the Salvation Army trained girls with the intention of sending them into service, this was not in fact the destination of the majority of girls referred to the home as a result of sexual abuse. A quarter of them were initially sent into service at 15 but, in half these cases, their behaviour was later deemed unsatisfactory. A quarter of the girls were sent home to live with relatives and often found employment in other industries: dress-making, the knitting factories, and munitions work (although the Army disapproved of the latter). Two of the girls were referred to hospitals for the 'feeble-minded'. In quantitative terms, very few of the girls ended up as the product so idealised by the charitable institution: the well-trained housemaid. In qualitative terms, despite those deemed unsatisfactory, the Army was possibly justified in claiming it had shone a light on troubled lives, providing loving care for a few of the most troubled youngsters of the day.

The Jewish Association for the Protection of Women and Children: the case of 'Leah'

Despite the development of specialist children's homes by Christian denominations after 1900, the sexually abused girl presented problems for Anglo-Jewry both before and after the turn of the century. To recognise her presence was to recognise the presence of immorality and corruption in the Jewish community. It was an especially loaded issue. Racist agitators during the 1890s stigmatised the Jews as physically, mentally and morally inferior; they claimed the Jews, as procurers, were responsible for the white slave trade.[74] Lara Marks has suggested that Anglo-Jewry was reluctant to acknowledge the existence of Jewish prostitutes in the 1880s because of the fear that this would damage the reputation of the Jewish community and incite anti-semitism.[75] Reticence over sexual abuse must be linked to the same concerns. Despite attempts to evade the problem, Jewish organisations were forced to face up to its reality and to adopt a reluctant strategy to provide for the 'fallen' child.

The first Jewish charities were set up in London's East End, under the auspices of the Jewish Board of Guardians,[76] in response to the huge influx of immigrants from Russia, Poland, Galicia and Romania between 1870 and 1914.[77] The Jewish Association for the Protection of Girls and Women was founded in 1885 by Constance Battersea (née Rothschild) as the first rescue society to cater for Jewish cases, many of them young mothers of 14 or 15. Battersea later described how she was roused to action one evening when she received news at her Hyde Park home that two young Jewish women had turned up at a Christian mission for fallen women:

> They frankly stated ... that they belonged to the unhappy sisterhood, and that even if they wished to abandon their present way of living it would be impossible, for every door would be shut against them. 'Our own people disown us,' they said, 'their Law forbids them to receive us, and we will not enter a Christian Home ... for, however bad we may be, we will not give up our Faith.'[78]

Prior to this, she had always deemed 'rescue work' unnecessary amongst the Jewish community.[79] Battersea mobilised her wealthy and prominent Jewish relatives to join the Ladies' Committee of the new Association: Battersea acted as honorary secretary with her cousin, Lady Rothschild, as president. A rescue home was founded in Mile End in August 1886 which moved to Charcroft House, Shepherd's Bush, the following year.

Chaim Bermant has drawn attention to the dominance of Jewish welfare institutions by an élite group of wealthy Anglo-Jewish families, the 'cousin-hood', closely aligned through marriage and business ties.[80] The Jewish Association was no exception; the opening pages of the Minute Book of the Ladies' Committee, dominated by the Rothschilds and Montefiores, reads as a list of exclusive West End addresses.[81] The linguistic, cultural and class-based divide between the West End Anglo-Jewish philanthropists and the East End Eastern European Jews, who were the recipients of their welfare work, became a point of tension, intensified by anti-semitism.[82] David Feldman has suggested that the Anglo-Jewish, attempting to assert their Englishness and patriotic loyalty to the empire, constructed the Jewish immigrants, whom they did not really welcome, as pre-civilised and 'other'.[83] In her *Reminiscences,* Battersea was careful to emphasise the moral respectability of the East End Jews, but she also drew attention to the exoti-cism of their dark physical appearance, dress and customs. In his 1892 novel, *Children of the ghetto,* Zangwill described, in the words of the socialist Simon Wolf, the cynicism with which the well-to-do reformers might have been regarded:

> Our philanthropists do but scratch the surface. They give the working man with their right hand what they have stolen from him with the left. ... The only way for our poor brethren to be saved from their slavery ... is for them to combine against the sweaters, and to let the West-End Jews go and hang themselves.[84]

The records of the Jewish Association for the Protection of Girls and Women show how the differences of social and class positioning – between the Jewish élite, their employees, and their charges (the poor girls of the East End) – led to structural and organisational weaknesses, which ulti-mately resulted in problems of control and discipline in the Charcroft House Rescue Home.[85]

In September 1885, 15-year-old Leah accused a 34-year-old friend of her father, Jacob Benjamin, of seducing her. The new Criminal Law Amendment Act had just come into operation, thereby raising the age of consent from 13 to 16, rendering the man's actions illegal for the first time. The matter came to light after a neighbour told Leah's mother how she had seen them together in the street, the man with his arm around the girl's waist. Both parties lived in a street off White Horse Lane, Mile End. Leah's father, a fish-monger, reported the matter to the police. At Thames Police Court, Benjamin, a traveller, who was living apart from his wife, admitted he had slept with her on several occasions, once at his sister-in-law's house. The girl agreed she had consented, although she stated he had once dragged her into a brothel in Maidment Street. Leah also told the court that Benjamin was not the first man she had sexual relations with; when she had been in service, her mistress's son had taken 'improper liberties with her'.[86] The case was committed to the Old Bailey for trial. Defence lawyer Mr Geoghegan invoked the 'saving clause', arguing that the man had reasonable cause to believe Leah was over 16.[87] He suggested that she had a reputation for behaving immodestly; that both her level of sexual experience and her appearance were more than would be expected of a girl of 15. The Recorder, in his summing up speech to the jury, expressed the opinion that 'the new act had turned immorality into crime'.[88] Benjamin, although a 34-year-old married man, was to be seen as the victim of this wayward girl. The prosecution never questioned why Benjamin, as a family friend, should be so ignorant of Leah's age and he was acquitted of the charge.

Leah's case was typical of many of those which came before the Central Criminal Court after the change in legislation in 1885: cases of girls, often from poorer areas of London who, although technically under the age of consent, evoked very little sympathy in judges, juries or even, as we shall see, in philanthropists. Although children in theory because of their age, they were seen as adult in knowledge and behaviour; the 'saving clause' was invoked throughout the late 1880s and 1890s to acquit men of the charges made by these children who were not really 'children'. These were cases which we might define now as sexual abuse, given the contrasting ages of the parties and the willingness of the men to take advantage of a young girl's precocity, but which in 1885 were construed as 'rescue' cases by philanthropists: cases of 'fallen' girls who needed to be reclaimed. It seems that Leah was seen as a 'problem' child by her parents who were prepared to hand her over to the Jewish Association and she was admitted to the Rescue Home at Mile End in November 1885.[89]

The Jewish Association was willing to accept 'fallen' girls but they were expected to be penitent and to reform their 'bad' ways; there was little sympathy for those with behavioural problems, who were not prepared to accept the discipline of the rescue home, or who were seen as 'fallen' too far for rescue. Leah was the only one out of four applicants who was accepted into the rescue home in November/December of that year as a 'fit' or suitable resident. The majority of girls who requested admittance were deemed unsuitable and referred on to other Christian refuges for prostitutes.[90] An applicant had to be 'fallen' in order to enter Charcroft House, but she must not be so 'fallen' as to be a corrupting influence on others.[91] Like the National Vigilance Association (NVA) on which it modelled its rescue work, it was very particular about its clients.

Leah's progress in the home was far from successful and she came to be regarded as a troublemaker. A few months after her arrival she 'escaped one morning [and] was brought back in a most unrepentant state by her father'. The committee minutes described her as 'a thoroughly deceitful girl', beyond the control of the matron or her assistant.[92] The Ladies' Committee decided that she should be removed to another (non-Jewish) refuge for fallen women. In December she was promised she would be allowed back if 'she proved herself amenable to good influences';[93] the Ladies' Committee continued to visit her in the non-Jewish refuge and to report back on her progress. Despite sending her away, they were concerned to maintain a relationship with her and it seems that Leah herself now thought of Charcroft House as 'home', begging to return. In November 1887 she was in the London Hospital 'in a very bad state of health' but, by 1888, aged 18, was finally back at Charcroft House, her father writing to request a visit in October of that year.[94] We have no record of what happened to her after 1888 although one would presume that a job in domestic service was her intended destination.

In her *Reminiscences*, Constance Battersea acknowledged the difficulty of reforming the girls who came to Charcroft House, attributing the problem to racial character rather than their degraded moral status:

> Although Jewish girls may be easy to touch for the moment, for they are generally emotional, excitable, and often full of real true feeling, they may be difficult to influence for any long period of time, and those who undertake this work must be prepared for many heart-breaking disappointments.[95]

A reading of the committee minutes reveals that there was a real problem with discipline in the home. Leah was not the only one to abscond.[96] In July 1887 the committee was busy getting quotes for a wooden screen at the end of the garden 'to prevent the girls from climbing over and getting away'.[97] Like Agnes Cotton's home, where girls were also absconding, the disciplinary regime seems to have been strained; perhaps a combination of 'excitable' temperament and the breakdown of authority and trust.

The Association seems to have had tremendous difficulty in finding effective staff. The work at Charcroft House got off to a bad start with the appointment of its first Jewish superintendent, Mrs R., in July 1886. The Association agreed to employ Mr R. as well, at a far greater salary than his wife, as a docks officer to meet ships of immigrants arriving in London and to escort young girls without pre-arranged 'respectable' destinations to the Association's lodging house. The Ladies' Committee became increasingly dissatisfied with their work. By March 1887 there were firm reports that Mrs R. was 'not a reliable person' and that her husband who 'makes himself very offensive to all those with whom he comes in contact' should be carefully watched over to ensure he did his duties.[98] The couple were finally dismissed in May 1887. The next appointment, Mrs L., was carefully selected and sent away for six months' training – three months in the Lock Hospital and three months in other London rescue homes; in her absence, a compromise was to be reached by employing a temporary Christian matron who was well-experienced in rescue work, together with a Jewish housekeeper who could attend to any religious duties.[99]

The staffing difficulties partly stemmed from sheer bad luck; partly, too, from the newness of the venture within the Jewish community and the impossibility, therefore, of finding Jewish women skilled in rescue work to act as matrons and superintendents of the homes; but also from the attitudes of the committee, who tended to employ superintendents on short-term contracts for trial periods and to sit in judgement rather than to work collaboratively with the superintendent of a home. The survival of sources probably presents a biased view: we hear the murmurs at committee level rather than discussions with the home's staff. The Salvation Army ledgers allow us to access a very different viewpoint: that of the carers who worked with children on a day-to-day basis. However, unlike the Salvation Army, the Jewish Association does appear to have run along the far more conventional lines associated with benevolent paternalism and patronage by the wealthy: rule by a self-appointed oligarchy.[100] It should be stressed that it was the Salvation Army rather than the Jewish Association that was unusual in its practices. The Jewish Association, with its drawing-room committees, was structured in exactly the same way as many middle-class welfare organisations, including the NVA with which it worked closely and which, as Deborah Gorham has pointed out, also had serious problems with errant girls escaping the confines of its adult rescue home.[101]

The problems of discipline also resulted from rescue home policies that treated adult women and teenage girls, accustomed to making their own way in life, as children. Gorham has drawn attention to the ways in which middle-class philanthropists based their attempts to reform 'fallen' girls on middle-class definitions of girlhood as a period of vulnerability requiring protection.[102] They were unwilling to allow the expressions of freedom and independence that the girls were used to, and their desire to 'protect' in fact became confused with the desire to 'control'.[103] Corporal punishment was condemned at Charcroft House but the system of incentives and deterrents – including money bribes – which took its place was patronising to the inmates, who, not surprisingly, rebelled. When Laura Ormiston Chant visited Charcroft House in 1887 she recommended that staff should 'treat the girls as children and reward good conduct by giving them a treat at a cooking lesson'.[104] She suggested that emotional outbursts were pathological rather than psychological in causation:

> Unreasonable fits of temper should be treated as physical, a dose of calming medicine to be given to quiet the nerves, an excellent prescription for this Mrs Chant has promised to send to the Matron.[105]

The troubled inmate was to be sedated rather than talked to; her emotions were to be seen as the irrational hysteria of adolescence rather than a very personal response, with its own internal logic, to experiences and surroundings.[106]

Leah's reaction to the Jewish rescue home seems to have been an ambiguous one – she was clearly unhappy there, and fought against its petty discipline; but, once she was released she begged the Ladies' Committee to let her back. Perhaps she was confused as to what she really wanted, rebelling against authority, but then touched by the interest that the ladies showed in her by visiting her in hospital. Rejected by her parents, the rescue home was her only chance; once over the fence, she found there was, in fact, nowhere to escape to. Her teenage years, as for many sexually abused or 'precocious' girls, were spent in a state of constant upheaval. Rejection by her parents was followed by continual moves from one home to another in the attempt by her rescuers to find a home suitable for her and to make her suitable for a home. Her experiences were very similar to those referred to the Waifs and Strays homes in their teens.

Montefiore House

From the turn of the century, the Jewish Association became increasingly concerned at the lack of care available for younger Jewish girl children, who were refused admission to Anglican industrial schools unless they converted to the Christian faith. The King Edward School, Hackney, was one of the few industrial schools willing to work with the Jewish community; in 1903 it had nine Jewish girl residents and allowed Jewish clergy and lady visitors to give religious instruction.[107] Yet the arrangement was far from satisfactory; the school rejected the Association's request for the appointment of a permanent Jewish teacher as too expensive, and, furthermore, was not prepared to accept 'fallen' girls or those with a dubious moral reputation. What was to become of Jewish girls 'too young to go into the rescue home but whose past rendered them unsuitable candidates for the majority of industrial schools?'[108] These included 'brothel children', who could be removed from 'immoral surroundings' under Ellice Hopkins's Act, and girls, some of whom might have been sexually abused, who would be classified as 'fallen'. The result of these discussions was the setting up of a new industrial school – Montefiore House – to be run by the Jewish Association, specifically for Jewish girls.[109] The hard grind of domestic work at Charcroft House was replaced at Montefiore House by a mixture of religious instruction, organised play, schooling and then industrial training.

The history of the home is a paradox, for, although its very foundation emerged from the express need to find a home for 'fallen' girl children, and indeed a number of its inmates clearly belonged to this category, the governing committee was persistently trying to change the rules to exclude such children from the home.[110] Its intentions were consistently frustrated, however, because there was simply nowhere else to send them (which was, of course, the reason why the home had been set up in the first place). In 1904 the committee had drawn up a policy for the projected home, stating that it was prepared to deal with children from 'immoral surroundings' but not 'vicious children' whom it deemed 'unsuitable for an industrial school'.[111] It would, therefore, accept 'fallen' or sexually abused children provided they were well-behaved, non-disruptive and unlikely to pass on their 'knowledge' to others.

When previously latent behavioural difficulties surfaced in the home, the committee's reaction was to seek transfer to another institution. In 1912, Esther, aged 13, was transferred from Montefiore House to Charcroft House because of what were described as 'immoral tendencies' (possibly a reference to masturbation) and because a doctor had examined her and found her 'fallen'.[112] The committee wished to change its admissions policy to a refusal to take 'fallen' girls, but was advised against doing so by the Home Office because the school was a 'sectarian one' (i.e. the only one offering care for Jewish girls).[113] Another girl, 14-year-old Rebecca, was deemed 'morally unfit for Montefiore House' in 1913 after she had both run away and been found 'corrupting' other children with her 'conversation'.[114] Her 'delinquency' was seen as too serious for an industrial school and a reformatory environment was gauged more appropriate. Yet the only two reformatories in the country prepared to take 'fallen' girls – the Church Army Home at Old Southgate and the Willows annexe of Mount Vernon Green Reformatory in Liverpool – would only admit Church of England children. Rebecca had to stay at Montefiore House since the Willows turned down the Association's application for her transferral.

Even after the setting up of Montefiore House, therefore, the provision for 'fallen' Jewish girls was far from adequate. The situation of the 'Leahs' of 1914 was, in many ways, similar to the experience of the 15-year-old in 1885. In 1914 Leah might have become a guinea pig for the latest medical treatment – hypnotic suggestion was being tentatively and controversially tried out by psychologist Dr Abelson on one of the Montefiore House girls – but she would still have been seen as a 'problem' to be sent elsewhere if possible.[115] Even the staffing difficulties continued, as a succession of matrons sought leave of absence because the job had taken too heavy a toll on their health.[116]

The Jewish Association demonstrated continued reluctance to get involved in the discussion of juvenile prostitution and child abuse. Its reticence in 1885 was matched by its distance, in the Edwardian period, from suffragette and purity campaigns to improve the treatment of child victims of sexual assault in courts of law. The Association's reticence must be attributed to its desire to maintain the morally spotless image of the Jewish community in face of wider anxieties about issues of 'race' and racism: it knew bad press could be used by anti-semitic opinion for its own purposes and, clearly, did not want to wash its dirty laundry in public. Unfortunately for the girls involved, it is doubtful that it got washed in private either.

The slow emergence of specialist residential homes for sexually abused girls has been delineated in relation to the problematic status of the 'fallen' child. The child's moral status prevented her admittance to ordinary institutions and necessitated the setting up of separate homes. Her moral status also meant that, in the Anglo-Jewish case, the desire to intervene was tempered by an understandable need to maintain appearances of respectability in the wake of anti-semitic accusations of Jewish 'immorality'. Age was also a crucial factor: the experiences of girls removed from their homes at a young age and those who were placed in rescue homes as teenagers remained very different. Homes for children under 12 developed therapies that aimed to provide love and emotional support as well as a disciplined structure to schooling, work and play. In the rescue home, however, where the stress was placed on training for outside employment, young women were infantilised and denied the personal autonomy to which they were already accustomed.

8 Conclusion

From 'corruption' to 'neurosis'?

By the end of the nineteenth century the view that children were essentially innocent was subject to sustained critique. Child psychologist James Sully argued in 1895 that 'the infant, though it has a nature capable of becoming moral or immoral, is not yet a moral being; and there is a certain impertinence in trying to force it under our categories of good and bad, pure and corrupt'.[1] Nevertheless, those involved in the day-to-day business of child-saving continued to express their concerns within a familiar Judaeo-Christian framework and to analyse moral development in terms of good and evil propensities. The sexual abuse of children was discussed in relation to notions of a moral economy based on the duality of innocence/corruption; it was an analysis that was closely related to notions of class and gender. Causation was discussed in terms of savagery and bestiality and was often linked to the close living conditions of the poor. The effects of abuse were gauged in terms of moral corruption and pollution. Treatment was framed in terms of moral reclamation and a return to a lost state of childhood innocence.

The dualistic model had a profound effect on the experiences of girls who found themselves involved in allegations of sexual abuse. They faced intensive cross-examination, both in and out of court, about their sexual knowledge and experience. Some were ostracised by friends and family. Others were removed from their home environments and transferred to a 'specialist' institution many miles away; most significantly, once institutionalised, they were taught to forget the past, to block out memories of abuse and to begin a new life in another part of the country.

The beginnings of a shift in attitude are discernible from the end of the First World War as the idea that victims of sexual abuse should be ghettoised in separate institutions for 'fallen' girls came under attack. The 1925 Departmental Committee on Sexual Offences against Children held that victims of sexual assault were 'no more a moral danger' than a girl who had been caught 'pilfering'.[2] The committee recommended that segregation should be avoided: most victims of sexual assault should be placed in ordinary homes.[3] The notion of 'moral corruption' was up for debate, a result of the popularisation of child psychology and a growing interest in psychoanalysis within certain 'expert' circles.

In 1920, representatives of the Medical Women's Federation – Mary Gordon, Jane Walker and Ethel Williams – produced an analysis of the trauma of sexual abuse that was clearly influenced by Freudian theory:

> To awaken or excite the dormant passion of a child or young person … prematurely is to confound its sense of right and wrong, and to give it a false view of human and social relationships and duties which it is very difficult to correct later. The physical and mental balance is often upset, and healthy development hindered. Not only unfortunate impressions but severe neurosis may persist in later life as a consequence of such experience.[4]

Their comments were judged so important that they were quoted at length in the report of the 1925 Departmental Committee.[5] The findings of this committee were potentially path breaking. The effects of sexual abuse were discussed as psychological trauma rather than moral damage. Treatment was delineated in terms of psychotherapy rather than religious conversion. The causes of abuse were interpreted in relation to the mental disorder of abusers although there was a continued emphasis on the living conditions of the poor.[6]

Freud's *The aetiology of hysteria*, published in German in 1896, had clearly associated the trauma of sexual abuse in childhood with neurosis in later life.[7] Controversy rages as to why Freud allegedly abandoned a model based on actual abuse or 'seduction' for a theory of sexual phantasy linked to the Oedipal complex. Masson's suggestion that Freud reneged his original theory as a result of pressure from friends, eminent members of the Viennese bourgeoisie whose children formed the client-base for his research, is still a matter of debate.[8] Despite Freud's apparent turn-around, his early theories influenced the work of Albert Moll, whose study *The sexual life of the child* was published in England in 1912 as the third volume of Havelock Ellis's *Studies in the psychology of sex*.[9] Moll wrote that: 'Freud … believes that sexual attempts on children may give rise … to severe neurosis – an idea which forms an important part of the etiological [sic] system put forward by this author.'[10] Moll's interpretation of the early Freud, which identified the psychological effects of actual abuse, was clearly echoed in the evidence given by the Medical Women's Federation.

There are few indications of the Freudian influence in Britain before 1912.[11] Carolyn Steedman has drawn attention to the work of psychoanalyst David Eder, who, working with Margaret McMillan, made notes on the 'nervous traumas' of his patients at the Deptford Camp School from 1911; he also translated Freud's *On dreams* in 1914.[12] While psychoanalysis might have made in-roads amongst advanced and radical thinkers, its influence was not apparent in the records of the NSPCC, the Jewish Association or the Waifs and Strays Society before the First World War. The course of 'hypnotic suggestion' which was given to one girl at Montefiore House in

1913, while radically new in method, was, in practice, simply a more severe version of the strategies of forgetting the past which were developed in other homes from the 1880s if not before.

Although the Departmental Committee of 1925 can be seen as a departure in thinking on the sexual abuse of children in the British context, its significance should not be overstated. A proliferation of viewpoints is apparent within medicine and psychology in the inter-war period. Whilst Gordon, Walker and Williams spoke of actual sexual trauma in childhood, others took a very different perspective. Dr Letitia Fairfield, employed by the London County Council to examine children appearing before the courts, told the Medical Women's Federation that, although incest was more common than suspected, children's evidence should be treated with extreme caution: 'children take to dirty practices among themselves or with boy companions; then some child weaves a phantasy of intercourse with an adult which she plants on to anyone whom chance brings along'.[13] Freudian theory (of both trauma and phantasy) remained extremely controversial. As one psychologist put it in 1923: 'much that is written today upon the influence of repressed sexual experiences may be dismissed as grotesque and untrue. ... There can be no doubt that Freud has exaggerated the part which sexual impulses play in causing neurosis.'[14]

The recommendations of the 1925 committee were largely ignored. As Pamela Cox has demonstrated in her important study of the treatment of girl delinquents, the segregation of 'fallen' and 'unfallen' children continued into the 1930s.[15] She has argued that religious beliefs and structures continued to shape life within the children's home where the impact of psychoanalysis seems to have been minimal.[16] In her examination of social work agencies in Boston, USA, Linda Gordon has suggested that psychiatric and psychoanalytic theories had their greatest impact during the 1940s and 50s: the theory of phantasy was widely used to ignore or 'explain away' complaints of incest and sexual abuse.[17] The child herself or her mother (rather than the father) became the figure of blame. In the influential work of John Bowlby, childhood neurosis was linked to the 'emotional attitude' of the mother towards the child; inappropriate mothering could lead to an increase in the child's 'sexual and aggressive impulses and phantasies'.[18] A detailed study of juvenile and adult courts, of children's homes and of NSPCC records – similar, indeed, to that undertaken for the 1830–1914 period – would be necessary before any significant claims could be made about the influence of psychoanalytic theory on twentieth-century legal and welfare practice in Britain. The work of Cox and Gordon suggests that the post-war period warrants extensive further investigation.[19]

Thus the dualistic structure of the religious/moral paradigm, although challenged by psychological and psychiatric theory, continued to hold sway for much of the twentieth century. And, indeed, it still permeates Anglo-American cultures at a popular level (despite Freud's 'discovery' of infantile sexuality). As Chris Jenks has pointed out, there is a significant tendency, evidenced most clearly in the mass media, to position children in relation to a traditional set of binary oppositions that include childhood/adulthood, innocence/corruption and victim/threat.[20] Continued moral panic about child criminals is testament to a cultural inheritance from the Victorian past. In a sensitive attempt to understand and explain the intense public shock and outrage surrounding the murder of toddler James Bulger by two 10-year-old boys in Liverpool in February 1993, poet Blake Morrison has suggested that: 'those nameless boys had killed not just a child but the idea of childhood'.[21] He has argued that 'there's an idea that some children are uniquely damaged, a race apart ... there's too much Us and Them, a denial of a shared humanity'.[22] The current panic is also, therefore, testament to a growing recognition that the ideal of childhood innocence is simply untenable. It seems that a radical shift in conceptual framework is required but it is not yet clear what an alternative framework might be. The Victorian conceptualisation of childhood/adulthood in terms of innocence and experience to some extent frames understandings of age in the legal and criminal justice systems today. Age-of-consent law in Britain, based on the 1885 Criminal Law Amendment Act, still delineates females between the ages of 13 and 16 as an intermediate category who, as somehow less innocent, require slightly lower levels of protection. This book has pointed to the specific circumstances, cultural and social, which shaped experiences and meanings of sexual abuse in the last century. Sociologists are also beginning to put current understandings of abuse, childhood, adulthood, sexual and social development, under a similar microscope.[23]

Notes

1 Introduction: 'the children of the poor'

1 M. Warner, *Monuments and maidens. The allegory of the female form* (London: Picador, 1987), pp. 146–77.

2 J. Hodge, *Up the steps of the Old Bailey* (London: Baron, 1944); S. Jackson, *The Old Bailey* (London: W. H. Allen, 1978).

3 A. Davin, 'Imperialism and motherhood', *History Workshop Journal* 5, 1978, pp. 9–65.

4 C. Steedman, *Strange dislocations. Childhood and the idea of human interiority 1780–1930* (London: Virago, 1995), p. 5.

5 J. Scott, 'Gender: a useful category of historical analysis', *American Historical Review* 5, 1986, pp. 1,053–75. Scott has discussed the operation of gender as both 'a constitutive element of social relationships based on perceived differences between the sexes' and 'a primary way of signifying power' (p. 1,067). She has argued that gender has been widely employed as a metaphor for all social and political relationships; my aim here is to demonstrate this presence within nineteenth-century legal institutions.

6 Warner, *Monuments and maidens*, p. xx.

7 Steedman, *Strange dislocations*, p. 9.

8 I use the word 'English' intentionally to acknowledge the differences between English and Scottish law. A long-established Scottish law against incest had no equivalent in England and Wales until 1908. See V. Bailey and S. Blackburn, 'The Punishment of Incest Act 1908: A case study of law creation', *Criminal Law Review* 1979, pp. 708–18.

9 I. Hacking, 'The making and molding of child abuse', *Critical Inquiry* 17, 1991, pp. 253–88. Key studies in the discovery and definition of sexual abuse have included (ordered chronologically); L. Armstrong, *Kiss daddy goodnight: a speak-out on incest* (New York: Pocket Books, 1978); D. Finkelhor, *Sexually victimised children* (New York: Macmillan, 1979); F. Rush, *The best kept secret: sexual abuse of children* (Inglewood Cliffs: Prentice-Hall, 1980); J. L. Herman, *Father–daughter incest* (London: Harvard, 1981); P. B. Mrazek and C. H. Kempe (eds), *Sexually abused children and their families* (Oxford: Pergamon, 1981); S. Butler, *Conspiracy of silence: the trauma of incest* (San Francisco: Volcan, 1985); A. Miller, *Thou shalt not be aware: society's betrayal of the child* (London: Pluto, 1985); D. E. H. Russell, *The secret trauma: incest in the lives of girls and women* (New York: Basic Books, 1986).

10 G. Behlmer, *Child abuse and moral reform in England 1870–1908* (Palo Alto, California: Stanford University Press, 1982); H. Ferguson, 'Cleveland in history: the abused child and child protection, 1880–1914', in *In the name of the*

child. Health and welfare 1880–1940, R. Cooter (ed.) (London: Routledge, 1992), pp. 146–99; C. Hooper, 'Child sexual abuse and the regulation of women: variations on a theme', in *Regulating womanhood*, C. Smart (ed.) (London: Routledge, 1992), pp. 54–77.

11 J. L. Casper, vol. 3 of *A handbook of the practice of forensic medicine based upon personal experience*, translated from the 3rd edn by G. W. Balfour (London: New Sydenham Society, 1864), p. 318.

12 Jan Lambertz, 'Sexual harassment in the nineteenth-century English cotton industry', *History Workshop Journal* 19, 1985, pp. 29–61, see p. 29.

13 1841 Act for Taking Away the Punishment of Death, 4 & 5 Vict., C. 56, S.3; 1861 Offences Against the Person Act, 24 & 25 Vict., C. 100, Ss 50 & 51; 1875 Offences against the Person Act, 38 & 39 Vict., C. 94, Ss 3 & 4; 1885 Criminal Law Amendment Act, 48 & 49 Vict., C. 69, S. 4 ; 1908 Punishment of Incest Act, 8 Ed. 7, C. 45.

14 See, for example, L. A. Jackson, 'Women professionals and the regulation of violence in inter-war Britain', in *Unguarded passions: gender, class and 'everyday' violence in Britain, c. 1850–c. 1950*, S. D'Cruze (ed.) (Harlow, England: Longman), in press.

15 'Trial and conviction of the ex-provost of Leith', *The Times*, 6 November 1855, p. 9.

16 This estimate is based on data collected for the present study.

17 J. M. Donovan, 'Combating the sexual abuse of children in France 1825–1913', *Criminal Justice History* 15, 1994, pp. 59–95 and J. M. Masson, *The assault on truth: Freud's suppression of the seduction theory* (Harmondsworth: Penguin, 1985), pp. 14–40, discuss the French forensic background.

18 For example, P. Coveney, *The image of childhood. The individual and society: a study of the theme in English literature* (Harmondsworth: Penguin, 1967); H. Cunningham, *Children and childhood in western society since 1500* (London: Longman, 1995).

19 Steedman, *Strange dislocations*. C. Jenks, *Childhood* (London: Routledge, 1996) pursues a similar line of argument by way of a sociological rather than a literary approach.

20 J. Rose, *The case of Peter Pan, or the impossibility of children's fiction* (London: Macmillan, 1985); C. Mavor, 'Dream rushes. Lewis Carroll's photographs of little Girls', in *Pleasures taken: performances of sexuality and loss in photographs* (London: I. B. Tauris, 1996), pp. 7–47.

21 P. King and J. Noel, 'The origins of "the problem of juvenile delinquency": the growth of juvenile prosecutions in London in the late-eighteenth and early-nineteenth centuries', *Criminal Justice History* 14, 1993, pp. 17–42; P. King, 'The rise of juvenile delinquency in England 1780–1840. Changing patterns of perception and prosecution', *Past and Present* 160, 1998, pp. 116–66; H. Shore, *Artful Dodgers: youth and crime in early nineteenth century London* (London: The Royal Historical Society, 1999).

22 L. Davidoff and C. Hall, *Family fortunes: men and women of the English middle class 1750–1850* (London: Century Hutchinson, 1987) and R. J. Morris, *Class, sect and party. The making of the British middle class: Leeds 1820–50* (Manchester: Manchester University Press, 1990).

23 Report of the Royal Commission on Children's Employment in Mines and Manufactories, PP 1842, XV, XVI & XVII; Report of the Special Assistant Poor Law Commissioners on the Employment of Women and Children in Agriculture, PP 1843, XII.

24 *Hansard Parliamentary Debates*, 3rd series, House of Commons, 31 July 1885, Col. 717, Mr Serjeant Simon.

25 M. Cale, 'Girls and the perception of sexual danger in the Victorian reformatory system', *History* 78, 1993, pp. 201–17; P. Cox, 'Rescue and reform: girls, delinquency and industrial schools 1908–33' (Ph.D. thesis, University of Cambridge, 1996); L. Mahood and B. Littlewood, 'The "vicious girl" and the "street-corner boy": sexuality and the gendered delinquent in the Scottish child-saving movement 1850–1940', *Journal of the History of Sexuality* 4, 1994, pp. 549–578.

26 H. Hendrick, *Child welfare. England 1872–1989* (London: Routledge, 1994), pp. 1–42.

27 Davidoff and Hall, *Family fortunes*, pp. 76–100, stresses the central importance of evangelical protestantism in the formation of middle-class identity. Similarly, Morris, *Class, sect and party*, p. 321, has written of the Leeds middle classes: 'If there was a dominant strand of ideology it was evangelical religion. This acted not so much as a basis of religious belief but as a vehicle for transmitting certain powerful views of social structure and social responsibility.'

28 T. Percival, *Medical jurisprudence or a code of ethics and institutes adapted to the professions of physic and surgery* (Manchester: printed for private circulation, 1794), p. 92. This text formed the basis of his *Medical ethics; or, a code of institutes and precepts, adapted to the professional conduct of physicians and surgeons* (Manchester: S. Russell, 1803) which was also reprinted in 1829 and 1849 (London: J. Churchill).

29 Percival, *Medical jurisprudence*, p. 93.

30 Percival, *Medical jurisprudence*, p. 82–3.

31 M. Wiener, *Reconstructing the criminal: culture, law and policy in England 1830–1914* (Cambridge: Cambridge University Press, 1990) discusses the influence of discourses of morality and respectability on the nineteenth-century criminal justice system.

32 Rush, *The best kept secret*; Susan Brownmiller, *Against our will: men, women and rape* (Harmondsworth: Penguin, 1986), first published 1975.

33 Brownmiller, *Against our will*, p. 15.

34 A. Clark, *Women's silence, men's violence: sexual assault in England 1770–1845* (London: Pandora, 1987), p. 2; S. D'Cruze, 'Approaching the history of rape and sexual violence', *Women's History Review* 1, 1992, pp. 376–96.

35 H. White, *Tropics of discourse: essays in cultural criticism* (Baltimore: The John Hopkins University Press, 1978), p. 92.

36 G. Walker, 'Rereading rape and sexual violence in early modern England', *Gender and History* 10 (1), 1998, pp. 1–25.

37 Ibid., p. 3.

38 Clark, *Women's silence*; Linda Gordon, *Heroes of their own lives. The politics and history of family violence* (London: Virago, 1989); J. Walkowitz, *City of dreadful delight. Narratives of sexual danger in late Victorian London* (London: Virago Press, 1992).

39 Gordon, *Heroes of their own lives*, p. vi.

40 M. Foucault, *Discipline and punish: the birth of the prison*, translated by A. Sheridan (Harmondsworth: Peregrine, 1977); M. Foucault, *An introduction*, vol. 1 of *The history of sexuality*, translated by R. Hurley (Harmondsworth: Penguin, 1990).

41 J. Butler, *Gender trouble – feminism and the subversion of identity* (London: Routledge, 1990); C. Ramazanoglu, *Up against Foucault. Explorations of some tensions between Foucault and feminism* (London: Routledge, 1993); L. McNay, *Foucault and feminism* (Cambridge: Polity, 1992); J. W. Scott, *Gender and the politics of history* (New York: Columbia University Press, 1988); C. Weedon, *Feminist practice and poststructuralist theory* (Oxford: Blackwell, 1987).

42 For a more detailed examination of Foucault's theories of power in relation to the issues of incest and domestic violence, see V. Bell, *Interrogating incest: feminism, Foucault and the law* (London: Routledge, 1993), pp. 57–72; S. D'Cruze, *Crimes of outrage. Sex, violence and Victorian women* (London: UCL Press, 1998), pp. 22–3; and D. and J. F. MacCannell, 'Violence, power and pleasure. A revisionist reading of Foucault from the victim perspective', in *Up against Foucault*, Ramazanoglu (ed.), pp. 203–39.

43 A. J. Hammerton, *Cruelty and companionship: conflict in nineteenth-century married life* (London: Routledge, 1992), p. 7; Gordon, *Heroes of their own lives*, p. vi.

44 J. Hearn, *Men in the public eye* (London: Routledge, 1992); J. Donzelot *The policing of families* (London: Hutchinson, 1982).

45 L. Davidoff, M. Doolittle, J. Fink and K. Holden, *The family story. Blood, contract and intimacy, 1830–1960* (Harlow, England: Addison Wesley Longman, 1999).

46 R. Samuel, *East End underworld: chapters in the life of Arthur Harding* (London: Routledge, 1981), quoted in A. Davin, 'When is a child not a child?', in *Politics of everyday life: continuity and change in work and the family*, H. Corr and L. Jamieson (eds) (London: Macmillan, 1990), p 54.

47 Jenks, *Childhood*, p. 7.

48 This account of Foucault's points, based on an interview in French, is taken from Bell, *Interrogating incest*, pp. 151–6.

49 Ibid.

50 Ibid.

51 J. Weeks, *Invented moralities: sexual values in an age of uncertainty* (Cambridge: Polity, 1995).

52 R. Evans, *In defence of history* (London: Granta, 1997), p. 51.

53 L. Gordon, 'The politics of child sexual abuse: notes from American history', *Feminist Review*, 28, 1988, pp. 54–64.

54 Davin, ' When is a child not a child?', pp. 37–61.

55 Both rape and carnal knowledge of a female 'within age' became misdemeanours in 1275 under the First Statute of Westminster, 3 Ed. 1, C. 13. In 1285 the Second Statute of Westminster, 13 Ed. 1, C. 34, made rape alone a felony. Both are cited and discussed in W. Blackstone, *Commentaries on the laws of England* (Oxford: Clarendon Press, 1773), p 212. Crimes were originally adjudged felonies if they entailed forfeiture of goods on death or execution.

56 18 Eliz. 1, C. 7, cited in Blackstone, *Commentaries*, p. 21?

57 Blackstone, *Commentaries*, p. 212.

58 Ibid.

59 A. E. Simpson, 'Vulnerability and the age of female consent: legal innovation and its effect on prosecutions for rape in eighteenth century England', in *Sexual underworlds of the Enlightenment*, G. S. Rousseau and R. Porter (eds) (Manchester: Manchester University Press), pp. 180–205.

60 A. S. Taylor, *Elements of medical jurisprudence*, 1st edn (London: 1844), p. 575, argued that 'carnal intercourse' with a girl aged 10–12 was a misdemeanour. See Public Record Office, London, Home Office Registers, H027/112, Yorkshire Assizes March 1855, for the case of HW, convicted of unlawfully carnally knowing a girl aged 10–12. Convictions for assault with intent to carnally know a female aged 10–12 were obtained in the case of TR, HO27/77, Yorkshire Assizes July 1845, and the case of BM, London Metropolitan Archive (LMA), Middlesex Quarter Sessions January 1855, Deposition MJ/SPE/1855 no. 3.

61 1828 Offences Against the Person Act, 9 George IV, C. 31, S. 17; 1875 Offences Against the Person Act, 24 & 25 Vict., C. 100, Ss 50 & 51.

62 1875 Offences against the Person Act, 38 & 39 Vict., C. 94, Ss 3 & 4. The felonies of rape and unlawful carnal knowledge were punishable through maximum sentences of life penal servitude or five years' imprisonment; the misdemeanours of indecent assault, attempted carnal knowledge or carnally knowing a girl aged 12–13 were punishable by up to two years' imprisonment.

63 1885 Criminal Law Amendment Act, 48 & 49 Vict., C. 69, S. 4. Similar punishments to the above were upheld.

64 The 1956 Sexual Offences Act, 4 & 5 Eliz. 2, C. 69, maintained the distinction between a 'felony' and an 'offence' in age of consent legislation. The present law states that it is a felony, punishable by life imprisonment, to have unlawful sexual intercourse with a girl under the age of 13; it is an offence, punishable by two years' imprisonment, to have intercourse with a girl between the ages of 13 and 16.

65 See, for example, *The Times*, 4 July 1860, p, 12, Middlesex Quarter Sessions, case of PF.

66 24 & 25 Vict., C. 100, S. 52. The 1861 Act seems to have had very little effect on Yorkshire prosecutions (see chapter 2), suggesting that, in some areas, the common law age of consent had always been upheld.

67 See also T. Hitchcock, *English sexualities 1700–1800* (Basingstoke: Macmillan, 1997), pp. 72–75, which cites A. Simpson, 'Masculinity and control: the prosecution of sex offenses in eighteenth-century London' (Ph.D. thesis, New York University, 1984); H. Cocks, 'Sodomy and the criminal law', paper presented at the Social History Society Conference, York, England, 1999.

68 A. S. Taylor, *A manual of medical jurisprudence*, 2nd edn (London: J. A. Churchill, 1846), p. 561, citing Archbold 409, noted that 'it is felony in the agent only'.

69 The 1880 Assault of Young Persons Act, 43 & 44 Vict., C. 45.

70 The 1922 Criminal Law Amendment Act, 12 & 13 Geo. 5, C. 56.

71 1908 Punishment of Incest Act, 8 Ed. 7, C. 45. Incest, within the prohibited degrees of consanguinity, was made punishable as a misdemeanour at the Assizes by penal servitude of 3–7 years or imprisonment for no more than two years. If the offence involved a girl under 13, the punishments for unlawful carnal knowledge, as laid down by the 1885 Criminal Law Amendment Act, were to apply. For a detailed discussion see Bailey and Blackburn, 'The Punishment of Incest Act'; S. Wolfram, 'Eugenics and the Punishment of Incest Act', *Criminal Law Review* 1983, pp. 308–16; Bell, *Interrogating incest*.

72 E. Bristow, *Vice and vigilance: purity movements in Britain since 1700* (Dublin: Gill & Macmillan, 1977).

73 London Society for the Protection of Young Females (and Prevention of Juvenile Prostitution), *Fourth annual report* (London: 1839).

74 For an empirical account of social purity campaigns see Bristow, *Vice and vigilance*. For 'heroic' interpretations of femininist campaigns see S. Jeffreys, *The spinster and her enemies: feminism and sexuality 1880–1930* (London: Pandora Press, 1985) and M. Jackson, *The real facts of life: feminism and the politics of sexuality c.1850–1940* (London: Taylor & Francis, 1994). Their work has been challenged by studies which argue that female reformers, whilst fighting the sexual double standard, were nevertheless caught up within a social purity discourse involving discipline, surveillance and protection. See J. Walkowitz, 'The politics of prostitution', *Signs* 6 (1), 1980, pp. 123–35; F. Mort, *Dangerous sexualities: medico-moral politics in England since 1830* (London: Routledge & Kegan Paul, 1987); L. Bland, *Banishing the beast: English feminism and sexual morality 1885–1914* (London: Routledge, 1995).

75 Reports of the Select Committees on the Administration and Operation of the Contagious Diseases Acts, PP 1868–9, VII.1; PP 1878–9, VIII.397; PP 1881, VIII.193; PP 1882, IX.1. Reports of the Select Committees of the House of Lords on the Law Relating to the Protection of Young Girls, PP 1882, XIII.823; PP 1881, IX.355.

76 PP 1881, IX.355, Q. 579.

77 PP 1882, XIII.823, Q. 45.

78 Walkowitz, *City of dreadful delight*; D. Gorham, 'The "maiden tribute of modern Babylon" re-examined. Child prostitution and the idea of childhood in late-Victorian England', *Victorian Studies* 21, 1978, pp. 353–79; A. Plowden, *The case of Eliza Armstrong: a child of 13 bought for £5* (London: Trinity Press, 1974).

79 Stead was sentenced to three months' imprisonment, without hard labour, for abduction and indecent assault.

80 Walkowitz, *City of dreadful delight*, pp. 85–102.

81 *Pall Mall Gazette*, 8 July 1885, p. 2.

82 W. T. Stead, *Speech delivered by Mr W. T. Stead at the Central Criminal Court on Wednesday November 24 1885, before Mr Justice Lopes* (London: Moral Reform Union, 1885).

83 J. Walkowitz, *Prostitution and Victorian society, women, class and the State* (Cambridge: Cambridge University Press, 1980), p. 17.

84 PP 1881, IX.355, Qs 221 & 910, evidence of Sir James Ingham, chief magistrate of the Metropolitan district, and William Hardman, chairman of the Surrey County Sessions.

85 PP 1881, IX.355, Q. 915, evidence of William Hardman.

86 See Mort, *Dangerous sexualities*, p. 132.

87 For example, Gorham, 'The "maiden tribute"', p. 366. Lord Cranmore and Browne did indeed comment that 'he believed that there were very few of their Lordships who had not, when young, been guilty of immorality. He hoped that they would pause before passing a clause within the range of which their sons might come' (*Hansard*, House of Lords, 24 June 1884, Col. 1,219). His remarks, however, were in the context of a clause involving the arrest of men for the soliciting of women; although clearly condoning both the double standard and male use of prostitutes, he did not publicly condone sexual relations with 12-year-olds.

88 Mort, *Dangerous sexualities*, p. 128. In addition to the age-of-consent clause, the bills proposed a whole list of measures to outlaw prostitution, soliciting, the keeping of brothels and gross indecency between males.

89 Mort, *Dangerous sexualities*, p. 132.

90 *Hansard*, House of Commons, 12 August 1880, Cols 1,082–6, Mr Hastings.

91 *Hansard*, House of Commons, 31 July 1885, Col. 721, Mr Macartney.

92 *Hansard*, House of Commons, 31 July 1885, Col. 717, Mr Sergeant Simon.

93 *Hansard*, House of Lords, 24 June 1884, Col. 1213, Lord Mount-Temple. For Mount-Temple's reputation as an evangelical reformer (he was brother-in-law to Lord Shaftesbury) see K. Heasman, *Evangelicals in action. An appraisal of their social work in the Victorian era* (London: Geoffrey Bles, 1962), p. 17.

94 The Central Criminal Court at the Old Bailey acted in place of an assize court for the whole of London, north and south of the River Thames, and for the county of Middlesex. Up until 1889 cases from the Greater London area north of the Thames were tried at the Middlesex Quarter Sessions; quarter sessions cases from areas south of the river were sent to the county sessions for Kent and Surrey. In 1889, with the formation of the London County Council, the County of London Sessions were created to take business for Greater London,

while the Middlesex Quarter Sessions continued to try cases for outlying areas only. The Yorkshire Assizes originally came within the Northern Assize Circuit; for the period 1864–76 they were included in the Midland Circuit and after 1876 in a newly created North Eastern Circuit.

95 The drop in the number of cases of sexual assault tried at the Middlesex Sessions after 1885 is explained by the creation of the County of London Sessions to take metropolitan business.

96 Clark, *Women's silence*, p. 98.

97 Ibid.

98 1908 Children Act, 8 Ed. 7, C. 67.

99 LMA, Thames Police Court, registers 1885–1910, PS.TH/A1 & A2. LMA, Hampstead Magistrates Court, minutes of evidence 1870–1914, PS/HAM/A1, and court registers 1880–1914, PS/HAM/B.

100 See, for example, *Hampstead and Highgate Express*, 2 June 1907, p. 6.

101 M. W. Beresford and G. R. Jones (eds), *Leeds and its region* (Leeds: British Association, 1967); D. Fraser, *A history of modern Leeds* (Manchester: Manchester University Press, 1980); D. P. Hudson, *The genesis of industrial capital: a study of the West Riding wool textile industry c. 1750–1850* (Cambridge: Cambridge University Press, 1986); A. Raistrick, *The making of the English landscape. West Riding of Yorkshire* (London: Hodder & Stoughton, 1970).

102 H. J. Dyos and M. Wolff (eds), *The Victorian city: images and realities* (London: Routledge & Kegan Paul, 1973); G. Stedman Jones, *Outcast London: a study in the relationship between classes in Victorian society* (Oxford: Clarendon Press, 1982).

103 E. J. Connell and M. Ward, 'Industrial development 1780–1914', in Fraser, *History of modern Leeds*, pp. 142–76, see p. 158.

104 The population of the West Riding of Yorkshire rose from 1.013 million in 1831 to 1.882 million in 1871 and 2.843 million in 1901. The population of London rose from 1.656 million in 1831, to 3.261 million in 1871 and 4.536 million in 1901. See B. R. Mitchell, *British historical statistics* (Cambridge: Cambridge University Press, 1988), pp. 30–3.

105 C. Emsley, *Crime and society in England 1750–1900*, 2nd edn (Harlow: Longman, 1996), p. 103.

106 This figure has been calculated using Judicial Statistics for England and Wales, PP 1890–1, XCIII.1 and population estimates contained in Mitchell, *British historical statistics*, p. 12.

107 Judicial statistics for each county were recorded in the Parliamentary Papers on a yearly basis. The population of Cornwall remained fairly static throughout the nineteenth century. A population of 301,000 in 1831 rose very slowly to 362,000 in 1871, dropping to 322,000 in 1901. See Mitchell, *British historical statistics*, pp. 30–3.

108 L. Kelly, *Surviving sexual violence* (Cambridge: Polity, 1988), pp. 162–5.

109 G. J. Hall and R. D. F. Martin, *Child abuse procedure and evidence* (London: Barry Rose, 1993), p. 7, cited in S. M. Edwards, *Sex and gender in the legal process* (London: Blackstone Press, 1996), p. 267.

110 *The Times*, 3 August 1875, p. 10, quoted in C. A. Conley, 'Rape and justice in Victorian England', *Victorian Studies* 29 (4), 1986, pp. 519–36, see p. 523.

111 Kelly, *Surviving sexual violence*; Finkelhor, *Sexually victimised children;* Russell, *The secret trauma*.

112 Edwards, *Sex and gender*, p. 269.

113 Hooper, 'Child sexual abuse', p. 55.

114 Cited in Ibid.

2 Family, neighbourhood and police

1 West Yorkshire Archive Service (Wakefield), QS1/234/2, case of VM, April 1895.

2 Ibid.

3 Walkowitz, *City of dreadful delight*. For a discussion of earlier versions of the aristocratic seduction myth, see A. Clark, 'The politics of seduction in English popular culture', in *The progress of romance: the politics of popular fiction*, J. Radford (ed.) (London: Routledge & Kegan Paul, 1986), pp. 47–70.

4 L. Rose, *The erosion of childhood: child oppression in Britain 1860–1918* (London: Routledge, 1991) has provided an essentially whiggish account of the development of child protection legislation in terms of humanitarian progress, using the evidence of parliamentary commissioners to depict the exploitation of children before the emergence of the child protection movement. Behlmer, *Child abuse*, has analysed government reports and parliamentary legislation as background to his main point of focus: the founding of the NSPCC. Neither of these accounts have examined the choices, strategies and childcare practices of working people.

5 Select Committee on the Bill to Regulate the Labour of Children in Factories, PP 1831–2, XV.1, quotation taken from Qs 2,887–8. Report of the Special Assistant Poor Law Commissioners on the Employment of Women and Children in Agriculture, PP 1843, XII.1, quotation taken from p. 73. Similar views were expressed by the Royal Commission on the Physical and Moral Condition of the Children and Young Persons Employed in Mines and Manufactures, PP 1842, XV.1. The term 'the labouring poor' was used interchangeably with 'the lower orders' and 'the working classes' to refer to both the urban and industrial proletariat; see K. Snell, 'Differential bitterness: the social outlook of the rural proletariat in eighteenth and nineteenth century England and Wales', in *Social orders and social classes in Europe since 1500: studies in social stratification*, M. L. Bush (ed.) (London: Longman, 1992), pp. 158–84.

6 For a detailed analysis of the political and social climate of the 1880s see Stedman Jones, *Outcast London*.

7 A. Mearns, *The bitter cry of outcast London* (London: Frank Cass, 1970), 1st edn 1883.

8 Ibid., p. 10.

9 Royal Commission on the Housing of the Working Classes, PP 1884–5, XXX.1. This quotation from Lord Shaftesbury's evidence was emphasised through inclusion in the main body of the report, p. 13.

10 A. Wohl, 'Sex and the single room: incest among the Victorian working classes', in *The Victorian family: structure and stresses* (London: Croom Helm, 1978), pp. 197–216, see p. 199. This tendency was also manifest in some early feminist accounts, such as Rush, *The best kept secret* as well as in the prurient, sensationalist and male-centred account of child prostitution provided in R. Pearsall, *The worm in the bud. The world of Victorian sexuality* (London: Penguin, 1969). For an important critique of the reports of commissioners investigating conditions in the mines, see A. V. John, *By the sweat of their brow: women workers at Victorian coal mines* (London: Croom Helm, 1980).

11 Walker, 'Rereading rape'; D'Cruze, *Crimes of outrage*.

12 See John Benson, *The working class in Britain 1850–1939* (London: Longman, 1989), pp. 116–19.

13 As Elizabeth Roberts, *A woman's place: an oral history of working-class women 1890–1940* (Oxford: Blackwell, 1984), p. 169 has pointed out, children often called neighbours 'aunt' or 'uncle' whether they were related by blood or not.

14 Benson uses the definition of community provided by R. Dennis, *English industrial cities of the nineteenth century: a social geography* (Cambridge: Cambridge University Press, 1984), p. 285: 'people from the same area sharing the same attitudes, beliefs and interests, and expressing their communality of interest through social action'. See Benson, *The working class*, p. 118. This chapter will demonstrate that a wider sense of community existed in a diasporic sense beyond the immediate 'neighbourhood'. Family and friends who had migrated provided links between different neighbourhoods. Furthermore, those who gave testimony in the court cases demonstrated a sense of reponsibility and duty towards all children, whether they knew them to be local or not.

15 PRO, HO 18/35, petition 15; London Metropolitan Archive (LMA), MJ/SPE/1865/09, no. 66; MJ/SPE/1865/13, no. 63; MJ/SPE/1870/16, no. 21; MJ/SPE/1875/21, no. 9; *Hampstead and Highgate Express*, 20 May 1882, p. 4; MJ/SPE/1880/12, no. 8; MJ/SPE/1880/30, no. 30; WYAS, QS1/229/5, case of EL; LMA, MJ/SPE/4 August 1900, no. 21; MJ/SPE/7 May 1910, no. 24.

16 WYAS, QS1/169/7, case of BS; LMA, MJ/SPE/14, no. 26.

17 M. Douglas, *Purity and danger: an analysis of the concepts of pollution and taboo* (London: Routledge, 1991), 1st edn 1966.

18 Ibid., p. 4.

19 M. Vicinus, 'Helpless and unfriended: nineteenth-century domestic melodrama', *New Literary History* 13, 1981, pp. 127–43, see p 139. See also P. Brooks, *The melodramatic imagination* (New Haven: Yale University Press, 1976) and C. Crosby, 'History and the melodramatic fix', in *The ends of history: Victorians and 'the woman question'* (London: Routledge, 1991), pp. 69–109.

20 Vicinus, 'Helpless and unfriended', p. 139.

21 LMA, MJ/SPE/1880/30, no. 30.

22 Vicinus, 'Helpless and unfriended', p. 139.

23 LBland, *Banishing the beast*; S. Kingsley Kent, *Sex and suffrage in Britain 1860–1914* (London: Routledge, 1990).

24 E. Ross, *Love and toil. Motherhood in outcast London 1870–1918* (Oxford: Oxford University Press, 1993), p. 19. Elizabeth Roberts's rich and detailed oral history study of Lancashire, *A woman's place*, provides evidence of similarities across regions. Although Roberts's work focuses on the early twentieth century, many of the practices she describes were clearly in place in nineteenth-century working-class neighbourhoods.

25 Ross, *Love and toil*, p. 8.

26 WYAS, QS1/189/12, case of JH.

27 LMA, MJ/SPE/1880/35, no. 12.

28 LMA, MJ/SPE/1870/08, no. 7.

29 C. Emsley has emphasised the continuities between eighteenth and nineteenth-century policing in *Crime and society in England 1750–1900* (London: Longman, 1987), pp. 216–47.

30 The Metropolitan Police Force was founded in 1829; attempts were made to extend the new police to provincial boroughs through the Municipal Corporations Act of 1835 and to counties through the Rural Constabulary Act 1839. Local authorities were finally compelled to set up police forces through the County and Borough Police Act of 1856. For more detailed studies of this legislation and its effect see C. Emsley, *The English police* (London: Harvester Wheatsheaf, 1991) and C. Steedman, *Policing the Victorian community: the formation of English provincial police forces 1856–80* (London: Routledge & Kegan Paul, 1984).

31 WYAS, QS1/204/15, case of SC.

32 LMA, MJ/SPE/5 August 1905, no. 9.

33 Ibid.
34 *Hampstead and Highgate Express*, 3 July 1886, p. 6.
35 Ibid. The gipsies, although commended, were infantilised and treated as figures of fun both in court and by the newspaper reporter. The newspaper drew attention to laughter in court after the man's final comment, which, it seems, was deemed ironic as inappropriate to his station.
36 LMA, MJ/SPE/1880/38, no. 11.
37 Ross, *Love and toil*, pp. 166–9.
38 WYAS, QS1/229/5, case of JG.
39 WYAS, QS1/244/1, case of WC.
40 *Hampstead and Highgate Express*, 26 August 1876, p. 3.
41 Judicial Statistics, PP 1890–1, XCIII.1; Mitchell, *British historical statistics*, p. 12.
42 See Kelly, *Surviving sexual violence*, pp. 59–60 for an overview of contemporary estimates. D. West (ed.), *Sexual victimisation* (Aldershot: Gower, 1986) has reported the results of a British survey in which 54 per cent of a sample of female students said they had experienced some form of sexual abuse as children (cited in Kelly, *Surviving sexual violence*, p. 59).
43 Emsley, *Crime and society*, pp. 21–32.
44 E. Bass and L. Thornton (eds), *I never told anyone: writings by women survivors of sexual abuse* (New York: Harper & Row, 1983); Russell, *The secret trauma*; K. Browne, 'Child sexual abuse', in *Male violence*, J. Archer (ed.) (London: Routledge, 1994).
45 R. Storch, 'The policeman as domestic missionary: urban discipline and popular culture in northern England 1850–1880', *Journal of Social History* 4, 1970, pp. 481–509. D. Philips, *Crime and authority in Victorian England* (London: Croom Helm, 1971).
46 R. Roberts, *The classic slum* (London: Penguin, 1971), p. 100.
47 Stedman Jones, *Outcast London*, p. 295.
48 Emsley, *Crime and society*, p. 113. The West Riding had seen clashes between working people and authorities as a result of the high level of Chartist activity in the 1840s. See *Leeds Mercury*, 21 March 1840, for trials of the Barnsley, Sheffield and Bradford Chartists at the Yorkshire Assizes.
49 See Samuel, *East End underworld*, p 2: 'The Nichol' was a maze of streets which 'was regarded by the working-class people of Bethnal Green as so disreputable that they avoided contact with its people'
50 C. A. Conley, *The unwritten law. Criminal justice in Victorian Kent* (Oxford: Oxford University Press, 1991); J. Davis, 'A poor man's system of justice: the London police courts in the second half of the nineteenth century', *Historical Journal* 27(2), 1984, pp. 309–35; J. Davis, 'Prosecutions and their context: the use of criminal law in later nineteenth-century London', in *Policing and prosecution in Britain 1750–1880*, D. Hay and F. Snyder (eds) (Oxford: Clarendon Press, 1989), pp. 397–426. For useful overviews of this historiography see D. Philips, ' "A just measure of crime, authority, hunters and blue locusts": the "revisionist" social history of crime and the law in Britain 1780–1850', in S. Cohen and A. Scull, *Social control and the state* (Oxford: Blackwell, 1985), pp. 50–74 and V. A. C. Gatrell, 'Crime, authority and the policeman-state', in vol. 3 of *The Cambridge social history of Britain*, F. M. L. Thompson (ed.) (Cambridge: Cambridge University Press, 1990), pp. 243–310.
51 Davis, 'Prosecutions and their context', p. 419.
52 In some areas police were drawn from the neighbourhoods they policed. Although the Metropolitan Police Force preferred to recruit non-Londoners in order to ensure impartiality, this policy seems to have become increasingly

untenable. H. Shpayer-Makov, 'A portrait of a novice constable in the London Metropolitan Police, c. 1900', *Criminal Justice History* 12, 1991, pp. 133–60, argues that, by the 1880s, half of all recruits had actually lived in London before joining the force and were drawn from 'the vast reservoir of the urban working class' (p. 139). There might be differences in status. Arthur Harding commented that one of his aunts was considered 'posh' because 'she married a police sergeant and lived in the building next to Bethnal Green police station' (Samuel, *East End underworld*, p. 13).

53 C. Booth, *Maps of London poverty*, vol. 5 of *Life and labour of the people in London. First Series: Poverty* (London, Macmillan, 1969), from revised edn 1902, 1st edn 1889 & 1891. Booth coloured the streets on his map in yellow to represent the 'wealthy', in red to represent the 'well-to-do middle classes', in pink for those 'fairly comfortable', and purple for areas which were 'mixed, some comfortable, others poor'. Streets coloured pale blue were 'poor', those coloured dark blue were 'very poor, casual [labour] and chronic want', while those marked in black were inhabited by the 'lower class, vicious, semi-criminal'. While these classifications obviously reflect Booth's own particular perceptions of wealth and poverty, his maps can, nevertheless, provide a general indication of the geographical location of different social groups within the metropolis. All Booth's categories, other than the most affluent, were represented by victims appearing at the Middlesex Sessions, including the slums of Clerkenwell and Whitechapel, which were shaded black on the maps.

54 *The Times*, 30 November 1865, p. 11 & 7 December, p. 11.

55 *The Times*, 30 November 1865, p. 11.

56 Ibid.

57 H. Mayhew, *The London street-folk*, vol. 1 of *London labour and the London poor* (New York: Dover, 1968), first published 1861–2, p. 256.

58 Booth, *Maps of London poverty*.

59 Booth, *Classification of Streets*, vol. 2 of *Poverty*, p. 82.

60 For assaults on alleged abusers see, for example: WYAS, QS1/234/2, case of VM; LMA, MJ/SPE/1870/05, no. 26; LMA, MJ/SPE/5 August 1905, no. 9. References to money payments are made in WYAS, QS1/204/12 case of JB; LMA, MJ/SPE/1870/14, no. 22. For a case in which a mother stopped her daughter from going to baby-sit because she suspected the girl was being molested by her employer see LMA, MJ/SPE/1875/01, no. 29.

61 Davis, 'Poor man's system of justice', p. 310.

62 Storch, 'The policeman as domestic missionary'.

63 *The Times*, 9 September 1830, p. 4c.

64 Ibid.

65 *Illustrated Police News*, 21 May 1870, p. 3.

66 Emsley, *Crime and society*, pp. 181–2.

67 See A. Clark, *The struggle for the breeches: gender and the making of the British working class* (Los Angeles: University of California, 1995), p. 44. For detailed studies of the ways in which the bodies of working women were sexually objectified by middle-class writers see L. Davidoff, 'Class and gender in Victorian England: the diaries of Arthur J, Munby and Hannah Cullwick', *Feminist Studies* 5 (1), 1979, pp. 87–141 and John, *By the sweat of their brow*.

68 *Leeds Mercury*, 8 December 1860, p. 4.

69 Ibid.

70 *West London Observer*, 27 February 1875, p. 3.

71 Ibid.

72 WYAS, QS1/224/7, case of FB.

73 Clark, *Struggle for the breeches*, pp. 220–32. See also S. O. Rose, *Limited livelihoods. Gender and class in nineteenth-century England* (London: Routledge, 1992), pp. 126–53.

74 J. Benson, *British coalminers in the nineteenth century: a social history* (Dublin: Gill & Macmillan, 1980), pp. 142–71.

75 Ross, *Love and toil*; D'Cruze, *Crimes of outrage*.

76 See V. A. C. Gatrell *The hanging tree: execution and the English people 1770–1868* (Oxford: Oxford Univerity Press, 1994) for further discussion of these petitions. Judicial Statistics for England and Wales, PP 1830, XII.1, p. 3, states that, out of 1,397 persons sentenced to death in 1830, as a result of petitioning, only 46 were executed. The success rate for petitions in rape cases was far lower than the overall average: of the nine men sentenced to death for rape in 1830, three were actually executed.

77 PRO, HO 18/29, no. 39.

78 Ibid.

79 PRO, HO 18/30, no. 29.

80 Both Justice Hawkins and the grand jury commented on the unprecedented number of cases of rape and indecent assault of children which came before the Yorkshire Winter Assizes 1885 (*Yorkshire Post*, 11 November 1885, p. 6). Out of the eighteen cases involving child victims, ten involved girls under the age of 13 and eight involved girls in the 13–16 age band.

81 Walkowitz, *City of dreadful delight*, p. 82.

82 *The Times*, 27 August 1885, p. 10.

83 Ibid.

84 *Yorkshire Post*, 31 July 1885, p. 5.

85 *Leeds Mercury*, 20 August 1885, p. 3.

86 *Yorkshire Post*, 17 December 1885, p. 5. The *Pall Mall Gazette*, 21 September 1885, p. 10, makes reference to a Manchester case in which a father, whose daughter had been 'outraged', increased his demand for cash settlement from 10s to £5 after reading Stead's story about the purchase of juvenile prostitutes in London.

87 P. Mrazek, M. Lynch and A. Bentovim, 'Sexual abuse of children in the United Kingdom', *Child abuse and neglect* 7, 1981, pp. 147–53 has estimated that 43 per cent of child sexual abuse is perpetrated within the family, 25 per cent by strangers and 32 per cent by non-family members who are nevertheless known to victims. J. Plotnikoff and M. Woolfson, *Prosecuting child abuse: an evaluation of the government's speedy progress policy* (London: Blackstone Press, 1995) has provided an analysis of 200 child sexual abuse cases that came before English magistrates' courts and crown courts 1990–2. In this study, 50 per cent of alleged abusers were relatives (including step-relations or parents' cohabitees), 7 per cent were strangers and 43 per cent were known to but unrelated to the victim.

88 Details of the relationship between victim and alleged abuser were traced in 194 of the Middlesex cases and 56 of the Yorkshire cases.

89 *The Times*, 21 May 1830, p. 4, 'The Hyde Park cases'.

90 See W. F. A. Archibald, J. H. Greenhalgh, J. Roberts, *The Metropolitan Police guide*, 3rd edn (London: HM Stationery Office, 1901), p. 1,009, for a discussion of the Parks Regulation Acts. For information about 'additional constables' appointed by dock or harbour boards, private factory and estate owners, see Steedman, *Policing the Victorian community*, pp. 45–6. A park constable in Regents Park, who gave evidence before Clerkenwell magistrates in 1870, produced a whole list of cases which he had reported to the local

police station, including three charges of indecency within the previous two months: LMA, MJ/SPE/1870/14, no. 19.

91 The term 'park pest' was actually used by the NSPCC; see *Child's Guardian* 21(11), 1907, p. 125.

92 WYAS, QS1/249/6, case of JG; QS1/244/4, case of JWF.

93 See J. Gillis, 'Servants, sexual relations and the risks of illegitimacy in London, 1801–1900', *Feminist Studies* 5, 1979, pp. 142–73.

94 D'Cruze, *Crimes of outrage*, Chapter 5, pp. 81–109 for a subtle analysis of violence against women and girls in the workplace.

95 The classic study of radicalism in the West Riding is of course E. P. Thompson's inspirational *The making of the English working class* (London: Penguin, 1968). Clark, *The struggle for the breeches*, is a powerful re-working of Thompson's project, which emphasises the role of gender and sexual politics in the development of radical and working-class cultures.

96 T. Eagleton, *The rape of Clarissa. Writing, sexuality and class struggle in Samuel Richardson* (London: Blackwell, 1982), p. 88.

97 Ibid., p. 4.

98 Clark, *Struggle for the breeches*, pp. 220–32.

99 D. Hay, 'Property, authority and the criminal law', in *Albion's fatal tree: crime and society in eighteenth-century England*, D. Hay, P. Linebaugh, E. P. Thompson *et al.* (London: Allen Lane, 1975), pp. 13–62.

100 WYAS, QS1/244/9, case of WH. A Wakefield confectioner, who was accused of abusing a 16-year-old servant in June 1905, was overheard telling her mother: 'You cannot do anything if you try as they will believe my tale before yours.'

101 Clark, *Struggle for the breeches*, p. 49.

102 Roberts, *The classic slum*, p. 44.

103 NSPCC, First annual report, 1885, p. 8.

104 There does appear to have been a divergence between legal theory and practice, since there are cases in which wives gave evidence against their husbands in police courts before 1889; see, for example, LMA, MJ/SPE/1875/16, no. 11 and WYAS, QS1/224/6, case of FM.

105 WYAS, QS1/224/6, case of FM.

106 WYAS, QS1/244/6, case of WL.

107 PRO, CRIM 1/8/2, case tried at the Old Bailey.

108 *The Times*, 14 March 1870, p. 11.

109 Ibid.

110 WYAS, QS1/224/6, case of FM.

111 Ibid.

112 WYAS, QS1/179/4, case of SP.

113 Gordon, *Heroes of their own lives*, p. 264.

114 *The Times*, 15 April 1835, p. 6, described an Old Bailey trial in which the common-law wife of a 63-year-old man, accused of indecently assaulting his stepdaughter, 'appeared on his behalf and attempted to impugn the veracity of her daughter'. *West London Observer*, 7 June 1890, p. 3, reported a case in which the wife was called into the magistrates' court but refused to give evidence against her husband.

115 Crosby, 'History and the melodramatic fix', p. 106.

116 LMA, MJ/SPE/1885/39, no. 2.

117 LMA, MJ/SPE/1865/11, no. 70; *The Times*, 24 June 1835, p. 6.

118 C. Chinn, *They worked all their lives. Women of the urban poor in England 1880–1939* (Manchester: Manchester University Press, 1988), p. 152.

119 Royal Commission on the Housing of the Working Classes, PP 1884–5, XXX.1, Qs 5,872–5.
120 Ibid., Q. 1,954.
121 Ibid., Q. 6,864. See also A. Davin, *Growing up poor. Home, school and street in London 1870–1914* (London: Rivers Oram Press, 1996), pp. 51–7.
122 Gordon, *Heroes of their own lives*, p. 280.

3 The child savers

1 Salvation Army, Children's History Book VI, no. 26. See also note 89.
2 Children's Society, Case Files, no. 47, Caroline G. See also note 88.
3 SA, Children's History Book VI, no. 248.
4 Behlmer, *Child abuse*; Hendrick, *Child welfare*; T. H. Ferguson, 'Protecting children in time: a historical sociological study of the abused child and child protection in Cleveland from 1880 to the "Cleveland affair" of 1987' (Ph.D. thesis, Cambridge University, 1992). The Society was originally founded as the London Society for the Prevention of Cruelty to Children (LSPCC) in 1884. In 1889 it became the National Society for the Prevention of Cruelty to Children and set up a number of regional Aid Committees to deal with business outside London. I use the term NSPCC broadly here to refer to the Society in both its pre- and post-1889 forms.
5 I. Pinchbeck and M. Hewitt, *Children in English society* (London: Routledge & Kegan Paul, 1969); Rose, *The erosion of childhood*.
6 Ferguson, 'Protecting children in time'.
7 For NSPCC instructions on the waiving of standard procedure in 'emergency' cases, see NSPCC, *Inspector's directory* (London: NSPCC, 1904), p. 21. This was a staff protocol manual rather than a directory of inspectors.
8 Gordon, *Heroes of their own lives*; Gordon, 'The politics of child sexual abuse'.
9 Gordon, *Heroes of their own lives*, p. 215.
10 For an analysis of early 'radical feminist' campaigns see Jeffreys, *The spinster and her enemies*, and Jackson, *The real facts of life*. For a more nuanced account of the complex and fluid interactions of feminist and social purity ideas see Bland, *Banishing the beast*.
11 Gorham, 'The "maiden tribute"'.
12 See also Hendrick, *Child welfare*, pp. 1–20.
13 *Edinburgh Society for the Protection of Young Females* (Edinburgh: 1842), p. 3. Auxiliary societies were set up in several large towns. The Society used the term 'juvenile prostitution' to refer to girls in the 12–16 age bracket.
14 Society for the Rescue of Young Women and Children, *Eighteenth annual report* (London: Unwin Brothers, 1870), pp. 21–2.
15 Ibid., pp. 20–1.
16 The NVA aimed to protect women and children from 'criminal vice and public immorality' and to act as an umbrella organisation for similar societies; see the *Sentinel*, 1885, p. 475. The Jewish Association was set up to carry out rescue work with 'fallen' girls and women within the Jewish community in England and to campaign against the 'white slave trade'. See C. Battersea, *Reminiscences* (London: Macmillan, 1922) for a contemporary account.
17 *Child's Guardian* 2(8), 1888, p. 73.
18 NSPCC, *Annual report 1908*, p. 14.
19 NSPCC, *Annual report 1911–12*, p. 27.
20 NSPCC, *Annual report 1912–13*, p. 20.
21 LSPCC, *Annual report 1885*, p. 13.
22 LSPCC, *Annual report 1887*, p. 9.

23 NSPCC, *Annual report 1889*, p. 57.
24 LSPCC, *Annual report 1885*, p. 6.
25 NSPCC, *East London branch annual report 1891*, p. 5.
26 Foucault, *Introduction* to *The history of sexuality*, p. 27.
27 E. Cohen, *Talk on the Wilde side* (London: Routledge, 1993), pp. 4–5.
28 NSPCC, *Annual report 1908*, p. 14.
29 Steedman, *Strange dislocations*, p. 9.
30 Walkowitz, *City of dreadful delight*.
31 B. Waugh and H. Edward, 'Child of the English savage', *Contemporary Review* 49, May 1886, pp. 687–700.
32 *Child's Guardian* 8(5), 1894, p. 65.
33 *Child's Guardian* 8(2), 1891, p. 13.
34 NSPCC, *Annual report 1908*, p. 14.
35 Behlmer, *Child abuse*, p. 176. See also Hendrick, *Child welfare*, p. 58.
36 NSPCC, *Blackheath branch annual report 1904*, p. 12.
37 R. J. Parr 'Assaults on and corruption of children', 1910, reprinted in *Child's Guardian* 25(1), 1911, p. 5.
38 NSPCC, *Annual report 1894*, p. 33.
39 NSPCC, *Annual report 1885*, p. 6.
40 NSPCC, *East London branch annual report 1891*, p. 5.
41 Hacking, 'The making and molding of child abuse'.
42 *Child's Guardian* 7(10), 1893, p. 134.
43 See S. Mitchell, 'Girls' culture: at work', in *The Girls' Own: cultural histories of the Anglo-American girl 1830–1915*, C. Nelson and L. Vallone (eds) (Athens: University of Georgia Press, 1994), pp. 243–58, see p. 243. Although by the late nineteenth century the term 'girl' was applied to single females over the age of 11 of all social classes, it also had specific connotations with regard to prostitution; prostitutes of all ages, even those who were mothers were referred to as 'girls'. Working-class females who turned to prostitution often described themselves as 'unfortunate girls'.
44 Very few NSPCC case records now exist for the late nineteenth century. Although Ferguson, 'Protecting children in time', was able to use records for the Stockton and Thornaby branches, those for London and the West Riding have not survived. The role of the NSPCC solicitor has been reconstructed in this chapter using newspaper reports of court cases, Old Bailey indictments (that list the name and address of the prosecuting lawyer on the back) and the *Law Lists*.
45 NSPCC, *Inspector's directory*, p. 47.
46 Reported in *Child's Guardian* 9(2), 1895, p. 14.
47 NSPCC, *Annual report 1912–13*, pp. 19–20.
48 Associate Institute for Improving the Laws for the Protection of Women, *First report* (London: 1846), gives details about its foundation.
49 *South London Press*, 15 May 1880, p. 6, prosecution of a man accused of stabbing his wife. *South London Press*, 17 July 1880, p. 6, case involving an 11-year-old girl accused of stealing a purse.
50 *The Times*, 11 September 1884, letter of A.A. O'Neill, Secretary of the Society for the Protection of Women and Children, cutting held in NSPCC Archive, London.
51 Minutes of Evidence of the Royal Commission on the Administration and Operation of the Contagious Diseases Acts: PP 1871, XIX.1, Q.19,608, evidence of William Shaen.
52 M. Shaen, *William Shaen: a brief sketch* (Longmans: London, 1912).

53 PP 1871, XIX.1, Q. 19,548, evidence of William Shaen. Shaen had also been engaged at the grass-roots level, defending women brought up in court under the Contagious Diseases Acts. Josephine Butler was reputed to have written after his death that: 'He was a true friend of woman, far-seeing, clear-headed and just; he had great legal knowledge, and with the most chivalrous feeling towards women (proved by his whole life's labours for them and for children) he combined strong love of liberty and a keen sense of the dangers which are threatening constitutional liberty and individual liberty in these days on many sides.' This quotation is cited in Shaen, *William Shaen*, p. 24, without further reference.

54 PP 1871, XIX.1, Q. 19,548, evidence of William Shaen.

55 See, for example, *Illustrated Police News*, 24 September 1870, p. 3.

56 Booth, *Streets and population classified*, vol. 2 of *Poverty*, p. 82.

57 *The Times*, 25 February 1865, p. 9 and 4 March 1865, p. 12.

58 PP 1871, XIX.1, Q. 19,547, evidence of William Shaen, referred to the 'Association for Enforcing and Improving the Laws for the Protection of Women'. Shaen, *William Shaen*, referred to the 'Society for the Protection of Women and Children'. Newspaper reports of court cases tended to refer to the 'Associate Institute for the Protection of Women and Children' but there was some variation. Continuity of personnel, in particular the dominance of solicitor William Shaen, indicates that they are all the same organisation.

59 *Child's Guardian* 3(4), 1889, p. 65.

60 Society for the Protection of Women and Children, *Annual report 1891*, quoted in the *Child's Guardian* 5(6), 1891, p. 59.

61 Behlmer, *Child abuse*, p. 59, refers to the 'Society for the Protection of Women and Children'.

62 Report of the Committee on the Employment of Women in Police Duties, PP 1920, XXII.1,087, Q. 2,503, evidence of William Clarke Hall: 'I have had a great deal to do with indecent assaults on children, because I was counsel for 25 years to the Society for the Prevention of Cruelty to Children, who used to prosecute in all those cases in London.'

63 NSPCC Archive, 29/2/1, contains Moreton Phillips' own personal copy of the 1904 *Inspector's directory*, which is both signed by him at the front and subsequently annotated. Suggestions for changes in the wording of the directory are marked, some of which seem to have been effected in the next edition of the *Inspector's directory*, published in 1910.

64 *South London Press*, 15 July 1905, p. 2 & 26 August 1905, p. 5.

65 *South London Press*, 26 August 1905, p. 5.

66 *Child's Guardian* 9(2), 1895 p. 14.

67 *Child's Guardian* 11(10), 1897, p. 126.

68 Ibid.

69 Fawcett Library, London, NVA Executive Committee Minutes, Box 194, 22 June 1886, p. 14 and 5 July 1887, p. 201.

70 NVA, Box 194, 7 August 1888, p. 332.

71 *Sentinel*, 1885, p. 475.

72 NVA, Box 194, 28 October 1901 p. 148 & 27 June 1905, p. 64.

73 See NSPCC, *Kensington branch annual report 1889*, p. 7. Behlmer, *Child abuse*, p. 173, has argued that 'though NSPCC inspectors were also imposed on communities, they were much more likely to be regarded as allies in the struggle of the poor to maintain neighborhood respectability'.

74 Parr, 'Assaults on and corruption of children', p. 3.

75 NSPCC, *Annual report 1890*, pp. 29–30.

76 Annual reports of the Bradford, Leeds, Wakefield, Craven, Keighley, Dewsbury and Halifax branches are available for consultation at the NSPCC Archive.

77 NSPCC, *Annual report 1890*, pp. 29–30; *East London branch annual report 1890*, p. 4.

78 NSPCC notices were pinned up in all London police stations and, in 1889, Chief Commissioner James Munro instructed all metropolitan police constables to inform the society of all cases of child cruelty coming to their attention: A. Morton, *Early days* (London: Thomas Knight, 1956), p. 19.

79 Report of the Departmental Committee on Sexual Offences Against Young Persons: PP 1924–5, XV.905.

80 Ibid., S. 111.

81 Ibid.

82 *Child's Guardian* 7(3), 1893, p. 36.

83 Behlmer, *Child abuse*, p. 175.

84 1866 Industrial Schools Amendment Act, 29 & 30 Vict., C. 118.

85 1880 Industrial Schools Amendment Act, 43 & 44 Vict., C. 15.

86 1885 Criminal Law Amendment Act, 48 & 49 Vict., C. 69.

87 1891 Custody of Children Act, 54 Vict., C. 3. See J. Heywood, *Children in care: the development of the service for the deprived child* (London: Routledge & Kegan Paul, 1959), p. 63 for a discussion of this legislation.

88 Children's Society Archives, London, Case Files. For this study all case files for the years 1885, 1890, 1895, 1900 and 1905 identified as referrals on 'moral' grounds (using the Case File Summary Books) were examined, producing a sample of fifty-six cases. A further fifty-one case files involving girls sent to the specialist homes at Leytonstone and The Mumbles were also examined to produce a total sample of 107 Waifs and Strays cases. Cases have been renumbered and names changed to preserve anonymity; they are referred to by the prefix 'CS'. A full schedule of cases sampled can be obtained from the author or from Ian Wakeling, the Archivist, the Children's Society. See M. Cale, ' "Saved from a life of vice and crime": reformatory and industrial schools for girls c.1854–c.1901' (Ph.D. thesis, University of Oxford, 1993) and Cox, 'Rescue and reform', for more detailed studies of the work of the industrial schools run by the Waifs and Strays Society.

89 The case records of the Nest are located at the Salvation Army Archive, London, Children's History Books VI & VII. The case records of all girls referred to the Nest 1902–14 were examined. They are referred to by the prefix 'SA', followed by the case reference number given in the Children's History Books.

90 The term 'lady philanthropists' is used to denote middle-class women of a certain rank and authority within their local communities, who used their influence to carry out welfare work in the district. Lady philanthropists who sent girls to the Nest included Mrs Barrow Cadbury of Birmingham (SA, Children's History Book VI, no. 176) and Miss Wickham, daughter of the Dean of Lincoln (SA, Children's History Book VI, no. 158). For an analysis of the involvement of women in welfare work see F. Prochaska, *Women and philanthropy in nineteenth-century England* (Oxford: Clarendon Press, 1980).

91 SA, Children's History Book VI, no. 204.

92 Ibid.

93 CS, no. 32, Edith H.

94 Ibid.

95 NSPCC, *Inspector's directory* (1904), p. 44.

96 NSPCC, *Inspector's directory* (1910), p. 71.

97 SA, Children's History Book VI, no. 121

98 Ibid.
99 SA, Children's History Book VI, no. 158.
100 Ibid.
101 SA, Children's History Book VI, no. 98.
102 Ibid.
103 CS, no. 25, Alice S.
104 Ibid. Cale, 'Girls and the perception of sexual danger'.
105 Many thanks to NSPCC archivist Nicholas Malton for suggesting these points. The 1908 Punishment of Incest Act in fact removed cases from both church and NSPCC hands, stipulating that all allegations of incest should be handled by the Director of Public Prosecutions.
106 PP 1924–5, XV.905, S. 111 (original emphasis).

4 Signs on the body: the medical profession

1 C. West, *Lectures on the disease of infancy and childhood*, 2nd edn (London: Longman, 1852), pp. 2–3.
2 Ibid., p. 2.
3 Steedman, *Strange dislocations*, p. 63–76, shows that the notion of a semiology of the infant body was apparent in the popular child care manuals produced for parents in the early nineteenth century.
4 T. R. Forbes, *Surgeons at the Bailey. English forensic medicine to 1878* (New Haven: Yale University Press, 1985) provides an overview of the history of medical evidence.
5 B. Campbell, *Unofficial secrets: child sexual abuse: the Cleveland case* (London: Virago, 1988).
6 A. S. Taylor, *Elements of medical jurisprudence*, 11th edn (London: J. & A. Churchill, 1886) cited articles on pederasty published by Tardieu and Toulmouche in the French journal *Annales d'Hygiene* during the 1850s and 1860s. Discussions of pederasty and sodomy began to figure in English works from the mid 1880s onwards, reflecting the outlawing of gross indecency in 1885 and the attempt by sexologists (such as Havelock Ellis) to categorise perversions. These discussions, however, ignored the crucial matters of age, consent and responsibility – issues of autonomy and control – which underpinned legal interpretations of the rape and abuse of girls. In a few rare cases doctors gave forensic evidence at the Middlesex and West Riding Sessions in cases of attempted sodomy on boys; in these cases anal dilation was seen as a crucial sign. See for example WYAS, QS1/229/5, case of JWG, October 1890.
7 E. Smith, *A practical treatise on disease in children* (London: J. & A. Churchill, 1884). J. F. Goodhart and G. F. Still, *The diseases of children*, 8th edn (London: J & A Churchill, 1905). E. Henoch, *Lectures on children's diseases: a handbook for practitioners and students*, 2 vols translated from the 4th edn by J. Thompson MB (London: New Sydenham Society, 1889). L. E. Holt, *The diseases of infancy and childhood for the use of students and practitioners of medicine* (New York: D. Appleton, 1897); J. M. Keating and W. A. Edwards (eds), *Encyclopaedia of the diseases of children*, 5 vols (London: Young J. Pentland & Thomas Lewin, 1891–1901). Comprising articles written by a combination of American, Canadian and British authors, the *Encyclopaedia* was described in the *Lancet*, 5 October 1901, p. 918, as 'the standard work on paediatrics'.
8 *Lancet*, 4 January 1890, p. 24.
9 C. Blake, *The charge of the parasols: women's entry to the medical profession* (London: Women's Press, 1990).
10 See, for example, LMA, MJ/SPE/1885/3 no. 39 & MJ/SPE/1865/15 no. 18.

11 Contemporary Medical Archives Centre, Wellcome Institute for the History of Medicine, London. Medical Women's Federation, SA/MWF/C.64, 'Women in police courts', letter from Dr Marion Elford to Dr Haslam 6 November 1913. By courtesy of the Wellcome Trustees.

12 N. H. Wells, 'Medical women and the police force', *Medical Press and Circular* 22, October 1941, pp. 317–19.

13 Medical Women's Federation, SA/MWF/D.15, 'Police court and women police surgeons'. See also Jackson, 'Women professionals and the regulation of violence'.

14 Cited in Taylor, *Medical jurisprudence* (1844), p. 575.

15 F. Carrington and J. Payne, vol. 5 of *Reports of cases argued and ruled at nisi prius in the courts of king's bench, common pleas and exchequer 1823–41* (London: Sweet, 1824–42), p. 321.

16 Taylor, *Medical jurisprudence*, 3rd edn (1849), p. 635.

17 Keating and Edwards, vol. 5, part 2 of *Encyclopaedia* (1899), p. 892. This western analysis served to construct the Hindu male as savage and brutish; see H. Bannerjee, 'Age of consent and hegemonic social reform', in *Gender and imperialism*, C. Midgley (ed.) (Manchester: Manchester University Press, 1998), pp. 21–44.

18 Dr Adams, letter to the *Lancet*, 25 March 1843, p. 933.

19 Ibid.

20 Taylor, *Medical jurisprudence* (1844), p. 576.

21 Taylor, *Medical jurisprudence*, 4th edn (1852), p. 578. The cases of Regina v. Jordon (1839) in Carrington and Payne, vol. 9 of *Reports*, p. 118 and Regina v. Lines (1844) in F. A. Carrington and A. V. Kirwaun, vol. 1 of *Reports of cases argued and ruled at nisi prius in the courts of queen's bench, common pleas and exchequer 1843–53* (London: Sweet, 1845–55), p. 393, were seen as decisive steps in the establishment of this legal precedent.

22 4 & 5 Vict. C. 56.

23 Taylor, *Medical jurisprudence* (1886), p. 689–90.

24 J. Y. Simpson, 'Clinical lectures on the disease of women', *Medical Times and Gazette*, 16 April 1859, p. 384.

25 See K. Taylor, 'Venereal diseases in nineteenth-century children', *Journal of Psychohistory* 12(4), 1985, pp. 431–64, see p. 432.

26 Keating and Edwards, vol. 5, part 2 of *Encyclopaedia*, p. 893.

27 Taylor, *Medical jurisprudence*, revised by F. J. Smith (1910), p. 126. Despite this acknowledgement, however, the text continued to talk of the 'ignorance' of parents and to interpret vaginal infections as a result of catarrh and leucorrhoea.

28 M. Ryan, *A manual of medical jurisprudence compiled from the best medical and legal works* (London: Sherwood, Gilbert & Piper, 1831), p. 188. Ryan attributed this passage to the printed lectures of surgeon Sir Astley Cooper.

29 Simpson, 'Clinical lectures', p. 384.

30 Smith, *A practical treatise on disease in children*, p. 776.

31 Taylor, 'Venereal diseases'. Given that Taylor does not consider either the paediatric discussion of genito-urinary diseases or the medical-legal exegesis of child rape, her conclusion that 'nineteenth-century doctors were not … prepared to discover that children acquired sexually transmitted diseases through sexual contact' (p. 439) needs to be qualified. Doctors acknowledged its possibility but preferred to describe it as rare rather than widespread.

32 See Smith, *A practical treatise on disease in children*, p. 203 and Holt, *Diseases of infancy*, pp. 105–3.

33 W. R. Wilde, *Medico-legal observations upon infantile leucorrhoea* (1853), pamphlet cited by W. B. Kesteven, 'On the evidence of rape on infants, with remarks on the case of Amos Greenwood', *Medical Times and Gazette* 18, 1859, pp. 361–3.

34 Wilde's comments on the Amos Greenwood cases were first published in *Dublin Quarterly Journal of Medical Science*, February 1858, cited in Taylor, *Medical jurisprudence*, 7th edn (1865), p. 995.

35 Kesteven, 'On the evidence of rape', p. 363. W. R. Wilde responded in 'Observations on Mr Kesteven's remarks on the evidence of rape on infants', *Medical Times and Gazette* 18, 1859, pp. 518–20, 544–6.

36 Taylor, *Medical jurisprudence* (1844), p. 574; (1886), p. 688.

37 Taylor, *Medical jurisprudence* (1886), p. 696.

38 Ibid.

39 Henoch, vol. 2 of *Lectures*, p. 184: 'I advise you not to be too ready to assume that there has been an assault, for it pretty often happens that the mothers who declare that there has been such a thing, are either themselves deceived, or are trying to impose on the physician in order to get from him a certificate which they may use for ulterior ends.' Henoch, as director of the department of children's diseases in the Royal Charité Hospital, Berlin, was obviously referring to the Prussian system of divorce. In England, deeds of separation could be passed by magistrates and adultery with incest was deemed grounds for divorce through the 1857 Matrimonial Causes Act. See also H. Aubrey Husband, *The student's handbook of forensic medicine and medical police* (London: E. & S. Livingstone, 1883), p. 116, for a discussion of the forging of signs of sexual abuse.

40 Taylor, *Medical jurisprudence* (1886), p. 692.

41 J. Brown, letter to the editor *Medical Times and Gazette* 18, 1859, p. 638.

42 R. Summers, 'History of the police surgeon', *Police Surgeon* 14, 1978, pp. 46–58. Police surgeons were paid separately for each case they were called to attend (p. 49).

43 Doctors' evidence is recorded in 89 of the 315 Middlesex and West Riding Quarter Sessions depositions transcribed in the sample. It seems that a medical witness was deemed unnecessary in the majority of quarter sessions cases. This situation was not replicated in the higher courts – assizes and Old Bailey – where the names of doctors were always given in the witness lists on the back of the indictments. The reason for this anomaly must lie in the different sort of charges which were tried at the two types of court. Cases of rape and unlawful carnal knowledge, which by definition required medical proof relating to the degree of penetration, were only triable at the assize level. Charges of indecent assault, tried at the quarter sessions, were applied to a wide range of forms of assault, from simple touching or stroking which left no visible mark on the body, to near penetration, which could result in severe physical injuries. Conviction, in relation to cases involving inappropriate touching, was dependent on the presence of other adult witnesses to the act instead of medical testimony.

44 See for example LMA, MJ/SPE/1865/15, no. 63, MJ/SPE/1870/02, no. 29 and MJ/SPE/1885/39, no. 21.

45 During the 1830s and 40s doctors in court identified rupture of the hymen as the sole indicator of rape; see WYAS, QS1/179/4, case of SP, April 1840. Marks of violence such as swelling and redness were seen as signs of indecent assault or assault with intent; see QS1/169/7, case of BS, July 1830.

46 LMA, MJ/SPE/1870/19, no. 52.

47 WYAS, QS1/204/08, case of JM. See also QS1/204/03, case of MW, February 1865.

48 WYAS, QS1/234/02, case of VM.

49 LMA, MJ/SPE/1870/15, no. 15.

50 LMA, MJ/SPE/1880/18, no. 3. The jury decided to convict and sentenced the man to four months' imprisonment.

51 PRO, CRIM 1/60/02. Samples of clothing were sent to the chemistry departments of the big London hospitals to establish the specific nature of stains; see e.g. LMA, MJ/SPE/,1870/08, no. 69 & MJ/SPE/1880/30, no. 30. Until the discovery of the gonoccocus, however, biochemistry was limited in the contribution it could make to forensic discussions.

52 LMA, MJ/SPE/1865/05, no. 42.

53 PRO, CRIM 1/8/2.

54 Ibid.

55 Ibid.

56 LMA, MJ/SPE/1870/20, no. 30.

57 *East London Observer*, 1 October 1870, p. 3.

58 LMA, MJ/SPE/1870/21, no. 53.

59 *Eastern Post*, 11 June 1870, p. 7. See also *The Times*, 23 June 1845, p. 8 and *The Times*, 6 November 1865, p. 11 for indecent assault cases involving doctors.

60 *Illustrated Police News*, 29 November 1890, p. 3.

61 *Illustrated Police News*, 6 December 1890, p. 3.

62 E. Moberly Bell, *Storming the citadel. The rise of the woman doctor* (London: Constable, 1953), p. 76. Thanks to Lesley Hall for this analogy.

63 J. Walker, 'Reports, with comments, of twenty-one cases of indecent assault and rape upon children', *Archives of Pediatrics* 3, 1886, pp. 269–86 & 321–41.

64 L. Tait, 'An analysis of the evidence in seventy consecutive cases of charges made under the new Criminal Law amendment Act', *Provincial Medical Journal*, 1 May 1894, pp. 226–33.

65 J. A. Shepherd, *Lawson Tait: the rebellious surgeon 1845–1897* (Kansas: Colorado Press, 1980). Tait was elected president of the British Gynaecological Society in 1885 but was noted for making enemies in high places. Shepherd (p. 214) comments that 'Analysis' was not well received because Tait's disclosures were 'thought to be rather sordid'.

66 Tait, 'Analysis', p. 228.

67 See K. Thomas, 'The double standard', *Journal of the History of Ideas* 20, 1959, pp. 195–216.

68 Tait, 'Analysis', p. 226.

69 Ibid., p. 227.

70 See Clark, *Women's silence* and Walkowitz, *City of dreadful delight*.

71 Tait, 'Analysis', p. 226.

72 Ibid., p. 231. Tait's obsession with women and girls seducing or blackmailing men may have resulted, as Shepherd has indicated, from an incident in c. 1887, when a nurse threatened to take action against him for alleged seduction and for fathering an illegitimate child. See Shepherd, *Lawson Tait*, p. 177 for the details of this case and p. 157 for his work in defence of other doctors charged with criminal assault.

73 Tait, 'Analysis', p. 231.

74 Ibid.

75 Ibid.

76 Ibid., p. 229.

77 Walker, 'Comments and reports', p. 274.

78 Ibid., p. 283.

79 Ibid., p. 329.

80 Ibid., p. 331.

81 Taylor, *Medical jurisprudence* (1873), p. 473.
82 See Casper, *Handbook*, vol. 3, p. 339.
83 Ryan, *Medical jurisprudence*, p. 191.
84 W. Acton, *The functions and disorders of the reproductive organs in youth, in adult age and in advanced life* (London: J. A. Churchill, 1856), p. 1.
85 Contradictions are obvious in any attempt to represent the child as 'naturally' clean or pure. As Anne Murcott has pointed out, the infant, because of its helplessness and social training in the first years of its life, has to be kept clean by its carers otherwise it could become infinitely dirty and polluting. Eating and excretory processes have to be managed and controlled. See A. Murcott, 'Purity and pollution: body management and the social place of infancy', in *The body: social process and cultural theory*, M. Featherstone, M. Hepworth and B. S. Turner (eds) (London: Sage, 1990), pp. 122–34, see p. 129.
86 Foucault, *Introduction* to *The history of sexuality*, p. 29.
87 See Walkowitz, *Prostitution and Victorian society*.
88 S. Shuttleworth, 'Female circulation: medical discourse and popular advertising in the mid-Victorian era' in *Body politics: women and the discourses of science*, M. Jacobus, E. F. Keller and S. Shuttleworth (eds) (New York: Routledge, 1990), pp. 47–68, see p. 47.
89 Ibid., p. 56.
90 Mort, *Dangerous sexualities*. See also P. Stallybrass and A. White, *The politics and poetics of transgression* (London: Methuen, 1986).
91 E. Wilson, *The sphinx in the city* (Berkeley: University of California Press, 1991), p. 37.
92 Tait, 'Analysis', p. 227.
93 Walker, 'Reports and comments', p. 329.
94 Wilson, *Sphinx in the city*, p. 39.
95 Walker, 'Reports and comments', p. 274.
96 Ibid., p. 331.
97 Douglas, *Purity and danger*, p. 121.
98 Walker, 'Reports and comments', p. 332.
99 Report on the International Congress of Forensic Medicine in Paris, in *British Medical Journal*, 1889, p. 451.
100 Ibid.

5 'Witnesses of truth?' Children in the courtroom

1 *South London Press*, 19 August 1905, p. 3. The grand jury met before each quarter sessions (or assize) to examine the depositions (witness statements) against each defendant and to consider whether there was a case to answer. They either agreed to the bill of indictment, allowing the trial to proceed or ignored it, dismissing the case.
2 See chapter 1.
3 Conley, 'Rape and justice'. See also Conley, *The unwritten law*.
4 Court depositions that record the parental occupation/employment circumstances of child victims can be used to provide a rough indication of social class. Conviction rates for trial on indictment rose from 50 per cent in cases involving the children of unskilled labourers, to 66 per cent where parents were semi-skilled, to 69 per cent where parents were skilled, and to 76 per cent amongst the lower middle-classes. Thus the higher the social class of the victim, the more likely it was that the defendant would be found guilty. Occupations have been assigned class categories using the Registrar General's Decennial Census Supplement of 1921, which is discussed fully in W. A.

Armstrong, 'The use of information about occupation', in *Nineteenth century society: essays in the use of quantitative methods for the study of social data*, E. A. Wrigley (ed.) (London: Cambridge University Press, 1972), pp. 203–23. For a selection of critical essays that analyse problems connected with the use of occupation as an indicator of social class, see Bush, *Social orders and social classes*. Most cases were brought by parents and children from the skilled labour category who perhaps felt most at ease in the courts (skilled labour made up 46 per cent of cases where parental occupation is known). Only 17 per cent of cases involved parents of the lower middle classes (shopkeepers, publicans, etc.) who almost invariably used the law to prosecute defendants of a lower social class, often employees; 83 per cent of defendants who can be identified as employees were found guilty. In circumstances where the child victim was employed by the defendant, on the other hand, only 54 per cent of cases tried ended in conviction. No cases were tried which involved the children of top professionals. If incest occurred among the middle classes, it was extremely unlikely to end up in court.

5 In 84 per cent of cases involving girl victims aged 2–8, convictions were obtained following trial on indictment. This figure fell to 75 per cent in cases involving girl victims aged 9–12 and to 58 per cent where girls were aged 13–15. Where female victims were aged 15 (over the age of consent for most of the century) a low conviction rate of 49 per cent was obtained.

6 Convictions were recorded in all of the nineteen cases tried by jury that involved boy victims under 12.

7 LMA, MJ/SPE/1865/11, no. 70.

8 For a fascinating and innovative discussion of court documents as genre see N. Zemon Davis, *Fiction in the archives: pardon tales and their tellers in sixteenth-century France* (Oxford: Polity, 1987).

9 LMA, MJ/SPE/1865/11, no. 70.

10 Blackstone, vol. 4 of *Commentaries*, p. 214.

11 Ibid. This point was also stressed by the Criminal Law Amendment Act of 1885, clause 4, which awarded children the statutory right to give evidence without being officially sworn: 'The evidence of such girl or other child of tender years may be received though not given upon oath, if, in the opinion of the court or justices [she] ... is possessed of sufficient intelligence to justify the reception of the evidence, and understands the duty of speaking the truth.'

12 LMA, MJ/SPE/1880/01, no. 40.

13 T. R. and J. B. Beck, *Elements of medical jurisprudence*, 7th edition (London: Longman, 1842), p. 97.

14 For a detailed examination of the NSPCC's campaign to abolish the oath for young children, see Behlmer, *Child abuse*, pp. 73–7.

15 *Weekly Dispatch*, 28 June 1835, p. 236.

16 Casper, vol. 3 of *Handbook*, p. 289. While the issue of false accusation was constantly discussed, it was generally evidenced in terms of hearsay. Psychological research was taking place on the continent from 1900 as to the reliability of adult and children's testimony, but these studies of the scientific bases of suggestibility were not translated into English and there was no comparative body of research in Britain. See S. Ceci and M. Bruck, 'Suggestibility of the child witness: a historical review and synthesis', *Psychological Bulletin* 113, 1993, pp. 403–39, for an extremely useful account.

17 *The Times*, 14 December 1890, p. 11.

18 LMA, MJ/SPE/7 May 1910, no. 24.

19 WYAS, QS1/204/15, case of WS; QS1/224/7, case of AB;QS1/204/7, case of ML; QS1/229/5, case of LS.

20 For example WYAS, QS1/204/12, case of JB (1865) and QS1/224/6, case of FM (1885); QS1/184/6, case of WC (1845) and LMA, MJ/SPE/1855/27, no. 28 (1855); QS1/224/3, case of HM.

21 LMA, MJ/SPE/1865/16, no. 42.

22 *The Times*, 25 October 1860, p. 9.

23 LMA, MJ/SPE/1860/07, no. 59.

24 Jenks, *Childhood*; Steedman, *Strange dislocations*; Cunningham, *Children and childhood*.

25 Coveney, *The image of childhood*; Cunningham, *Children and childhood*.

26 For the emergence of delinquency as a social problem see King and Noel, 'The origins of "the problem of juvenile delinquency"'; King, 'The rise of juvenile delinquency in England'; Shore, *Artful dodgers*. For the growth of the reformatory system see M. May, 'Innocence and experience: the evolution of the concept of juvenile delinquency in the mid nineteenth century', *Victorian Studies* 17(1), 1973, pp. 7–29.

27 For the development of the idea of 'adolescence' from the 1880s onwards see J. Neubauer, *The fin-de-siècle culture of adolescence* (New Haven: Yale University Press, 1992).

28 The concept of the working-class child as scholar, which replaced the notion of the working-class child as labourer, only properly emerged from 1870 onwards with the introduction of compulsory education. See Hendrick, *Child welfare*, p. 29. There were, however, ways of flouting the school attendance officer. E. F. Hogg, 'School children as wage-earners', *Nineteenth Century* 42, 1897, pp. 235–44, pointed to patterns of absence (higher in girls than boys) as a result of paid work or baby-minding.

29 J. H. Gillis, 'The evolution of delinquency in England 1890–1914', *Past and Present* 67, 1975, pp. 96–126; H. Hendrick, *Images of youth. Age, class and the male youth problem, 1880–1920* (Oxford: Clarendon Press, 1990); S. Humphries, *Hooligans or rebels? An oral history of working-class childhood and youth 1889–1939* (Oxford: Blackwell, 1981).

30 Cale, 'Girls and the perception of sexual danger'; Cox, 'Rescue and reform'.

31 Mahood and Littlewood, 'The "vicious girl" and the "street-corner boy"'.

32 LMA, MJ/SPE/1865/11, no. 70.

33 See chapter 1 for a discussion of age-of-consent legislation.

34 PRO, HO17/70, Mv 19.

35 Ibid.

36 Ibid.

37 Ibid.

38 *The Times*, 6 May 1850, p. 7.

39 *The Times*, 31 October 1855, p. 9.

40 Mahood and Littlewood, 'The "vicious girl" and the "street-corner boy"', pp. 564–70.

41 LMA, MJ/SPE/1860/07, no. 9; *Yorkshire Post*, 24 March 1890, p. 6.

42 *The Times*, 4 December 1850, p. 7 & 23 November 1850, p. 7.

43 WYAS, QS1/204/7, case of ML.

44 WYAS, QS1/224/3, case of HM.

45 *West London Observer*, 16 February 1895, p. 2.

46 *Illustrated Police News*, 11 June 1910, p. 6.

47 PRO, HO17/70, Mv 19. My italics.

48 *The Times*, 28 September 1830, p. 4.

49 *Child's Guardian* 27(9), 1913, p. 104. The society's journal, campaigning for sex abuse cases to be heard *in camera*, received a disturbing letter from a doctor who had attended a police court to give medical evidence in a case of criminal

assault on an 11-year-old girl: 'This unfortunate child was made to stand upon a chair, before a full bench of magistrates ... and in full view of a number of people in the court, also the Press, the witnesses in this and two other cases, and give *full* details of everything that happened to her. The sight was very painful to me, and I was disgusted. ... Certainly women were asked to retire, but I can see no reason why a number of dirty old men should be allowed to remain in court and gloat over the details.' The Society also campaigned, at the same time, for the presence of women, in court, to accompany the child and offer her support and sympathy in the giving of evidence.

50 M. Poovey, *The proper lady and the woman writer. Ideology as style in the works of Mary Wollstonecraft, Mary Shelley and Jane Austen* (Chicago: University of Chicago Press, 1984), pp. 3–47.
51 Ibid., p. 26.
52 Ibid.
53 Ibid.
54 R. J. McMullen, *Male rape: breaking the silence on the last taboo* (London: GMP Publishers, 1990).
55 PRO, HO18/35, petition 15. The file contains a transcript of court testimonies.
56 Ibid.
57 This summary of developments is informed by Tim Hitchcock's extremely useful overview of eighteenth-century attitudes to homosexuality in *English sexualities*, pp. 58–75. See also A. D. Harvey, 'Prosecutions for sodomy in England at the beginning of the nineteenth century', *Historical Journal* 21(4), 1978, pp. 939–48 and R. Trumbach, 'Sex, gender and sexual identity in modern culture: male sodomy and female prostitution in Enlightenment London', *Journal of the History of Sexuality* 2, 1991, pp. 186–203.
58 *The Times*, 21 May 1830, p. 4, 'The Hyde Park cases'.
59 In 1830, twenty-five cases of 'unnatural practices' or 'assault with unnatural intent' on males were tried at the Old Bailey, compared to fifteen cases of rape or sexual assault on females. At the Middlesex Quarter Sessions in 1840, twenty cases of 'buggery', 'unnatural crime', or its attempt were tried compared to twenty-two cases of sexual assault on females. During the 1850s, 60s, 70s and 80s, prosecutions for sexual assault on adult males then dropped off in the London courts. The pattern of trials for buggery and related offences was not reflected in Yorkshire, where the profile for the 1830s and 40s was overwhelmingly assault by males on females (and continued to be so). It is unclear whether this is because of the lack of an active and visible 'homosexual' sub-culture in Yorkshire or because policing strategies did not develop in the same way as London; the answer probably lies in a combination of both factors.
60 Hitchcock, *English sexualities*, p. 2, pp. 60–72. Hitchcock's work, which draws on the thesis study of Anthony Simpson, provides a useful corrective to the emphasis which nineteenth-century historians have placed on the criminalisation of homosexuality in the 1890s.
61 J. Weeks, 'The construction of homosexuality', in *Sex, politics and society* (Harlow: Longman, 1989), pp. 96–121. The term 'homosexual' did not appear until the end of the nineteenth century.
62 F. B. Smith, 'Labouchère's amendment to the Criminal Law Amendment Bill', *Historical Studies* 67 (1976), pp. 165–75.
63 Cohen, *Talk on the Wilde side*; E. K. Sedgwick, *Epistemology of the closet* (Hemel Hemsptead: Harvester Wheatsheaf, 1991); A. Sinfield, *The Wilde century: effeminacy, Oscar Wilde and the queer movement* (London: Cassell, 1994).

64 Conley, *The unwritten law*, p. 17, has argued that 'the law against sexual assaults on a male person did not specify age' in the period 1859–80. While this is true in terms of statute law, case law indicates there was some notion of age of consent for males which was being consolidated 1840–80.

65 Taylor, *Elements of medical jurisprudence* 2nd edn (1846), p. 561. Simpson, 'Vulnerability and the age of consent', p. 186, has demonstrated that an age of consent of 14 for boys was in place throughout the eighteenth century.

66 Reg. v. Wollaston, Court of Criminal Appeal, 27 April 1872, in vol. 12 (1871–4) of *Reports of cases in criminal law argued and determined in all the courts in England and Ireland*, E. W. Cox (ed.) (London: Horace Cox, 1875), pp. 180–2; Reg. v. Lock, Court of Criminal Appeal, 23 November 1872, in ibid., pp. 244–7. Confusion had arisen over indecent assault because some lawyers and judges argued that, since an assault was by nature an unwanted intrusion, it was not possible to consent but only to resist; if there was no resistance there was no assault.

67 LMA, MJ/SPE/1870/23, no. 30.

68 Ibid.

69 WYAS, QS1/244/4, case of JH

70 Hitchcock, *English sexualities*, p. 60.

71 PRO, HO18/33, petition 15.

72 L. A. Jackson, 'The child's word in court: cases of sexual abuse in London 1870–1914', in *Gender and crime in modern Europe*, M. L. Arnot and C. Usborne (eds) (London: UCL Press, 1999), pp. 222–37.

73 LMA, MJ/SPE/1870/27, no. 44.

74 PRO, HO18/35, petition 15. The sentence of death was commuted to two years' imprisonment with life transportation.

75 Acton's depiction of women as essentially asexual was refuted by a long list of contemporaries. See Weeks, *Sex, politics and society*, pp. 40–1 and R. Porter and L. Hall, *The facts of life: the creation of sexual knowledge in Britain, 1650–1950* (New Haven, Connecticut: Yale University Press, 1995).

76 *The Times*, 13 September 1860, p. 11.

77 *Leeds Mercury*, 3 April 1865, p. 4.

78 Ibid. Despite the judge's stern response, the priest was sentenced to twelve months' imprisonment.

79 Both indecency and indecent assault charges were pursued in the following cases: PRO, Central Criminal Court Sessions Rolls, CRIM 4/997, indictment no. 150, tried October 1885; CRIM 4/1054, indictment no. 28, tried March 1890; CRIM 4/1053, indictment no. 52, tried February 1890. (There are many other examples.)

80 Minutes of Evidence of the Select Committee of the House of Lords on the Protection of Young Girls, PP 1881, IX.355, Q. 650.

81 Ibid., Qs 650 & 654.

82 Ibid., Qs 651–3.

83 J. Weeks, 'Inverts, perverts and Mary-Annes: male prostitution and the regulation of homosexuality in England in the nineteenth and twentieth centuries', in *Up against nature: essays on history, sexuality and identity* (London: Rivers Oram, 1991), pp. 10–45.

84 Ibid.

85 Smith, 'Labouchère's amendment'.

86 *Hansard*, 28 February 1890, col. 1534. Cited in Smith, 'Labouchère's amendment', p. 172.

87 Smith, 'Labouchère's amendment', pp. 172–3.

88 *The Times*, 21 November 1885, p. 2.

6 Masculinity, 'respectability' and the child abuser

1 *Child's Guardian* 27(9), 1907, p. 101.
2 Booth, *Life and labour*.
3 S. Smiles, *Self-help: with illustrations of conduct and perseverence* (Harmondsworth: Penguin, 1986), p. 203. 1st edn 1859.
4 This figure is based on the study sample of sexual assault cases tried at the Old Bailey, Middlesex Quarter Sessions, County of London Sessions, Yorkshire Assizes and West Riding Quarter Sessions where the victim is known to have been a child.
5 Conley, 'Rape and justice'; see also Conley, *The unwritten law*.
6 L. Zedner, *Women, crime and custody in Victorian England* (Oxford: Clarendon Press, 1991).
7 *Leeds Mercury*, 25 July 1840, p. 6.
8 A. McLaren, *The trials of masculinity. Policing sexual boundaries 1870–1930* (Chicago: University of Chicago Press, 1997) has examined how masculinity was policed through the definition of 'deviant' male types in law and medicine.
9 Four of the fourteen female defendants were charged in relation to adult victims; three for procuring females over 16, and one for indecently assaulting an adult male.
10 These names have been retained in their original form because the case became so famous. For the full story see Plowden, *The case of Eliza Armstrong*.
11 *Illustrated Police News*, 22 January 1910, p. 7.
12 *Child's Guardian* 19(9),1905, p. 103.
13 Zedner, *Women, crime and custody*, p. 56.
14 J. Tosh, 'Authority and nurture in middle-class fatherhood: the case of early and mid-Victorian England', *Gender and History* 8 (1), 1996, pp. 43–64.
15 PRO, CRIM/1/60/02.
16 Men's letters to Marie Stopes during the inter-war period revealed incidents in which they had been molested as children by female servants in the family home. See L. Hall, *Hidden anxieties. Male sexuality 1900–1950* (Cambridge: Polity, 1991), pp. 41–2.
17 A number of reports have drawn attention to the female sexual abuser. See S. Barwick, 'Not only men', *Spectator* 226 (8,499), 1991, pp. 8–10. For an account of the case of Rosemary and Frederick West see G. Burn, *Happy like murderers* (London: Faber & Faber, 1998).
18 E. Welldon, 'Mothers who learn to hate', *Guardian* 23 November 1995, p. 9. The term 'perversion' should be used carefully in any historical context.
19 LMA, MJ/SPE/1880/30 no. 30. In September 1880 two women who found a weeping child by the roadside automatically checked the child's underclothing and, finding it wet, assumed she had been assaulted: 'when the child cried I examined her clothes and saw that her drawers were wet, and wet as the result of sexual intercourse'. The ethics of their actions were not grounds for contestation.
20 Ross, *Love and toil*.
21 L. Davidoff, 'Silence and serendipity in feminist history', paper presented at a meeting of the London Women's History Network, October 1996, has highlighted this point.
22 J. Hearn 'Child abuse and men's violence', in *Taking child abuse seriously*, Violence Against Children Study Group (ed.) (London: Unwin Hyman, 1990), pp. 63–85. Contemporary statistical profiles, for both Britain and the USA, show that between 80 and 95 per cent of defendants accused of sex abuse are male; see Browne, 'Child sexual abuse'. The discrepancy in figures over time

would suggest either that slightly more women are now abusing children or that women were slightly less likely to be reported at the turn of the century.

23 I focus on the 'construction' of male sexuality because I assume that any essentialist notion of an inherent biological basis for rape must be ruled out. See P. R. Sanday, 'Rape and the silencing of the feminine', in *Rape: a historical and social enquiry*, S. Tomaselli and R. Porter (eds) (Oxford: Basil Blackwell, 1986), pp. 84–101.

24 *Pall Mall Gazette*, 8 July 1885. See also Walkowitz, *City of dreadful delight*, for a detailed reading of the *Pall Mall Gazette* articles.

25 H. M. Richardson, 'The outcasts', *Englishwoman*, September 1909, p. 4, quoted in Zedner, *Women, crime and custody*, p. 56. This particular article purported to describe life in the Birmingham slums.

26 Bland, *Banishing the beast*.

27 Clark, *Women's silence*, p. 6.

28 Clark, *Women's silence*, has found that only 33 per cent of rape cases forwarded to the Western Assize circuit between 1770 and 1799 actually resulted in trials; in the period 1800–1829 a more sizeable percentage of 54 per cent of all cases were tried.

29 Zedner, *Women, crime and custody*.

30 M. Girouard, *The return to Camelot. Chivalry and the English gentleman* (New Haven: Yale University Press, 1981); Davidoff and Hall, *Family fortunes*; J. A. Mangan and J. Walvin (eds), *Manliness and morality: middle-class masculinity in Britain and America 1800–1940* (Manchester: Manchester University Press, 1987); M. Roper and J. Tosh (eds) *Manful assertions: masculinity in Britain since 1800*, (London: Routledge, 1991); J. Tosh 'What should historians do with masculinity? Reflections on nineteenth-century Britain', *History Workshop Journal* 38, 1994, pp. 179–202, see p. 191.

31 Mangan and Walvin, *Manliness and morality*, p. 1, describe this in terms of change from 'a concern with a successful transition from Christian immaturity to maturity' in the early Victorian period to an emphasis on 'neo-Spartan virility' in the late Victorian period.

32 Tosh, 'What should historians do with masculinity?'.

33 Clark, 'The politics of seduction'.

34 For example, an article 'The overcrowded poor – A frightful depravity', in *Lloyd's Weekly Newspaper*, 6 January 1861, described an indecent assault case involving an 11-year-old girl which had recently come before the Guildhall Petty Sessions. The reporter commented: 'an outline of some of the principal facts may serve to show the dreadfully demoralising effects of the indiscriminate huddling together of the sexes among the poorer classes'.

35 Walkowitz, *Prostitution and Victorian society*.

36 J. E. Hopkins, *The White Cross Army. A statement of the Bishop of Durham's movement* (London: Hatchards, 1883), p. 17. Hopkins claimed that the movement attracted meetings of 1,000 to 2,000 men of all classes in Durham and other parts of the country.

37 See G. Dawson, *Soldier heroes. British adventure, empire and the imagining of masculinities* (London: Routledge, 1994), p. 146, for the rise of adventure fiction for boys. R. L. Stevenson's *Treasure Island* had been published in 1883; H. Rider Haggard's *King Solomon's mines* was published on 30 September 1885.

38 *Pall Mall Gazette*, 6 July 1885, p. 2.

39 B. Waugh, *William T. Stead: a life for the people* (London: H. Vickers, 1885), quotes taken from pp. 3–8. W. T. Stead, although examined here as a 'child saver', also features in the sample of defendants as a result of his trial at the

Old Bailey in 1885 for the indecent assault of 13-year-old Eliza Armstrong. See Plowden, *The case of Eliza Armstrong*.

40　*William T. Stead*, p. 7.

41　Mort, *Dangerous sexualities*, p. 132.

42　Tosh, 'What should historians do with masculinity?', p. 182.

43　Walkowitz, *City of dreadful delight*, p. 82.

44　*Leeds Mercury Supplement*, 1 August 1885.

45　V. Bailey, 'In darkest England and the way out: the Salvation Army, social reform and the Labour movement 1885–1910', *International Review of Social History* 29(2), 1984, pp. 133–71. P. Walker, 'Pulling the devil's kingdom down: gender and popular culture in the Salvation Army 1865–1895' (Ph.D. thesis, Rutgers University, 1992), p. 4. By 1883 there were 528 Salvation Army corps in the UK, 1,340 officers, sitting accommodation for nearly half a million people, and a circulation figure of 400,000 for the Army's periodical *War Cry*.

46　P. Walker, ' "I live but not yet I for Christ liveth in me": men and masculinity in the Salvation Army 1865–90', in *Manful assertions*, Roper and Tosh (eds), pp. 92–112.

47　Ross, *Love and toil*, see for example, p. 23.

48　Contemporary doctors suggested that puberty and the onset of menstruation occurred between 13 and 16 for girls during the 1880s. See C. Brown, 'Education and the nervous system', in *The book of health*, M. A. Morris (ed.) (London: 1883), p. 322, quoted in Davin, *Growing up poor*, p. 218 (note).

49　J. Kincaid, *Child-loving. The erotic child and Victorian culture* (London: Routledge, 1992), p. 4.

50　'The child prostitute', in *Pall Mall Gazette*, 8 July 1885, p. 2. Walkowitz, *City of dreadful delight*, p. 85, has drawn attention to the pornographic overtones of the 'Maiden tribute' articles generally.

51　Mavor, 'Dream rushes'.

52　Clark, *Women's silence*.

53　Kincaid, *Child-loving*, p. 225 has suggested that, in the nineteenth century, there was 'not as yet that much interest in child erotica, a form that develops along with the cultural strength of the erotic child and does not reach full flower until this century'. Further research needs to be done to substantiate these claims since erotic images of the child were undoubtedly already in circulation during the 1850s. Mid-nineteenth-century erotic photographs of the nude child are reproduced in G. Ovenden and R. Melville, *Victorian children* (London: Academy Press, 1972). In his *Sexual life of the child* (London: George Allen & Co, 1912, translated by E. Paul), p. 222, Albert Moll made clear links between sexual abuse and the eroticisation of innocence: 'We know that also in the case of the normal sexual inclination of the male, innocence on the part of the female exerts a notable stimulus ... whether ... a result of conventional opinions or ... an inborn mental disposition.' He went on to suggest that it was a psychological factor in the predisposition to paedophilia.

54　Of the sample cases tried at the Middlesex Quarter Sessions, County of London Sessions, Old Bailey, West Riding Quarter Sessions and Yorkshire Assizes, occupations were traced for a total of 696 defendants. Of these, 33 per cent can be identified as unskilled labour, 54 per cent as semi-skilled or skilled, 11 per cent as small-scale employers or lesser professions and only 2 per cent as top professionals or men of property. The majority of defendants were aged between 18 and 40; six cases involved boys of 14 and one involved a boy of 12.

55　Simpson, 'Vulnerability and the age of female consent', p. 193. The 1884 case cited in Hall, *Hidden anxieties*, p. 183, n. 16 (reported in the *Lancet*,

1884, p. 963) was an unusual exception. Medical and legal texts continued to refer to this belief as common (see, for example, Casper, *Handbook*, p. 301) but it is probable that, by the nineteenth century, such comments were less indicative of an actual belief and rather more illustrative of 'urban myths' regarding the folklore of the poor.

56 LMA, MJ/SPE/1870/08, no. 54.
57 LMA, MJ/SPE/1880/18, no. 3.
58 See for example *The Times*, 10 December 1845, p. 8.
59 WYAS, QS1/204/12, case of JB; QS1/244/1, case of WC.
60 *West London Observer*, 16 February 1895, p. 2; *Illustrated Police News*, 11 June 1910, p. 6.
61 *The Times*, 20 August 1855, p. 9; LMA, MJ/SPE/1860/19, no. 2; *The Times*, 19 April 1865, p. 11; MJ/ SPE/1870/14, no. 36; *Illustrated Police News*, 27 March 1875, p. 3; MJ/SPE/1880/36, no. 38; *South London Press*, 19 July 1910, p. 5.
62 *The Times*, 8 June 1870, p. 11.
63 LMA, MJ/SPE/29 November 1890, no. 16.
64 *Hampstead and Highgate Express* 7 April 1888, p. 7.
65 J. Fayrer, *On preservation of health in India* (London: Macmillan, 1894), p. 42. See also M. Harrison, 'Tropical medicine in nineteenth-century India', *British Journal for the History of Science* 25, 1992, pp. 299–318.
66 F. Buettner, 'Conceptualizing British childhoods in nineteenth- and twentieth-century India: scientific and cultural dimensions of colonial upbringing', paper presented at Northern Victorian Studies Colloquium, Leeds, England, 1996. M. Sinha, *Colonial masculinity: the 'manly Englishman' and the 'effeminate Bengali' in the late nineteenth century* (Manchester: Manchester University Press, 1995), pp. 147–9.
67 WYAS, QS1/229/3, case of JG.
68 J. De Groot, ' "Sex" and "race": the construction of language and image in the nineteenth century', in S. Mendus and J. Rendall (eds) *Sexuality and subordination. Interdisciplinary studies of gender in the nineteenth century* (London: Routledge, 1989), pp. 89–130.
69 S. Gilman, *Difference and pathology: stereotypes of sexuality, race and madness* (New York: Cornell University Press, 1985). Sinha, *Colonial masculinity*, pp. 18–19 & 138–72.
70 See Dawson, *Soldier heroes*, for a thought-provoking analysis of the cultural significance of the imperial adventure hero.
71 WYAS, QS1/239/5, case of GWU.
72 *Hampstead and Highgate Express*, 8 September 1888, p. 6.
73 LMA, MJ/SPE/1880/14, no. 49.
74 LMA, MJ/SPE/1880/26, no. 18.
75 *East London Observer*, 29 August 1885, p. 7.
76 Donzelot, *The policing of families*.
77 For changes in law on rape in marriage see *Guardian*, 15 March 1991, p. 6 and 24 October 1991, p. 1. For discussion of incest legislation see Bailey and Blackburn, 'The Punishment of Incest Act 1908'.
78 Hammerton, *Cruelty and companionship*, p. 7; Gordon, *Heroes of their own lives*, p. vi.
79 Hammerton, *Cruelty and companionship*, p. 32, has discussed the 'feelings of guilt over treatment of wives' which emerged in working-class dialect prose of the 1850s and 1860s and which point to an internalised conflict between a newer notion of companionate marriage and an older model of patriarchal marriage.
80 WYAS, QS1/204/12, case of JB. See also WYAS, QS1/224/3, case of HM.

81 WYAS, QS1/244/6, case of WL.

82 WYAS, QS1/224/6, case of FM.

83 WYAS, QS1/244/6, case of WL; QS1/179/10, case of SP; *Leeds Mercury*, 26 July 1845, p. 10; *Leeds Mercury*, 25 July 1840, p. 6.

84 LMA, MJ/SPE/1865/11, no. 70.

85 WYAS, QS1/244/6, case of WL.

86 L. A. Jackson, 'Family, community and the regulation of sexual abuse: London 1870–1914', in *Childhood in question*, A. Fletcher and S. Hussey (eds) (Manchester: Manchester University Press, 1999).

87 *Illustrated Police News*, 22 January 1910, p. 7.

88 Ibid.

89 Ibid.

90 LMA, MJ/SPE/1885/36, no. 63. The barrister's pocket book is enclosed with the depositions.

91 Gatrell, *The hanging tree*, pp. 497–541.

92 D. Duman, *The judicial bench in England 1727–1875. The reshaping of a profes-sional élite*. (London: Royal Historical Society, 1982).

93 See Duman, *The judicial bench*, p. 53, for a full social breakdown. Although in theory the legal profession was now open to talent regardless of social origin, only 7 per cent of judges appointed between 1850 and 1875 came from an artisanal background as compared to 2 per cent between 1727 and 1760.

94 A. Crew, *The Old Bailey: history, constitution, functions, notable trials* (London: Ivor Nicholson & Watson, 1933), pp. 73–4. Kerr sat at the Old Bailey in his capacity as Judge of the Sheriff's Court of the City of London 1859–1901. Rentoul held the post of Deputy Judge of the Sheriff's Court 1902–1919.

95 *The Times*, quoted in *Dictionary of National Biography. 1931–40 Supplement* (London: Oxford University Press, 1949), p. 211.

96 PRO, HO 45/9739/A55202, Cases of Rape on Children under 16. Memo on Principle which Should Govern Decisions, 1894.

97 Ibid. In practice, sentences were rarely served to their full term. The Home Office frequently granted licences for release after a convict had completed two-thirds of his sentence, or, in cases of life penal servitude, after ten or more years.

98 See PRO, HO 144/955/A63222, Corporal Punishment in Cases of Sexual Assault 1896–1914, for the comments of Justices Phillmore, Jelf and Wills. See *Child's Guardian* 24(12), 1910, p. 141, for Justice Bucknill's comments to the grand jury at the Derby Assizes.

99 *Child's Guardian* 28(3), 1914, p. 28. For suffragette and feminist campaigns on lenient sentencing see Bland, *Banishing the beast*, p. 252.

100 Conley, *The unwritten law*.

101 Armstrong, 'The use of information about occupation'; Bush, *Social orders and social classes*.

102 Wiener, *Reconstructing the criminal*, p. 46

103 R. McWilliam, *Popular politics in nineteenth-century England* (London: Routledge, 1998), p. 63. Thompson, *The making of the English working class*, provided an account of the transforming influence of methodism, which emphasised temperance, self-discipline and self-respect, amongst working men. This account of 'respectability' has recently been re-written by Clark, *The struggle for the breeches*, with a specific focus on gender dynamics; Clark has argued that 'respectability' also entailed the restriction of women's sphere within the home as part of the working-class ideal. Victor Bailey, 'In darkest England', has drawn attention to cultures of respectability in the later nineteenth-century socialist movement.

104 See *The Times*, 12 July 1845, p. 7 for the Lord Chief Baron's interventions in the jury's decision-making process. See also Emsley, *Crime and society*, p. 197.

105 For example *The Times*, 4 March 1865, p. 12: Lord Norbury was found guilty of common assault only and fined £5.

106 According to PRO, HO 45/9739/A55202, judges and juries continued to define sexual assault by fathers, guardians and figures of authority as the worse form of abuse. See also PRO, HO45/9907/B20738, Bill to Amend the Criminal Law Amendment Act of 1885 (1896), letter from Sir John Bridge to the Home Office, 20 April 1896. This did not mean that cases involving fathers were more likely to be convicted. Only 63 per cent of sampled cases in which the defendant can be identified as the father of a child victim resulted in a guilty verdict.

107 *The Times*, 9 July 1840, p. 7.

108 *The Times*, 6 February 1845, p. 8.

109 Conley, 'Rape and justice', p. 9.

110 *The Times*, 27 November 1860, p. 9.

111 Ibid.

112 *The Times*, 20 February 1835, p. 4.

113 *The Times*, 26 March 1835, p. 6

114 E. Chadwick, *Report on an inquiry into the sanitary conditions of the labouring population of Great Britain* (Edinburgh: Edinburgh University Press, 1965); Mayhew, *London labour and the London poor*, 1st edn 1842; Mearns, *The bitter cry of outcast London*; W. Booth, *In darkest England and the way out* (London. Carlyle Press, 1890). For more detailed analyses of the construction of the nineteenth-century urban poor as immoral see Stallybrass and White, *The politics and poetics of transgression*; Mort, *Dangerous sexualities*, and Wilson, *The sphinx in the city*.

115 *The Times*, 11 July 1850, p. 7.

116 *Yorkshire Post*, 29 April 1885, p. 3.

117 *The Times*, 23 June 1845, p. 8. See also the comments of West Riding Quarter Sessions Chairman Francis Darwin in *Yorkshire Post*, 9 April 1895, p. 8.

118 *News of the World*, 19 May 1895, p. 4.

119 See *The Times*, 7 November 1855, p. 11, for an unsympathetic response: 'The Assistant judge told the prisoner he was a drunken beast, and the sooner he was out of the court the better. Had the evidence been sufficient to convict him he would have gone away for some time to come.'

120 *The Times*, 8 June 1870, p. 11.

121 Wiener, *Reconstructing the criminal*, pp. 269–76. These mitigating pleas were not always successful. See, for example, *The Times*, 7 June 1870, p. 11.

122 *The Times*, 8 April 1880, p. 4.

123 *The Times*, 15 July 1875, p. 11.

7 Specialist homes for 'fallen' girls

1 PRO, HO 45/9887/B17147, Leytonstone Industrial School 1882–97. *The Good Shepherd Children's Home, Leytonstone*, pamphlet published 1885, p. 3.

2 Reformatory and Refuge Union, *The classified list of child-saving institutions* (London: Mahcarg & Sons, 1912).

3 The State performed a supervisory role in relation to certified industrial and reformatory schools. They were subject to an annual Home Office inspection after 1860 and *per capita* grants were provided for cases referred by magistrates. See May, 'Innocence and experience' and Cale, 'Girls and the perception of sexual danger'. For the role of evangelical religion in philanthropic welfare

work, see Heasman, *Evangelicals in action*; Prochaska, *Women and philanthropy*; and Heywood, *Children in care*.

4 PRO, HO 45/9888/B1721, St Vincent's Industrial School: complaint re conduct of masters.

5 Minutes of Evidence of the Royal Commission on Reformatory and Industrial Schools, PP 1884, XLV.1, Qs 7,621–2.

6 Report of the Departmental Committee on Sexual Offences Against Young Persons, PP 1924–5, XV.905, S. 97. The committee heard that boys had been neglected in 'preventive work' but advised against the separation of 'fallen' from 'unfallen'.

7 L. Mahood, *Policing gender, class and family. Britain 1850–1940* (London: UCL Press, 1995).

8 M. Cale, 'Working for God? Staffing the Victorian reformatory and industrial school system', *History of Education* 21 (2), 1992, pp. 113–27, p. 116.

9 See also Davidoff, *The family story*, pp. 4–5.

10 London Society for the Protection of Young Females and Prevention of Juvenile Prostitution, *Fourth annual report* (London: 1839).

11 Ibid., p. 13.

12 Rescue Society, *Extract from the twentieth annual report* (London: Rescue Society, 1872).

13 Ibid.

14 PRO, HO 45/9887/B17047, Letter from Agnes Cotton to Rt Hon. Sir William Vernon Harcourt, 4 February 1882.

15 Cooter, *In the name of the child*, p. 9.

16 *Our Waifs and Strays*, November 1886, p. 3.

17 Ibid.

18 CS, no. 25, case of Alice S. See chapter 3, note 88, for full details of Children's Society cases sampled.

19 *Our Waifs and Strays*, February 1901, p. 2.

20 Cale, 'Girls and the perception of sexual danger'; Cale, 'Saved from a life of vice'; Cox, 'Rescue and reform'.

21 Rescue Society, *Twentieth annual report*, p. 5. For the distinction that adult Magdalen Hospitals made between hardened 'prostitutes' and 'seduced' women see L. Nead, *Myths of sexuality: representations of women in Victorian Britain* (London: Blackwell, 1988), p. 96.

22 E. Hopkins, *Drawn unto death: a plea for the children coming under the Industrial Schools Act Amendment Act* (London: Hatchards, 1880), p. 9.

23 Cale, 'Girls and the perception of sexual danger', p. 207; Reports of the Inspectors of Reformatory and Industrial Schools of Great Britain, PP 1886, XXXV.1. As certified industrial schools, these homes received Home Office payments for residents committed by magistrates under the industrial schools acts.

24 S. Mumm, '"Not worse than other girls": the convent-based rehabilitation of fallen women in Victorian Britain', *Journal of Social History* 29 (3), 1996, pp. 527–546, see p. 530. Convent-based homes were rarely publicised and there is less surviving information since they were neither in receipt of Home Office money nor subject to inspection. The Waifs and Strays Society records make reference to the St John the Baptist Mission, Newford, Monmothshire and St Margaret's Mission, Cardiff. See CS, nos 81 (case of Beatrice T.) & 84 (Maria D.).

25 CS, no. 25, case of Alice S.

26 CS, no. 47, case of Caroline G.

27 Ibid.

28 CS, no. 32, case of Edith H., received into St Chads Girls Home, Far Headingley, Leeds, 1895.

29 Reformatory and Refuge Union, *The classified list*.

30 PRO, HO 45/10377/162475, Criminal Assaults on Children Under 16, 1908.

31 For the details of the setting up of new industrial schools for 'fallen' girls see PRO, HO 45/9887/B17047, Correspondence between the Home Office and the Church of England Penitentiary Society on the Criminal Assault of Children.

32 PRO, HO 45/10662/214154, Special Schools for Morally Difficult Girls, Circular to Justices.

33 Ibid.

34 Report from the Inspectors of Reformatory and Industrial Schools for Great Britain: PP 1914, XLVII.349, p. 13.

35 Report of the Departmental Committee on Sexual Offences Against Young Persons: PP 1924–5, XV.905, S. 111.

36 CS, no. 106, case of Lily W.

37 Ibid.

38 PRO, HO 45/9887/B17147, *The Good Shepherd Children's Home*, p. 5.

39 Ibid., p. 4.

40 Ibid., p. 6.

41 Ibid., p. 4.

42 PRO, HO 45/9887/B17147, Inquiry, 27 September 1894.

43 PRO, HO 45/9887/B17147, letter from Agnes Cotton, to A. V. Garland, clerk to the Industrial School Committee of the London School Board, 24 September 1894.

44 PRO, HO 45/9887/B17147, 29 October 1894, Report on Recent Inquiry.

45 Ibid.

46 Ibid.

47 CS, no. 106, case of Lily W.

48 Ibid.

49 CS, no. 58, case of Annie H.

50 CS, no. 70, case of Elizabeth B.

51 CS, no. 100, case of Pamela N.

52 CS, no. 89, case of Bertha C.

53 SA, Children's History Book VI, no. 96. See chapter 3, note 89, for full details of Salvation Army cases sampled.

54 H. R. Haggard, *Regeneration, being an account of the social work of the Salvation Army in Great Britain* (London: Longmans, 1910), p. 112.

55 SA, Children's History Books VI and VII. The books contain the names and records of those admitted after the home opened (rather than those transferred) and who were still resident from 1906 onwards.

56 See also Cale, 'Girls and the perception of danger'.

57 Salvation Army, *Climbing. Annual report of the social work of the Salvation Army* (London: Salvation Army, 1925), p. 13.

58 *Deliverer*, August 1908, p. 119.

59 Salvation Army, *Jewels for the king. A brief report of the rescue work of the Salvation Army* (London: Salvation Army, 1887), p. 4.

60 Ibid.

61 Ibid., p. 9.

62 SA, Children's History Book VI, no. 96.

63 Ibid.

64 Ibid.

65 L. L. Whyte, *The unconscious before Freud* (New York: Basic Books, 1960), p. 169; C. Steedman, *Childhood, culture and class in Britain. Margaret McMillan 1860–1931* (London: Virago, 1990), pp. 203–14; Steedman, *Strange dislocations*.
66 SA, Children's History Book VI, no. 168.
67 SA, Children's History Book VI, no. 66.
68 Cale, 'Girls and the perception of sexual danger', p. 209. The reference to Bertha's retelling of her story at The Mumbles is an unusual one.
69 F. A. McKenzie, *Waste humanity: being a review of part of the social operations of the Salvation Army in Great Britain* (London: Salvation Army, 1908), pp. 84–5.
70 *Annual report 1925*, p. 14.
71 Kelly, *Surviving sexual violence*, pp. 143–5.
72 Ross, *Love and toil*.
73 SA, Children's History Book VI, no. 96.
74 L. Marks, 'Jewish women and Jewish Prostitution in the East End of London', *Jewish Quarterly* 34 (126), 1987, pp. 6–10.
75 Ibid.
76 Beatrice Potter (later Webb) compared the role of the Jewish Board of Guardians to that of the Charity Organisation Society (Minutes of Evidence of the Select Committee of the House of Lords on the Sweating System: PP 1888, XX Pt 1.1, Q. 3,333).
77 D. Feldman, 'Jews in London 1880–1914', in *Minorities and outsiders*, vol. 2 of *Patriotism – the making and unmaking of British national identity*, R. Samuel (ed.) (London: Routledge, 1989), pp. 207–29, see p. 208, has cited the increase in the Russian and Polish population of London from 5,000 in 1871 to 63,000 in 1911 as an indicator of the scale of Jewish immigration. Immigrants congregated in Whitechapel, Mile End and Bethnal Green where they were absorbed, as cheap labour, into the 'sweated' textile industries. Leeds also saw a considerable influx at this time; see Fraser, *A history of modern Leeds* (records of the Leeds Jewish Board of Guardians are not available for this period).
78 C. Battersea, *Reminiscences* (London: Macmillan, 1922), p. 418.
79 Ibid.
80 C. Bermant, *The cousinhood* (London: Eyre & Spottiswoode, 1971); see also T. M. Endelman, 'Communal solidarity among the Jewish elite of Victorian London', *Victorian Studies* 23 (3), 1985, pp. 491–526.
81 Jewish Care archive (JC), Hartley Library, Southampton, Jewish Association for the Protection of Girls and Women, 2/1/1, Ladies' Committee Minute Book 1885–8.
82 L. Marks, *Model mothers: Jewish mothers and maternity provision in East London 1870–1939* (Oxford: Clarendon Press, 1994), pp. 26–43.
83 Feldman, 'Jews in London', pp. 210–2.
84 I. Zangwill, vol. 2 of *Children of the ghetto* (London: W. Heinemann, 1892), pp. 98–99.
85 L. Marks, ' "The luckless waifs and strays of humanity": Irish and Jewish immigrant unwed mothers in London 1870–1939', *Twentieth Century British History* 3(2), 1992, pp. 113–37.
86 *East London Observer*, 1 November 1885, p. 2.
87 *The Times*, 21 November 1885, p. 2.
88 Ibid.
89 JC, 2/1/1, 20 November 1885.
90 JC, 2/8/1, Minute Book of the Home Committee 1885–89.
91 Ibid., 4 April 1888.
92 Ibid., 7 May 1886.

93 Ibid., 23 November 1886 & 9 December 1886.
94 Ibid., 4 October 1888.
95 Battersea, *Reminiscences*, p. 423.
96 JC, 2/8/1, 21 December 1886.
97 Ibid., 5 July 1887.
98 JC, 2/1/1, 1 March 1887.
99 Ibid., 4 May 1887.
100 Stedman Jones, *Outcast London*, p. 252; Morris, *Class, sect and party*, pp. 161–203.
101 Gorham, 'The "maiden tribute"', p. 375.
102 Ibid.
103 Ibid., p. 355.
104 JC, 2/8/1, 21 January 1887.
105 Ibid.
106 See E. Showalter, *The female malady* (London: Virago, 1987) for the construction of hysteria as a form of madness brought on by women's reproductive function.
107 JC, Minutes of Council, 2/3/1, 26 April 1903.
108 Ibid., 4 July 1904.
109 Claude Montefiore offered the use of his large property at Stamford Hill for a nominal annual rent, and the first inmates of Montefiore House took up residence in 1905, an extra wing being added in 1909 to increase the capacity from 30 to 56.
110 See also Cale, 'Girls and the perception of sexual danger', p. 11.
111 JC, 2/3/1, 4 July 1904.
112 JC, Montefiore House General Committee Minutes 1912–16, 2/8/4, 5 November 1912.
113 Ibid., 2 March 1913.
114 Ibid., 4 July 1912.
115 Ibid., 1 July 1914.
116 Ibid., 7 April 1913.

8 Conclusion: from 'corruption' to 'neurosis'?

1 J. Sully, *Studies of childhood* (London: Longmans, 1895), p. 229.
2 Report of the Departmental Committee on Sexual Offences Against Young Persons: PP 1924–5, XV.905, S. 114.
3 Ibid.
4 Minutes of Evidence of the Joint Select Committee on the Criminal Law Amendment Bill, Criminal Law Amendment Bill (2) and Sexual Offences Bill: PP 1920, VI.851, Q. 455.
5 PP 1924–5, XV.905, S. 93.
6 Ibid., S. 76: Witnesses argued 'that many of these offences are committed by men who are insane or mentally defective'. Although the committee held that this 'general impression' was not corroborated by hard evidence, it did suggest that defendants should be sent for mental examination. Interpretations of abusive behaviour in terms of mental deficiency and feeble-mindedness became dominant in later decades; see Jackson, 'Women professionals and the regulation of violence'.
7 J. M. Masson, *The assault on truth: Freud's suppression of the seduction theory* (Harmondsworth: Penguin, 1985); A. Miller, *Thou shalt not be aware. Society's betrayal of the child* (London: Pluto Press, 1981); A. Scott, 'Feminism and the seductiveness of the "real event"', *FR* 28, 1998, pp. 88–102.

8 H. Israels and M. Schatzman, 'The seduction theory', *History of Psychiatry* 4 (13), 1993, pp. 23–59.
9 A. Moll, *The sexual life of the child*, translated from the German by Dr Eden Paul (London: George Allen & Co., 1912).
10 Ibid., p. 226.
11 D. Rapp, 'The early discovery of Freud by the British general public', *Social History of Medicine* 3, 1990, pp. 217–43.
12 Steedman, *Childhood, culture and class*, p. 209.
13 Medical Women's Federation, SA/MWF/D7, notes from Letitia Fairfield, 9 March 1925: by courtesy of the Wellcome Trustees.
14 H. C. Cameron, *The nervous child* (London: Hodder & Stoughton, 2nd edn 1923), p. 198.
15 Cox, *Rescue and reform*, p. 33; Cox, 'Girls, deficiency and delinquency', in *From idiocy to mental deficiency. Historical perspectives on people with learning difficulties*, D. Wright and A. Digby (eds) (London: Routledge, 1996), pp. 184–206, see p. 194.
16 Cox, *Rescue and reform*, pp. 50–4; Cox, 'Girls, deficiency and delinquency', p. 192.
17 Gordon, 'The politics of child sexual abuse', p. 60.
18 J. Bowlby, 'The influence of early environment in the development of neurosis and neurotic character', *International Journal of Psycho-analysis* 21, 1940, p. 10.
19 See also D. Thom, 'Wishes, anxieties, play and gestures. Child guidance in inter-war England', in Cooter, *In the name of the child*, pp. 200–19 and C. Urwin and E. Sharland, 'From bodies to minds in childcare literature. Advice to parents in inter-war Britain', in Cooter, *In the name of the child*, pp. 174–99.
20 Jenks, *Childhood*, pp. 123–31.
21 B. Morrison, *As if* (London: Granta, 1997), p. 21.
22 Ibid., p. 243.
23 For example, Jenks, *Childhood*.

Further reading

Sexuality

Bland, L. *Banishing the beast: English feminism and sexual morality 1885–1914* (London: Penguin, 1995).

Bristow, E. *Vice and vigilance; purity movements in Britain since 1700* (Dublin: Gill & Macmillan, 1977).

Clark, A. 'The politics of seduction in English popular culture 1748–1848'. In *The progress of romance: the politics of popular fiction*, J. Radford (ed.) (London: Routledge & Kegan Paul, 1986), pp. 47–70.

Cohen, E. *Talk on the Wilde side* (London: Routledge, 1993).

De Groot, J. ' "Sex" and "race": the construction of language and image in the nineteenth century'. In *Sexuality and subordination. Interdisciplinary studies of gender in the nineteenth century*, S. Mendus and J. Rendall (eds) (London: Routledge, 1989), pp. 89–130.

Foucault, M. *An introduction*, vol. 1 of *The history of sexuality*, translated by R. Hurley (Harmondsworth: Penguin, 1990), 1st published 1976.

Gillis, J. H. 'Servants, sexual relations and the rise of illegitimacy in London, 1801–1900'. In *Sex and class in women's history*, J. Newton, M. Ryan and J. Walkowitz (eds) (London: Routledge & Kegan Paul, 1983), pp. 114–45.

Gilman, S. *Difference and pathology: stereotypes of sexuality, race and madness* (New York: Cornell University Press, 1985).

Harvey, A. D. 'Prosecutions for sodomy in England at the beginning of the nineteenth century'. *Historical Journal* 21, pp. 939–48, 1978.

Hitchcock, T. *English sexualities 1700–1800* (Basingstoke: Macmillan, 1997).

Jeffreys, S. *The spinster and her enemies. Feminism and sexual morality 1880–1930* (London: Pandora, 1985).

Kingsley-Kent, S. *Sex and suffrage in Britain 1860–1914* (London: Routledge, 1990).

McClintock, A. *Imperial leather: race, gender, and sexuality in the colonial contest* (London: Routledge, 1995).

Mort, F. *Dangerous sexualities: medico-moral politics in England since 1830* (London: Routledge & Kegan Paul, 1987).

Nead, L. *Myths of sexuality. Representations of women in Victorian Britain* (Oxford: Blackwell, 1988).

Porter, R. and L. Hall *The facts of life: the creation of sexual knowledge in Britain, 1650–1950* (New Haven, Connecticut: Yale University Press, 1995).

Sedgwick, Eve Kosofsky *Epistemology of the closet* (Hemel Hempstead: Harvester Wheatsheaf, 1991).

Sinfield, A. *The Wilde century: effeminacy, Oscar Wilde and the queer movement* (London: Cassell, 1994).

Trumbach, R. 'Sex, gender and sexual identity in modern culture: male sodomy and female prostitution in Enlightenment London'. *Journal of the History of Sexuality* 2, pp. 186–203, 1991.

Walkowitz, J. *City of dreadful delight. Narratives of sexual danger in late-Victorian London* (London: Virago Press, 1992).

—— *Prostitution and Victorian society, women, class and the state* (Cambridge: Cambridge University Press, 1980).

Weeks, J. 'Inverts, perverts and Mary-Annes: male prostitution and the regulation of homosexuality in England in the nineteenth and twentieth centuries'. In *Against nature: essays on history, sexuality and identity* (London: Rivers Oram Press, 1991), pp. 10–45.

—— *Sex, politics and society*, 2nd edn (Harlow: Longman, 1989).

Masculinities

Clark, A. *The struggle for the breeches: gender and the making of the British working class* (Los Angeles: University of California, 1995).

Dawson, G. *Soldier Heroes. British adventure, empire and the imagining of masculinities* (London: Routledge, 1994).

Girouard, M. *The return to Camelot. Chivalry and the English gentleman* (New Haven: Yale University Press, 1981).

Hall, L. *Hidden anxieties. Male sexuality 1900–1950* (Cambridge: Polity, 1991).

Hearn, J. *Men in the public eye* (London: Routledge, 1992).

Mangan, J. A. and J. Walvin (eds) *Manliness and morality: middle-class masculinity in Britain and America 1800–1940* (Manchester: Manchester University Press, 1987).

McLaren, A. *The trials of masculinity. Policing sexual boundaries 1870–1930* (Chicago: University of Chicago Press, 1997).

Roper, M. and J. Tosh (eds) *Manful assertions: masculinity in Britain since 1800* (London: Routledge, 1991).

Sinha, M. *Colonial masculinity: the 'manly Englishman' and the 'effeminate Bengali' in the late-nineteenth century* (Manchester: Manchester University Press, 1995).

Tosh, J. 'What should historians do with masculinity? Reflections on nineteenth-century Britain'. *History Workshop Journal* 38, pp. 179–202, 1994.

Walker, P. ' "I live but not yet I for Christ liveth in me": men and masculinity in the Salvation Army 1865–90'. See Roper and Tosh (eds), 1991, pp. 92–112.

Medicine and the body

Armstrong, D. *Political anatomy of the body: medical knowledge in Britain in the twentieth century* (Cambridge: Cambridge University Press, 1983).

Blake, C. *The charge of the parasols. Women's entry to the medical profession* (London: Women's Press, 1990).

Clark, M. and C. Crawford *Legal medicine in history* (Cambridge: Cambridge University Press, 1994).

Cooter, R. (ed.) *In the name of the child. Health and welfare 1880–1940* (London: Routledge, 1992).

Douglas, M. *Purity and danger* (London: Routledge & Kegan Paul, 1970).

Forbes, T. R. *Surgeons at the Bailey. English forensic medicine to 1878* (New Haven: Yale University Press, 1985).

Harrison, M. 'Tropical medicine in nineteenth-century India'. *British Journal for the History of Science* 25, pp. 299–318, 1992.

Shepherd, J. A. *Lawson Tait: the rebellious surgeon 1845–1897* (Kansas: Colorado Press, 1980).

Shuttleworth, S. 'Female circulation: medical discourse and popular advertising in the mid-Victorian era'. In *Body politics: women and the discourses of science*, M. Jacobus, E. F. Keller and S. Shuttleworth (eds) (New York: Routledge, 1990), pp. 47–68.

Stallybrass, P. and A. White *The politics and poetics of transgression* (London: Methuen, 1986).

Steedman, C. 'Bodies, figures and physiology: Margaret McMillan and the late ninteenth-century remaking of working-class childhood'. See Cooter (ed.), 1992, pp. 19–44.

Summers, R. 'History of the police surgeon'. *Police Surgeon* 14, pp. 16–38, 1970.

Taylor, K. 'Venereal disease in nineteenth-century children'. *Journal of Psychohistory* 12, pp. 431–64, 1985.

Wilson, E. *The Sphinx in the city: urban life, the control of disorder and women* (Berkeley: University of California Press, 1991).

Childhood and child welfare

Arnot, M. L. 'Infant death, child care and the state: the baby-farming scandal and the first infant life protection legislation of 1872'. *Continuity and Change* 9 (2), pp. 271–311, 1994.

Behlmer, G. *Child abuse and moral reform in England 1870–1900* (Palo Alto, California: Stanford University Press, 1982).

Coveney, P. *The image of childhood. The individual and society: a study of the theme in English literature* (Harmondsworth: Penguin, 1967).

Cunningham, H. *Children and childhood in western society since 1500* (London: Longman, 1995).

—— *The children of the poor: representations of childhood since the seventeenth century* (Oxford: Blackwell, 1991).

Davin, A. *Growing up poor. Home, school and street in London 1870–1914* (London: Rivers Oram Press, 1996).

—— 'When is a child not a child?' In *Politics of everyday life: continuity and change in work and the family*, H. Corr and L. Jamieson (eds) (London: Macmillan, 1990), pp. 37–61.

Ferguson, T. H. 'Protecting children in time: a historical sociological study of the abused child and child protection in Cleveland from 1880 to the "Cleveland affair" of 1987' (Ph.D. thesis: Cambridge University, 1992).

—— 'Cleveland in history: the abused child and child protection, 1880–1914'. See Cooter (ed.), 1992, pp. 146–99.

Fletcher, A. and S. Hussey (eds) *Childhood in question. Children, parents and the state.* (Manchester: Manchester University Press, 1999).

Gorham, D. 'The "maiden tribute of modern Babylon" re-examined. Child prostitution and the idea of childhood in late-Victorian England'. *Victorian Studies* 21, pp. 353–79, 1978.

Hendrick, H. *Child welfare. England 1872–1989* (London: Routledge, 1994).

Heywood, J. *Children in care: the development of the service for the deprived child* (London: Routledge & Kegan Paul, 1959).

Jenks, C. *Childhood* (London: Routledge, 1996).

Jordanova, L. 'Children in history: concepts of nature and society'. In *Children, parents and politics*, G. Scarre (ed.) (Cambridge: Cambridge University Press, 1989), pp. 3–24.

Rose, L. *The erosion of childhood: child oppression in Britain 1860–1918* (London: Routledge, 1991).

Steedman, C. *Childhood, culture and class in Britain – Margaret McMillan 1860–1931* (Cambridge: Virago, Goodfellow & Egan, 1990).

—— *Strange dislocations. Childhood and the idea of human interiority 1780–1930* (London: Virago, 1995).

Crime and police

Arnot, M. L. and C. Usborne (eds) *Gender and crime in modern Europe* (London: UCL Press, 1999).

Conley, C. A. *The unwritten law: criminal justice in Victorian Kent* (Oxford: Oxford University Press, 1991).

Davis, J. 'A poor man's system of justice: The London police courts in the second half of the nineteenth century'. *Historical Journal* 27 (2), pp. 309–35, 1984.

—— 'Prosecutions and their context: the use of criminal law in later nineteenth-century London'. In *Policing and prosecution in Britain 1750–1880*, D. Hay and F. Snyder (eds) (Oxford: Clarendon Press, 1989), pp. 397–426.

D'Cruze, S. (ed.) *Unguarded passions. Gender, class and 'everyday' violence in Britain, c. 1850–1950* (Harlow: Addison Wesley Longman, in press).

Duman, D. *The judicial bench in England 1727–1875. The reshaping of a professional élite.* (London: Royal Historical Society, 1982).

Emsley, C. *Crime and society in England 1750–1900*, 2nd edn (Harlow: Longman, 1996), 1st edn 1987.

Gatrell, V. A. C. 'Crime, authority and the policeman-state'. In vol. 3 of *The Cambridge social history of Britain*, F. M. L. Thompson (ed.) (Cambridge: Cambridge University Press, 1990), pp. 243–310.

—— *The hanging tree. Execution and the English people 1770–1860* (Oxford: Oxford University Press, 1994).

Jones, D. *Crime, community and police in nineteenth-century Britain* (London: Routledge Kegan Paul, 1982).

Philips, D. *Crime and authority in Victorian England* (London: Croom Helm, 1971).

—— '"A just measure of crime, authority, hunters and blue locusts": the "revisionist" social history of crime and the law in Britain 1780–1850'. In *Social control and the state*, S. Cohen and A. Scull (Oxford: Blackwell, 1985), pp. 50–74.

Steedman, C. *Policing the Victorian community: the formation of English provincial police forces 1856–80* (London: Routledge & Kegan Paul, 1984).

Storch, R. 'The policeman as domestic missionary: urban discipline and popular culture in northern England 1850–1880'. *Journal of Social History* 4, pp. 481–509, 1970.

Wiener, M. J. *Reconstructing the criminal: culture, law and policy in England 1830–1914* (Cambridge: Cambridge University Press, 1990).

Zedner, L. *Women, crime and custody in Victorian England* (Oxford: Clarendon Press, 1991).

Juvenile delinquency

Cale, M. 'Girls and the perception of sexual danger in the Victorian reformatory system'. *History* 78, pp. 201–17, 1993.

—— '"Saved from a life of vice and crime": reformatory and industrial schools for girls c.1854 –c.1901' (Ph.D. thesis: Oxford University, 1993).

Cox, P. 'Girls, deficiency and delinquency'. In *From idiocy to mental deficiency. Historical perspectives on people with learning difficulties*, D. Wright and A. Digby (eds) (London: Routledge, 1996), pp. 184–206.

—— 'Rescue and reform: girls, delinquency and industrial schools 1908–33' (Ph.D. thesis: University of Cambridge, 1996).

Davies, A. '"These viragoes are no less cruel than the lads": young women, gangs and violence in late-Victorian Manchester and Salford'. *British Journal of Criminology* 39 (1), pp. 72–89, 1999.

Gillis, J. H. 'The evolution of delinquency in England 1890–1914'. *Past & Present* 67, pp. 96–126, 1975.

Hendrick, H. *Images of youth. Age, class and the male youth problem, 1880 1920* (Oxford: Clarendon Press, 1990).

Humphries, S. *Hooligans or rebels? An oral history of working-class childhood and youth 1889–1939* (Oxford: Blackwell, 1981).

King, P. 'The rise of juvenile delinquency in England 1780–1840. Changing patterns of perception and prosecution'. *Past & Present* 160, pp. 116–66, 1998.

King, P and J. Noel 'The origins of "the problem of juvenile delinquency": the growth of juvenile prosecutions in London in the late eighteenth and early nineteenth centuries'. *Criminal Justice History* 14, pp. 17–42, 1993.

Mahood, L. and B. Littlewood 'The "vicious girl" and the "street-corner boy": sexuality and the gendered delinquent in the Scottish child-saving movement 1850–1940'. *Journal of the History of Sexuality* 4, pp. 549–78, 1994.

May, M. 'Innocence and experience: the evolution of the concept of juvenile delinquency in the mid-nineteenth century'. *Victorian Studies* 17 (1), pp. 7–29, 1973.

Shore, H. *Artful Dodgers: youth and crime in early nineteenth century London* (London: The Royal Historical Society, 1999).

—— 'The trouble with boys: gender and the "invention" of the juvenile offender in early nineteenth-century Britain'. See Arnot and Usborne (eds), 1999, pp. 75–92.

Rape and domestic violence

Chaytor, M. 'Husband(ry): narratives of rape in the seventeenth century'. *Gender and History* 10 (1), pp. 1–25, 1995.

Clark, A. *Women's silence, men's violence: sexual assault in England 1770–1845* (London: Pandora, 1987).

—— 'Rape or seduction? A controversy over sexual violence in the nineteenth century'. In *The sexual dynamics of history: men's power, women's resistance*, London Feminist History Group (eds) (London: Pluto, 1983), pp. 13–27.

Conley, C. A. 'Rape and justice in Victorian England'. *Victorian Studies* 29, pp. 519–37, 1986.

D'Cruze, S. 'Approaching the history of rape and sexual violence'. *Women's History Review* 1, pp. 376–96, 1992.

—— *Crimes of outrage. Sex, violence and Victorian women* (London: UCL Press, 1998).

Eagleton, T. *The rape of Clarissa. Writing, sexuality and class struggle in Samuel Richardson* (London: Blackwell, 1982).

Gordon, L. 'Family violence, feminism and social control'. *Feminist Studies* 12 (3), pp. 453–78, 1986.

—— *Heroes of their own lives. The politics and history of family violence* (London: Virago, 1989).

Hammerton, A. J. *Cruelty and companionship: conflict in nineteenth-century married life* (London: Routledge, 1992).

Lambertz, J. 'Sexual harassment in the nineteenth-century English cotton industry'. *History Workshop Journal* 19, pp. 29–61, 1985.

McMullen, R. J. *Male rape: breaking the silence on the last taboo* (London: GMP Publishers, 1990).

Simpson, A. E. 'Vulnerability and the age of female consent: legal innovation and its effect on prosecutions for rape in eighteenth century England'. In *Sexual underworlds of the Enlightenment*, G. S. Rousseau and R. Porter (eds) (Manchester: Manchester University Press), pp. 180–205.

Tomaselli, S. and R. Porter (eds) *Rape: a historical and social enquiry* (Oxford: Basil Blackwell, 1986).

Tomes, N. 'A "torrent of abuse": crimes of violence between working-class men and women in London'. *Journal of Social History* 11, pp. 328–45, 1978.

Walker, G. 'Rereading rape and sexual violence in early modern England'. *Gender and History*, 10 (1), pp. 1–25, 1998.

Incest and child sexual abuse

Bailey, V. and S. Blackburn 'The Punishment of Incest Act 1908: a case study of law creation'. *Criminal Law Review*, pp. 708–18, 1979.

Bannerji, H. 'Age of consent and hegemonic social reform'. In *Gender and imperialism*, C. Midgley (ed.) (Manchester: Manchester University Press, 1998), pp. 21–44.

Bell, V. *Interrogating incest: feminism, Foucault and the law* (London: Routledge, 1993).

Donovan, J. M. 'Combating the sexual abuse of children in France 1825–1913'. *Criminal Justice History* 15, pp. 59–95, 1994.

Gordon, L. 'The politics of child sexual abuse: notes from American history'. *Feminist Review* 28, pp. 56–64, 1988.

Hooper, C. 'Child sexual abuse and the regulation of women: Variations on a theme'. In *Regulating womanhood*, C. Smart (ed.) (London: Routledge, 1992), pp. 54–77.

Jackson, L. A. 'The child's word in court: cases of sexual abuse in London 1870–1914'. See Arnot and Usborne (eds), pp. 222–37.

—— 'Family, community and the regulation of sexual abuse: London 1870–1914'. See Fletcher and Hussey (eds), 1999.

—— 'Women professionals and the regulation of violence in inter-war Britain'. See D'Cruze (ed.), in press.

Humphries, S. and P. Gordon *Forbidden Britain: our secret past 1900–1960* (London: BBC, 1994).

Israels, H. and M. Schatzman 'The seduction theory'. *History of Psychiatry* 4 (13), pp. 23–59, 1993.

Kincaid, J. *Child-loving. The erotic child and Victorian culture* (London: Routledge, 1992).

Masson, J. M. *The assault on truth: Freud's suppression of the seduction theory.* (Harmondsworth: Penguin, 1985).

Mavor, C. 'Dream rushes. Lewis Carroll's photographs of little girls'. In *Pleasures taken. Performances of sexuality and loss in photographs* (London: I.B. Tauris, 1996), pp. 7–42.

Miller, A. *Thou shalt not be aware: society's betrayal of the child* (London: Pluto Press, 1985).

Plowden, A. *The case of Eliza Armstrong: a child of 13 bought for £5* (London: Trinity Press, 1974).

Scott, A. 'Feminism and the seductiveness of the "real event"'. *Feminist Review* 28, pp. 88–102, 1998.

Wohl, A. 'Sex and the single room: incest among the Victorian working classes'. In *The Victorian family: structure and stresses* (London: Croom Helm, 1978), pp. 197–216.

Wolfram, S. 'Eugenics and the Punishment of Incest Act 1908'. *Criminal Law Review*, pp. 308–16, 1983.

The family and the state

Davidoff, L., M. Doolittle, J. Fink, K. Holden *The family story. Blood, contract and intimacy, 1830–1960* (Harlow, England: Addison Wesley Longman, 1999).

Davidoff, L. and C. Hall *Family fortunes: men and women of the English middle class 1750–1850* (London: Hutchinson, 1987).

Davin, A. 'Imperialism and motherhood'. *History Workshop Journal* 5, pp. 9–65, 1978.

Donzelot, J. *The policing of families* (London: Hutchinson, 1980).

Doolittle, M. 'Missing fathers: assembling a history of fatherhood in mid-nineteenth century England' (Ph.D. thesis, University of Essex, 1996).

Koven, S. and S. Michel (eds) *Mothers of a new world: maternalist politics and the origins of welfare states* (London: Routledge, 1993).

Lewis, J. *The politics of motherhood: child and maternal welfare in England 1919–39* (London: Croom Helm, 1980).

Mahood, L. *Policing gender, class and family. Britain 1850–1940* (London: UCL Press, 1995).

Roberts, E. *A woman's place: an oral history of working-class women 1890–1940* (Oxford: Blackwell, 1986).

Ross, E. *Love and toil. Motherhood in outcast London 1870–1918* (Oxford: Oxford University Press, 1993).

Tosh, J. 'Authority and nurture in middle-class fatherhood: the case of early and mid-Victorian England'. *GH* 8 (1), pp. 43–64, 1996.

—— *A man's place: masculinity and the middle-class home in Victorian England* (New Haven, Connecticut: Yale University Press, 1999).

Vicinus, M. 'Helpless and unfriended: nineteenth-century domestic melodrama'. *New Literary History* 13, pp. 127–43, 1981.

Religion and philanthropy

Bailey, V. 'In darkest England and the way out: the Salvation Army, social reform and the Labour movement 1885–1910'. *International Review of Social History* 29 (2), pp. 133–71, 1984.

Ball, G. 'Practical religion: a study of the Salvation Army's services for women 1884–1914' (Ph.D. thesis, University of Leicester, 1987).

Bermant, C. *The cousinhood* (London: Eyre & Spottiswoode, 1971).

Cesarani, D. *The making of modern Anglo-Jewry.* (Oxford: Blackwell, 1990).

Endelman, T. M. 'Communal solidarity among the Jewish élite of Victorian London'. *Victorian Studies* 23 (3), pp. 491–526, 1985.

Feldman, D. 'Jews in London 1880–1914'. In *Minorities and outsiders*, vol. 2 of *Patriotism – the making and unmaking of British national identity*, R. Samuel (ed.) (London: Routledge, 1989), pp. 207–29.

Heasman, K. *Evangelicals in action: an appraisal of their social work in the Victorian era* (London: Geoffrey Bles, 1962).

Marks, L. 'Jewish women and Jewish prostitution in the East End of London'. *Jewish Quarterly* 34 (126), pp. 6–10, 1987.

—— ' "The luckless waifs and strays of humanity": Irish and Jewish immigrant unwed mothers in London 1870–1939'. *Twentieth Century British History* 3 (2), pp. 113–37, 1992.

—— *Model mothers: Jewish mothers and maternity provision in East London 1870–1939* (Oxford: Clarendon Press, 1994).

Morris, R. J. *Class, sect and party. The making of the British middle class: Leeds 1820–50* (Manchester: Manchester University Press, 1990).

Mumm, S. ' "Not worse than other girls": the convent-based rehabilitation of fallen women in Victorian Britain'. *Journal of Social History* 29 (3), pp. 527–46, 1996.

Prochaska, F. K. *Women and philanthropy in nineteenth-century England* (Oxford: Clarendon Press, 1980).

Walker, P. ' "Pulling the devil's kingdom down": gender and popular culture in the Salvation Army 1865–1895' (Ph.D. thesis: Rutgers University, 1991).

Name index

Subject index

London Society for the Protection of
  Young Females 14, 133

McNaughton rules 130
magistrates 22–3, 30, 33, 46, 64, 90,
  126, 130
'maiden tribute of modern Babylon,
  The' (Stead) 15–16, 42, 56, 111,
  115–16
manliness 40, 107–8, 111–14, 116,
  118–19, 123, 125, 131
masculinity 33, 40, 54; of child abuser
  107–31
masturbation 86
medical evidence 90, 98
medical profession 71–89
medical texts 72, 79, 87
Medical Women's Federation 73, 153
melodrama 15–16, 28, 32–4, 45 6, 48
mental illness 130–1
Metropolitan Police Force 44, 78, 101,
  105
middle-class: attitudes 28–9, 36, 55,
  70, 73, 95–6, 148; identity 6–8;
  incest 50; *see also* respectability
Middlesex: relationship of
  defendant/victim 43–4; sexual
  assault cases 18–22, 30, 36
'minx' or 'victim' 83–5, 87
misdemeanour 13, 17, 96, 99
molly houses 101, 105
Montefiore House 149–50, 153
moral codes 36–7, 40, 50
moral economy 6–7, 52, 58, 89, 152
'moral miasma' 88
moral panic 7, 31, 41–3, 106, 155
moral purity 111
morality 12, 35, 85–9, 97, 97–9, 107,
  114
mothers 22, 33–5, 69, 76–7, 80–1, 83,
  109–11, 117, 121, 154
Mumbles, The, Swansea 66, 135–6, 140

National Vigilance Association 15, 54,
  63, 146, 148
neglect 59, 66–8
neighbours 28–50, 64
Nest, The, Clapton 51, 66–9, 136,
  140–3
neurosis, sexual abuse and development
  of 152–5
Newgate Prison 1
NSPCC (National Society for the

Prevention of Cruelty to Children)
  16, 25, 31, 46, 51–7, 59–68, 70, 93,
  100, 113, 124, 140, 153
number of abuse cases 3–5, 24, 29–31

oath 93
occupation 8, 125–6, 131
Offences against the Person Act (1861)
  13–14, 30
Old Bailey v, 1, 19, 21
original sin 5, 95
orphanages 66
ostracisation 49
other: male abuser as 108, 112; victim
  as 112, 114–16, 119
overcrowding 21, 29, 49–50, 54, 57,
  112, 121, 152 3

paediatrics 72, 87
paedophilia 114
parents 52, 65–9, *see also* fathers;
  mothers
park constables 44–5, 101
Parks Regulation Act (1872) 44
patriarchy 10, 112, 120, 122
perjury 93
phantasy theory 153–4
philanthropy: boys 100; child savers 11,
  53, 64–8, 70; custody law 120;
  homes for 'fallen' girls 132, 135–6,
  145–6, 148; moral imposition 114,
  status of child 13
police: boys 104–5; child savers 59–60,
  62–4; courts 22–3; social regulation
  28, 30–1, 33 4, 36, 38–40, 44–5;
  surgeons 72–3, 77–8; surveillance 16
pollution 6, 32, 56, 58, 69, 73, 85–9,
  152
Poor Law 46; officials 64, 67
pornography 115–16
poverty: body signs 84, 87–8; child 2;
  child savers 57, 60–1, 64, 70;
  delinquency and 95; homes for
  'fallen' girls 141; moral codes 37;
  psychology 152–3; respectability
  112; social class 129
power 8–10, 12, 120–2
precocity, sexual 6, 17, 53, 58, 68, 84,
  86–7, 96–7, 99, 103, 132, 135, 146
Prevention of Cruelty to Children Act
  (1889) 47
prevention strategies 37, 47

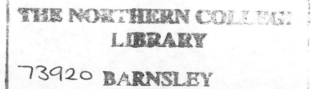